MERCKX: HALF MAN, HALF BIKE

WILLIAM FOTHERINGHAM

MERCKX: HALF MAN, HALF BIKE

YELLOW JERSEY PRESS
LONDON

Published by Yellow Jersey Press 2012

2 4 6 8 10 9 7 5 3

First published in Great Britain in 2012 by
Yellow Jersey Press
Random House, 20 Vauxhall Bridge Road,
London SW1V 2SA

www.vintage-books.co.uk

Addresses for companies within The Random House Group Limited can be found at:
www.randomhouse.co.uk/offices.htm

The Random House Group Limited Reg. No. 954009

A CIP catalogue record for this book
is available from the British Library

ISBN 9780224074483 (hardback)
ISBN 9780224091954 (trade paperback)

Printed and bound in Great Britain by
Clays Ltd, St Ives plc

This book is dedicated to the late Laurent Fignon, a man who loved la course en tête

CONTENTS

LIST OF ILLUSTRATIONS

All photos courtesy of Offside, unless stated.

Wambst, dead and Merckx with lasting back problems (courtesy of Getty Images).

9. Flair and flares on the Bald Mountain: Merckx climbs to the Ventoux observatory en route to victory in the 1970 Tour.

10. The 1971 Tour is in the great man's pocket a day from Paris. True to his character, he is still looking for chances to attack in the Chevreuse valley.

11. Pictures of Merckx smiling were said to be rare: above he celebrates victory in the 1971 Milan–San Remo, his fourth win there in six years, below he relaxes at the dinner table with his team during the 1974 Tour (both courtesy of Getty Images).

12. In 1973, Merckx landed his second victory in Paris–Roubaix. Here he is retrieved by the front group led by the Belgian Walter Planckaert before making his final move.

13. Roger de Vlaeminck was Merckx's great rival in the Classics: he is struggling to hold The Cannibal in the 1975 'The Hell of the North', although at the finish the order would be reversed (courtesy of Getty Images).

14. A typical masterstroke late in the 1974 Tour: the solo attack that sealed victory in the Vouvray to Orleans stage.

15. Tour starts in the 1970s were low-key affairs: Merckx pedals away into the rain at Dieppe in the 1974 race (courtesy of Getty Images).

16. The 1977 Tour, The Cannibal's last: he is fighting against time – in both senses – in the mountain time trial from Morzine to Avoriaz (courtesy of Getty Images).

17. Sick and exhausted, Merckx slumps over his bike at the Alpe d'Huez finish in the 1977 Tour. After this, retirement was only a matter of time (courtesy of Getty Images).

ACKNOWLEDGMENTS

For sharing memories of Merckx on various occasions I should like to thank: Jørgen Leth, Jean-Luc Vandenbroucke, Gian-Paolo Ormezzano, Bob Addy, Ian Banbury, Sean Kelly, Michael Wright, Jiří Daler, Joël Godaert, Giorgio Albani, Bernard Thévenet, Ole Ritter, Vittorio Adorni, Ernesto Colnago, Sid Barras, Emile Daems. Particular thanks should go to Jos Bruyère, Guillaume Michiels and Bob Lelangue, all of whom were generous with their time when discussing their years at Merckx's side.

During research for a future book on Flandrian cycling, the name Merckx inevitably came up when I interviewed Rik Van Looy, Patrick Sercu, Walter Godefroot, Herman Van Springel and Frans Verbeeck. I would like to thank all of these greats for their help.

For providing telephone numbers and general advice, I should like to thank Stéphane Thirion, Marc Ghyselinck, Marco Pastonesi and Philippe Bouvet. Their names seemed to open doors wherever I looked.

Other valuable assistance came from Chris Boardman and Peter Keen, both of whom provided insights into their Hour Records and that of Merckx. I am indebted to my brother Alasdair for helping with interviews with Raphael Geminiani and Txomin Perurena, and to Barbara Rumpus at *l'Equipe* for sourcing one particular piece of writing. Jacinto Vidarte and Javier de Dalmases were generous with their memories of José Manuel Fuente while Joël Godaert provided insights into the final months of Merckx's career and supplied extracts from his book *Eddy Merckx La Roue de la Fortune*, reproduced in *La Dernière Heure*. Many thanks to Tim Harris and Jos Ryan for good coffee, encouragement and the loan of their spare bed in East Flanders while I was interviewing. My son Patrick will remember this book for his first paid writing assignment – Merckx's palmares – for which many thanks.

My agent John Pawsey and my sports editor at the *Guardian*, Ian Prior, have both provided valuable backing over many years now. At Yellow Jersey Press my editor Matt Phillips was a tower of strength from start to finish, while thanks are also due to James Jones in design for the cover, Bethan Jones in publicity, Phil Brown in production, the copy editor, Richard Collins and the proof reader, Myra Jones.

As ever, I owe the biggest and most enduring debt to Caroline, Patrick and Miranda, who have been unstinting in their love and support in the face of yet more absences in foreign parts and many days when my heart and mind were in Flanders or the Dolomites.

INTRODUCTION

Eddy Merckx made his first attack as the five leaders went under the small triangle of red cloth hanging from a long string over the road that marked a kilometre to ride until the finish line at the Avoriaz ski station. Suddenly, he dived up the right-hand side of the narrow corridor of road between the crowds of cycling fans. After that there were only three of them: Merckx, riding in the rainbow jersey of world champion, the Dutchman Joop Zoetemelk in the blue of Gan-Mercier, and the stocky Frenchman Bernard Thévenet, the man in the yellow jersey, leader of the 1975 Tour de France. It was Thévenet who retrieved Merckx when he attempted to get away a second time, 250 metres from the line, but when the world champion went again immediately, having given the Frenchman no time to recover, Thévenet let him go. The three attacks gained Merckx third place behind the winner Vicente López Carril of Spain, and allowed him to finish two seconds ahead of Thévenet.

Given that Merckx had won close to five hundred races, the third place was insignificant. Given that Thévenet enjoyed an advantage of nearly three minutes, the seconds looked meaningless. But for a man who had broken his jaw that morning the series of brutal accelerations and the minuscule time gain were truly remarkable. He should have been in hospital, or lying on a sofa nursing the double fracture that had left his face swollen and bruised. Instead, he had fought his way over three massive Alpine passes, through 225 kilometres in the blazing sun, he had led the way down the descent to Morzine, the resort at the foot of the final climb – Thévenet was a clumsy descender, and it was worth pushing him to the limit – in a style that can only be described as heroic. It was futile. It was also self-destructive. It was glorious.

At first sight, the crash could hardly have been more innocuous. They were not even racing at the time. At the start of the stage in the little Alpine town of Valloire, as the Tour de France peloton progressed slowly from the assembly point on to the lower slopes of the Col du Télégraphe, the Dane Ole Ritter moved suddenly to avoid colliding with another rider. The speed was slow, but Eddy Merckx, who was riding alongside, could not miss Ritter's handlebars: they became entangled with his. He could no longer control the bike: down he went, forwards and sideways. It could have been *rien de grave*, as the Tour commentators usually say: but just this once, the impact was not absorbed by an outstretched arm or knee. Merckx fell on his face.

Even when the race doctor Pierre Dumas arrived to treat him, the real extent of his injuries was not immediately apparent. His face over the left cheekbone swelled up as if he had received a right hook in a pub brawl. Dumas smeared painkilling ointment over his cheek, making it look as if a sickly white mould was growing there. He was dazed and probably concussed: he spoke in Flemish to a Spanish rider he knew well, hardly the behaviour of a lucid man. He was advised, urged, implored to quit the race, the chorus led by Dumas, echoed by his teammates and his manager, Bob Lelangue. He kept pedalling. Why? He still cannot put his finger on it.

He was made to talk to television after that stage finish as he shivered in his transparent Adidas race cape, the arm of the loud-shirted interviewer placed protectively around his shoulder. The words slurred together as he tried to limit the movement in his jaw, but the sentences still came out fluently, courteously. The interrogation lasted five minutes. Why had he continued? Why had he made the pace down the final descent? Might he abandon in the morning? Was the Merckx era over? Did he feel he had few friends in the peloton? Did he feel Bernard Thévenet would be a worthy winner of the Tour de France? And finally, as he walked away to nurse his wounds, he was called back. Look, here was Thévenet, could he talk about Merckx, and could Merckx talk about him? And could they shake hands, please, for the cameras? A lesser man would have thrown a blue screaming hissy fit, raged about the need to get medical treatment. The stoicism of the man who had dominated cycling for seven years is a wonder to behold.

That evening X-rays showed he had broken his cheekbone – further tests after the race showed a double fracture, with a bone splinter floating near his sinuses. He had virtually no sensation in his jaw: he could only take fluids. Dumas and his medical team advised that if he continued the Tour, he did so at his own risk. The race was lost: before the crash, Thévenet had opened a gap of nearly three minutes which, even if Merckx had been in one piece, would have been impossible to close. 'Almost any other rider would have accepted this abundant excuse and abandoned the Tour.' Instead, Merckx continued. It was a Calvary, as the French call it, which lasted six days: out of the Alps through Châtel and Thonon-les-Bains, north-west to Chalon-sur-Saône after 256 kilometres, nine hours in the saddle and into Paris to the Champs-Elysées.

Rather than nursing his injuries, Merckx contested the rest of the race with Thévenet as he had fought at the finish at Avoriaz. To that first brace of seconds, he added fifteen in the next day's time trial at Châtel, and a further sixteen on the stage to Senlis when the Frenchman fell off near the finish. With Merckx fighting on in this way instead of opting for passive acquiescence, no one could question Thévenet's right to win the race. No one could argue that the Frenchman had had an easy ride. 'I didn't believe I was going to win the Tour until two laps from the finish on the Champs-Elysées,' Thévenet told me. 'I felt I couldn't leave the door open for him for a moment, he might jump. I didn't have a peaceful time.'

By staying in the race and contesting it to the finish, 'Merckx granted Thévenet a total triumph,' said one eyewitness. 'Had he retired, that victory would have been questionable.' Quite why he remained in that Tour Merckx himself could not say, although with hindsight he felt it was a foolish act that had hastened his eventual decline. One factor was the prize money that would make a massive difference to the incomes of the teammates who were dependent on him. His own explanation, to the television interviewer, was simple: 'Getting off by the side of the road is not my way.' The most simple explanation is this, however: the odds might have been heavily against him, but he still had a chance of winning. If he had gone home, and then Thévenet had fallen off in his turn or fallen ill, how would he have felt?

For years fans and media had looked on as Merckx dominated the sport with inexorable power. His feats were so hard to convey, to understand, that it was more straightforward to dismiss him as an automaton, a superhuman figure, 'the monster', 'the crocodile', 'the Cannibal'. Avoriaz and its aftermath showed facets of Merckx which had always been there, in spadefuls, but which had been overlooked. Professional conscience, all-consuming determination, unwillingness to submit to the dictates of fate, a sheer blind love for his métier, fear of doing something he would regret: he put all these things into public view in those six days. That explained why when he eventually reached Paris in second place – the first time in eight years he had finished a major Tour anywhere other than first – he was more popular than he had ever been. Half man, half bike, one writer had called him: after Avoriaz he was all too human.

It was twenty years between the day Eddy Merckx first entered my world, and the day I finally met him. On 13 July 1977 I came out of school in Exeter to find my father waiting in the car listening to the Tour de France commentary from the Alps on French radio. It had, he told me, been an extraordinary day on the race: thirty backmarkers eliminated, Eddy Merckx dropped by the leaders and suffering like a dog to stay in contention. That had coincided with the gift of the paperback of Geoffrey Nicholson's account of the 1976 Tour: *The Great Bike Race*, a book which I have read to pieces over the last thirty-five years. Nicholson painted an evocative picture of the greatest cyclist in the history of the sport. He described a distant man, with 'the graven features of a totem pole', who was so serious, so much of the time, that it had become a game among newspaper journalists to find pictures of him smiling. Merckx took his métier so seriously that no one was surprised at the chain of events that had kept him out of the 1976 race. An injury in the Giro d'Italia left Merckx to choose between his own desire to win six Tours, and professional obligation, which dictated he should continue the Giro even though he had no chance of winning. It was, said Nicholson, utterly typical that he chose the latter course.

At the close of 1997, I travelled to Belgium to interview Merckx and was struck by two things I had not expected. He had taken the trouble to wait for me at Brussels airport for my delayed flight with no sign of impatience let alone annoyance. He could have let me find my own way, or delegated the task to a minion; but no: we had an appointment and he was going to keep it. If that was a surprise, so was his height. In the old photographs I had seen, he had always looked no bigger than average for a cyclist. They were the classic pictures: Merckx bent over his bike in Paris–Roubaix 1970, Merckx being picked up off his bike after breaking the Hour Record in 1972, Merckx seeming to punch the pedals as he attacked yet again for yet another win. There was nothing to prepare me for the sight of the greatest cyclist in the world towering over the majority of the crowd in the arrivals hall.

Merckx's surprising height is an apt metaphor for a man who bestrides his sport, and world sport. The man waiting – surprisingly unrecognised by the public – at Zaventem that day was one of the most prolific winners ever seen in any field. In cycling, he will remain unique for the quantity of his victories as well as their quality. For several years, he managed the seemingly impossible feat of making this most volatile of sports as close to being predictable as it could ever be. The rate at which he won races in his best years will never be equalled: 250 wins in 650 starts between 1969 and 1973. In some years he was close to winning one in two races that he started. The tally is colossal: five Tours de France, five Tours of Italy – three times the magic 'double' of both races in the same year – three world road race championships, the record for stage wins in the Tour de France and for the number of days spent wearing the prestigious yellow jersey, the prized Hour Record and over thirty wins in one-day Classic races. It is a scale of achievement that was completely stunning at the time, and which will never be matched.

Merckx changed the standards by which cycling is judged, setting the bar impossibly high. He raced in a new way, always attacking, taking every race on from start to finish. His approach brooked no compromise, no matter where the race, what its context and no matter what the weather. He was the first rider to dominate the Tour, consistently, day by day, in the style followed later by Bernard Hinault, Miguel Indurain and Lance

Armstrong. Their Tour triumphs are sometimes compared to Merckx or considered greater but the Merckx victories have to be seen in their context. Each was part of a kaleidoscope of domination of an entire season, just as each season was part of a bigger picture of seven years' total ascendancy over his sport. In his status as the nonpareil of cycling, the eternal reference point, Merckx is the two-wheeled equivalent of Muhammad Ali, Pelé, Ayrton Senna.

There are other sides to Merckx as well. Like Pelé, like George Best, like Ali, he is a visual icon as well as a man who dominated his sport. There are the unforgettable images – Merckx like a crucified Christ after being punched by a spectator in the 1974 Tour, Merckx with his head angled as his full body strength is used to push the pedals round, Merckx with his arms and shoulders covered with snow in the Tour of Belgium in 1970. But the film footage is also extensive: *La Course en Tête*, *Stars and Watercarriers*, *The Greatest Show on Earth*. If Fausto Coppi is the cyclist whose life was a novel, Merckx's would be a film, but a documentary rather than a romance.

The sequence that best captures the visual essence of Merckx comes from *La Course en Tête*, where he is seen training on static rollers at his home near Brussels: the sweat drips down his nose and cheeks to gather in a puddle on the floor, the long legs whirl faster and impossibly faster again, the tyres rock back and forth, but the Elvis Presley quiff above the mod sideboards remains pristine. Like Fausto Coppi, Merckx is a style icon, but one for the 1970s: those sideburns and cheekbones, matched with white polo-neck jumpers, sharp suits, wide collars. He is one of the few men who have ever looked good in flares.

Capturing the essence of such a visual, sporting and human icon poses particular issues for a journalist. Ours is a reductive art: stripping what we are presented with to an immediate bite. The issues have to be explored within a limited window of time. You can't cover them all. The question I was mulling over all the way to Brussels was the same one I would have asked Senna, Ali or Pele, and which I was lucky enough, later, to be given the opportunity to ask other huge, and in some cases, prolific winners: the jockey Tony McCoy, Sir Chris Hoy, Serge Blanco, Lennox Lewis. What I wanted to know was not how Merckx became the greatest. The question in my mind was why?

Why the years of total focus? When defeat happened, why was the only solace to be found in victory, the only way that the sheet could be wiped clean? What had inspired in this man a need to win on such an epic scale, confined only by the sheer physical limitation of what one human body could achieve before it finally ran up the white flag? Why, when he had won a Classic such as Milan–San Remo five times, did he still want to win it again? Why, when you have an impregnable lead in the Tour de France, do you make a 140-kilometre solo escape, and add another eight minutes to your margin, as Merckx did at Mourenx in the 1969 Tour? Why, in short, was this man so insatiable?

With Merckx, it was clear that if his body had not eventually given way, he would have kept winning. Indeed, closer examination of his career suggests that he began to feel his physical limitations as early as the third year of his dominance. As the ride to Avoriaz and its aftermath showed, he was truly unstoppable, to the point of recklessness, in the same way that the true greats of mountaineering seem to ignore the potential consequences of their actions. The self-destruction that marked the end of Merckx's career was the cycling equivalent of the climber who continues towards the top of Everest or K2 knowing death is not far away. Rational thinking does not come into it.

I didn't expect a clear-cut answer from Eddy, but I got the beginnings of one. 'Passion, only passion' was the reply to my question, the word repeated like a mantra. 'At school they asked me what I wanted to do and I said "I want to be a racing cyclist". They said "but that's not a job". I don't know why it was [I felt like that]. There were no cyclists in my family. It really was just passion. I don't know how to explain it.' It was, he said, not merely a question of winning, but of fulfilling what you were given, to the best of your ability.

Human genius takes many forms, but it is not restricted to art, science or industry. Sport is a hobby to most of the world, but its supreme practitioners are as driven and creative as a Mozart or a Brunel, a Dickens or a Shakespeare. All seem to be possessed by their métier in the same way. The French writer Pierre Chany saw this, producing the perfect riposte for those who criticised Merckx for making cycling predictable: 'has anyone wondered whether Molière damaged theatre, Bach harmed music, Cézanne was detrimental to painting or Chaplin ruined cinema?'

What Merckx created in his eight years at the top of cycling was a series of little masterpieces. His escape to Mourenx, the Hour Record, or his attack to win his seventh Milan–San Remo were works of sporting genius. They were not born of brute force and ignorance, but each was the culmination of a lengthy process: countless hours of training, sleepless nights of worry, experience, acquired knowledge. They were not mere stunts to earn prize money. Famously, Merckx never knew what cash might be on offer for any given event. And as the 1975 Tour de France's denouement showed, he could lose in style. Cycling was about more than merely winning, or earning a good living.

Merckx is not an expansive man, but he was clearly capable of waxing lyrical in his guttural *Bruxellois* French about passion.

That intrigued me, because other greats of cycling I had met, most notably Bernard Hinault, were almost dismissive about their cycling careers. Others had regrets that seemed to consume them. Others had raced hard and didn't delve into the whys and wherefores. Merckx had expanded on it elsewhere: 'It's the most beautiful thing that there is in the whole world. If nature has given you exceptional ability it would be a shame not to use it. You have to work on what you are given. Otherwise you will have achieved nothing in your life and wasted what you have in you.' What drove him, he said in another interview, was 'dreaming [in my view another term for 'passion']. It was stronger than me. I was a slave to it. There was no reasoning involved.'

Passion was Merckx's word for what drove him, and it provided a perfectly adequate sound-bite answer for a magazine interview, but it didn't completely get to the heart of the question. Passion is a catch-all term for enthusiasm, drive, motivation. Merckx described it as the most beautiful thing in the world. With that veneration came a sense of his respect, duty and his fear of the guilt that would come were that duty not fulfilled. Merckx told me: 'As well as being the best, crossing the line in first place, the fact that you are making your living out of your passion is very important. When something is your passion and you can make it into your profession, that is the most beautiful thing anyone can have.' These are words that could have been spoken by a genius in any field of human endeavour, from Ernest Shackleton to Albert Einstein. Therein lies the eternal fascination with such figures.

As sports fans and sports writers, we spend our lives watching legends from a distance. We know what they do and how they do it. We rarely meet them. Some of us know the facts and statistics in more detail than may be entirely healthy. We marvel at the little strokes of genius produced by a Dan Carter or a

George Best, shake our heads at the insatiable urge of a McCoy, a Michael Schumacher or a Merckx, and perhaps hope that some of it may rub off on our own attempts to be the best we can. But we rarely understand why our idols are so driven.

For the bulk of the human race, 'the why' is the hardest thing to understand when we look at heroes who achieve on the scale of Merckx. That is because, as normal human beings, we are satisfied with what we can get, within certain limits. Most of us keep our lives in proportion. What we strive to comprehend is what drives these people to go beyond the limits of what is physically or psychologically reasonable. These men visit places that are out of reach of 99.9 per cent of the human race. Hence the eternal fascination.

Perhaps, first time round, I had dismissed the 'how' a little too readily. The how and the why are conjoined. The Merckx story is about competition pure and simple. Within cycling, Merckx is one of the few greats where the passion relates solely to two wheels. Coppi had his 'White Lady', a sexual intrigue that convulsed his country, and his place in Italian history as an icon of post-war reconstruction. Tom Simpson's tale was that of a tragically premature death in cycling's greatest drugs scandal. The story of Lance Armstrong encompasses cancer and controversy; Jacques Anquetil's drugs and sex as well as five Tour wins. A lack of 'reason' is the only side to Merckx, whose story was described by the French writer Philippe Brunel as 'a vocation fulfilled in exemplary style'.

The 'why' and the 'how' are not just about the man in question: they encompass the motivations that drive men to compete, what makes some better than others, and what made one man much better than all the rest. For once, it actually is about the bike.

PART ONE

THE 1960s

FATHER AND SON

He was too small to have any chance of winning. That was the feeling among the group of teenage cyclists, maybe fifteen strong, when the little lad attacked as they sped across the old market place in Enghien, a small town south-west of Brussels. The boy was aged sixteen years and four months, a couple of years younger than most of the others, and was riding a smaller gear, pedalling at a furious cadence on his single-speed bike. He would never keep it up. The local youths had put their heads together before the start and had decided that one of them should win; the attacker was not a local, indeed they had no idea who this youngster was in the red jersey on the blue bike. But he looked too small to hang on to the finish line located across the Brussels highway, a few hundred yards down the road, outside the Café Alodie – known as the Pink Café – in Petit-Enghien. Or so they thought.

The race on 1 October 1961 was just one of seven such events run in Enghien each year by the local cycling club, *Pedale Petit-Enghiennoise*, and one of thousands of circuit races held across Belgium between March and October. They were usually organised to add a bit of pizzazz to a local fair, or *kermis*, with signing-on, start and finish at the local café. The Enghien race was over eight laps of a small circuit taking in the town centre, with *primes* – intermediate prizes – in front of each of the three cafés as the race went past. *Kermis* circuits, some claim, are specially designed so that the lap time is just long enough for the spectators to pop inside after the bunch has passed, order a round of brown beers, and get outside again to catch the next lap. For this race, a tombola had enabled the cycling club to put up 6000 francs in prize money, with 400 to the winner. The bouquet and cup were handed to the victor by a local girl, Marianne Leyre, daughter of the local police chief who was making sure the race was run safely. She was a friend of the organisers' two daughters and it just happened to be her turn that day. She was a little put out because her platinum-blonde hair had been poorly dyed chestnut.

Petit-Enghien was the first of eighty victories that Edouard Merckx – as the brief report in the *Courrier d'Escaut* newspaper called him – would take as an amateur, the first of a total of 525 wins he would land in more than 1800 races he would start in his career. It was not a particularly auspicious event. He had raced a dozen times since his first outing in July, at Laeken, the location of the bike shop run by the former professional Félicien Vervaecke where he had bought his blue bike. He had abandoned four times, come close to winning in a couple. His studies and his work in his parents' grocer's shop left him little time to train: he estimated he had put in two training runs of twenty kilometers, plus the daily trip to and from school. He was felt to be too frail to use the same gear as the others, so he rode a smaller one in order not to put too much strain on his young legs. It put him at a disadvantage.*

The Merckx family were proud of their boy. Jenny Merckx, Edouard's mother, took the photograph of him smiling shyly alongside Marianne Leyre, bouquet and cup in his hand. Even then, in spite of his lack of success, young Edouard had two *supporters* – used in Flemish the English word implies a following more obsessive than in most sports – and so the vegetable merchant and the neighbour who lived above the bookshop

---

* Aficionados might like to know that the usual underage gear was 49x17; young Merckx was using 50x18.

across the road were invited for dinner that night. Although the following weekend Edouard Merckx was brought back to reality when he finished eighteenth in his last race of the season, he and his advisers drew confidence from that first victory. And no one would ever consider him 'too small to win' again.

Young Eddy had also been dismissed as too fat. Guillaume Michiels still smiles about that, more than half a century on. In the mid-1950s, Michiels was a professional cyclist who lived a few hundred yards away from the Merckxs' grocery, up what was then a steep hill but is now a gently sloping lawn in front of a block of flats. His mother helped the Merckx family in the shop, cleaning, cooking items while they manned the counter; they in turn helped her feed her four children with items from the business which was no longer quite good enough to sell, but could still be eaten. Michiels did not have a car – his father had died a few years earlier and the family was short of cash – so occasionally Eddy's father, Jules Merckx, a cycling fan, would help Guillaume get to races with a lift. On Sundays, when the shop closed at lunchtime, the family would come as well if the *kermis* was close by. It is likely that these were Eddy Merckx's first encounters with cycle racing.

One day, as they stood in the shop door, Eddy said to Guillaume – who was only ten years older than him – *'moi, je vais faire coureur* – I'm going to be a bike racer too.' Michiels laughs as he remembers it, at his own reaction rather than the youth's words. 'I said *"le foitie"'* – this is something he cannot translate from *Bruxellois* dialect, but it relates to corpulence – '"in five years you won't get through that door, Eddy, given how fat you are".' Ten, fifteen, twenty years later, they would joke about the exchange as Michiels drove Eddy from race to race, the small plump boy now the greatest cyclist the world had ever seen.

Even now, Woluwe is a curious mix of suburbia with hints of deep countryside. The villas and semi-detached houses cluster close together on the gentle slope, where the British Army placed an anti-aircraft battery after retaking the Belgian capital in 1944. The little suburb's centre with its avenue, vast Catholic church and its school is just over the crest of the hill. The great triumphal arch that marks the road to Brussels stands in one direction. Down the other way lies the deep forest that used to surround the Belgian capital. Just a few streets below where the Merckx family made their home above their grocery shop on Place des Bouvreuils, the vast old trees survive in thick knots now broken up with roads, parkland, new housing, motorways and business parks.

From his eighth-floor flat in Woluwe, Michiels paints a bucolic if hard-working picture of life in the Brussels suburb in the late 1940s and 1950s. The community is only a few kilometres to the south-east of the centre of Brussels, but in those days it had not quite been subsumed into the capital. Where there are now ranks of apartment blocks and houses, there were fields with peasants growing strawberries and beetroot and tending cattle. Children could be sent out to play in perfect safety. It was quite a contrast with what Jules and Jenny had experienced not long before they moved here with their one-year-old son in 1946. The greatest cyclist in the word was brought up in a very green suburb but he had been born in a community that had been ripped to shreds by atrocities of a ferocity and scale that are now barely imaginable.

Meensel-Kiezegem is a pair of small villages of some five hundred people fifty kilometres south-east of Brussels, in the peaceful rural heart of Flemish Brabant. It amounts to two little huddles of brick-built houses less than a mile apart on the top of a gently rolling hill. There have been many Merckxs in Kiezegem, the smaller of the two hamlets. Along with the name Pittomvils, Merckx is the most common on the stones in the small graveyard next to the brick-built church close to the road junction at the heart of the hamlet. One particular branch of the Merckx family, Rémy, his wife and their children, lived in no. 4 Kerkstraat, right next to the church at the cross-roads where the lines of houses converge. When war came and the Germans marched through Belgium, Rémy Merckx's family, and another landowner, Félix Broos, sided with the occupiers. Gaston Merckx, the third oldest of the sons, was a member of Vlaamse Wacht, a Flemish paramilitary organisation sympathetic to the Nazis.

By July 1944 the tide had turned in favour of the Allies and the resistance became more confident, more open in its actions. There was the occasional 'liquidation' of a collaborator: these were isolated events, not always followed up by the Germans and their local allies, but in Meensel-Kiezegem it was different. On 30 July 1944, as he was walking to the nearby fair at Altenrode, Gaston Merckx was shot dead, a little distance from the village, right at the end of Kerkstraat, where his family lived.

Reprisals from the German SS and the local paramilitaries were swift and deadly. There were two round-ups, on 1 and 11 August, when most of the male population was gathered in the playing field of the school in Meensel. In total ninety-one people, some from outside the villages, but sixty-three from Meensel and fifteen from Kiezegem, were transported to prisons in Leuven and Brussels where they were tortured before seventy-one of them were taken to Germany, mainly to the concentration camp at Neuengamme, near Hamburg. Only eight returned. The detainees were mainly men: a large propor-tion of the male inhabitants of Meensel in particular was detained, and deported.

Just under ten months later, the man who would make the name Merckx a byword for immense achievement, colossal physical and mental courage and an unstinting work ethic was born into this devastated community. His father, Jules, was a distant cousin of Rémy Merckx. Jules had married Eugénie (Jenny) Pittomvils, a farmer's daughter, on 24 April 1943. Edouard was their first child, born at 29 Tieltstraat on the outskirts of Kiezegem on 17 June 1945. The house is several hundred yards down the hill from the church, the last in the road heading north to the fields and the neighbouring village of Tielt-Winge; the village football pitch lies opposite. The birth was a difficult one; Jenny Merckx was initially assisted by neighbours and a local midwife. When the doctor eventually arrived, he had to use forceps, which left marks on the boy's forehead. He was christened Edouard Louis Joseph; the name Edouard ran in the family.

By the time of his birth, peace had been declared in Europe, but that did not leave Meensel-Kiezegem at peace. This was a small community: every face was known, memories were long where even minor events were concerned. The impact of the events of August 1944 was immense and long-lasting. Jules Merckx, father of young Edouard, appears to have been blameless. He is said to have hidden in a septic tank which fortunately had been cleaned out just before the Germans began searching the village. It can be assumed that if he had had any allegiance to Rémy Merckx and that branch of the Merckx family, he would not have concealed himself.

Guilt or innocence was only one part of the lasting issue, however. Before the Allies appeared Gaston Merckx's three brothers, Maurice, Marcel and Albert, had escaped, most probably to Germany, and no one knew where they were: they were never seen again. There was no immediate closure. There were two waves of reprisals in Meensel-Kiezegem, one following liberation in September 1944, and a second when the few survivors of the round-ups returned to the villages from May 1945.

As in other communities across Europe, there was harassment and violence and destruction of property. Armed men searched houses at dead of night for collaborators who had escaped. In August 1945, one of the handful of men who had survived the concentration camps returned to the village and heard rumours that one of the Merckx brothers might be hiding on a farm owned by a member of the Pittomvils family, Louis. A group of former resistance men gathered by night and burned the place. Louis Pittomvils was shot dead, although he was innocent of any misdeed. The perpetrators were never brought to justice.

Jules, Jenny and young Edouard moved to the Brussels suburbs a year after the war ended. The events of 1944 and 1945 in Meensel-Kiezegem may or may not have played a part in the decision, but they are there in the background nonetheless. The community had been ripped to pieces by the atrocities, and the family had suffered. Two of Jenny's brothers, Petrus and Josef, had been deported to Germany. Josef died in Bergen-Belsen on 14 March 1945. Petrus was a 110-kilo colossus when he left but returned a wraith of just thirty-eight kilos, his legs deeply scarred from beatings by the Gestapo. His doctors said it was better that he did not discuss his experiences. Two other members of the wider Pittomvils family had died in Neuengamme.

In those difficult post-war years, the opportunity to lease the grocer's shop must have been too good to pass up on. Jules had left his family farm to work as a carpenter in the nearby town of Leuven but did not get on with his boss and was unhappy. Jenny's sister had a shop in the Brussels suburb of Anderlecht and Jenny went there regularly to help her so she knew what was involved. It was Jenny who heard about the grocer's shop being up for lease; speaking to the writer

Stéphane Thirion, she said, 'I wanted something else, for us and our son.' The chance for her son to learn French also mattered. Jules was less enthusiastic, she said, and 'accepted out of love'.

Jenny Merckx was also the driving force behind the running of the shop. It was not far from her sister, and also within reach of Jenny's parents, who remained in Kiezegem: the family returned to visit the farm at weekends. Eddy Merckx himself makes the point that they were warmly welcomed. He raced there at least twice in his early years; once in an event that has never been recorded when he was about twelve, the second a race in his first season, 1961, which he did not finish.

The grocer's shop opened by Jules and Jenny in September 1946 in Place des Bouvreuils, Woluwe-Saint-Pierre, was in a tiny square, barely fifty metres across, well away from the bustle of Woluwe's commercial centre. It lay on the south side of the square, which still boasts a newsagent's in another of the buildings: a small plaque in the traffic island in the middle of the street denotes the fact that Eddy Merckx was brought up here. They had moved a mere fifty kilometres – nowadays a rapid run down the motorway that passes the university town of Leuven – but the Merckx family did more than merely move house: they crossed the language divide, from a Flemish-speaking area, Brabant, to one where French was spoken, leaving the grandparents behind.

Belgium is a linguistic and cultural patchwork, divided between the largely Flemish-speaking north, Flanders, and the French-speaking south, Wallonia, with French-speaking enclaves to the west, Hainaut Occidental, and in the centre, the region around Brussels. It would be inaccurate to say that Walloons and Flandrians are completely separate: during research for this book, I kept meeting couples who were bilingual. The distinction between the various areas is clear, however. Like most Flandrians, Jules spoke only Flemish, although Jenny was fluent in French, having been taught the language by her grandmother. As well as crossing the language divide, they were also crossing a social divide: they were country people in a relatively rich suburb.

The move from Meensel-Kiezegem to Brussels had an important effect on young Edouard's future career, his identity, and the impact he would make on his divided nation. Most fundamentally, the name that is now synonymous with world domination in cycling would probably not have been Eddy. Merckx, with its consonants, is a Dutch name. The contraction of Edouard to Eddy is a customary French nickname. Had he been a pure Flandrian, it would probably have been shortened to Ward.

Had Edouard become Ward rather than Eddy, he would probably still have been a racing cyclist, given that Meensel-Kiezegem had its own champion, the double Paris–Roubaix winner, Georges Claes, who ran a local bike shop and took groups of youngsters from the area out riding on Sundays. That alternative trajectory would have made Merckx another member of a generation of cyclists from Belgium's Flemish-speaking regions that was arguably the most talented produced by a single nation at any time in cycling history. Merckx's contemporaries included stars such as Walter Godefroot, Herman Van Springel, Eric Leman, Roger De Vlaeminck and Freddy Maertens. Ward Merckx might still have turned out to be the strongest of the lot, but he might not have ended up a cycling demi-god.

Young Eddy was a hyperactive child who wanted to be outdoors, something his mother struggled with, especially when the twins Michel and Micheline were born in May 1948. He spent hours in the little hills and woods of the south-east Brussels suburbs and loved to spend time on his grandmother's farm at Meensel-Kiezegem helping to look after the animals. Woluwe must have been a child's paradise with lakes and deep forests just a couple of blocks away. It was no wonder that Eddy sometimes stayed out longer than he should and returned covered in scratches from his adventures. 'It was permanent anguish,' Jenny said. On one occasion he went fishing, and was out so long that the police were called and he got into trouble – the worst of it being, from Eddy's point of view, that he was grounded. He was kept in for a day after climbing a crane when his parents were having gutters installed and, on another occasion, he began playing in a building site with his friends as night fell: they had a climbing race up another crane, and he was twenty metres higher than the next youth by the time they were stopped.

That set the pattern for a conflicted childhood and adolescence. Eddy would try to escape constraints such as school and the confines of the shop, which became cramped as the family expanded, with all the children sharing one room and a lodger occupying another. His mother would try to restrain him. Jules would grumble at him that he would never be any good at anything, Guillaume Michiels recalls, for example, when he was carrying empty bottles out of the shop, and dropped one or two. Eventually, thanks to the bike, he would escape for good and become a nomad, living almost constantly on the road, either training, racing or travelling.

Eddy took after his father, who had been a good runner and a better than average footballer, and remained a cycling fan. Merckx junior was not the healthiest child, suffering from earache, headaches, growing pains and cramps, but that didn't restrain him. Any sport would do: Eddy would try them all – boxing, basketball, table tennis, lawn tennis, and football as

well as races on his bike round the local streets. He played
lawn tennis for his school, and inside-right for the junior side
of the local team which later became Royal White Star Woluwe
(motto today *Be The Best*). After one match, he was made to
stay behind so he could be given a full set of kit as a reward
for scoring several goals. A photograph in the Merckx family
album, reprinted in Pierre Thonon's account of his early years
(*Eddy Merckx, l'Irrésistible Ascension d'un Jeune Champion*)
shows him borne shoulder-high by his peers after winning a
local boxing tournament, one glove punching the air in the
style of Muhammad Ali.

   Such successes mattered. He was an immensely competitive
child. He loved playing cards, and was extremely unhappy if
he didn't win a table-tennis match or if he lost at dominoes.
Later, he was just as competitive in poker games in race hotels
while killing time with his teammates. He had a love of mechanical things from early on, making soapbox carts and sometimes
stripping his first racing bike and repainting it. He was curiously
sensitive – he cried when his younger brother and sister told
him Father Christmas did not exist, and his mother confirmed
the devastating news. All these traits would shine through in
the man and the champion.

   The Merckxs were a Catholic family. There was mass on
Sunday – something young Eddy found difficult because of
the need to keep still for more than a short while – and prayers
in May in front of the statue of Mary at the end of the road.
It was a hard-working environment. Sunday was a busy day in
the shop, because competing businesses were closed, so young
Eddy had to help out cutting ham and cheese, weighing fruit
and serving behind the counter, while his friends were playing.

   Later, Eddy would insist that they were not a rich family.
These things are relative. The accommodation above the shop
was cramped – Jules's comment when Jenny told him she was

expecting twins was 'where shall we put them?' – but the Merckxs were by no means poor. They certainly did not experience the near-starvation that was the background to the early lives of Fausto Coppi, Federico Bahamontes, Rik Van Steenbergen, or even a contemporary such as Luis Ocaña, who walked four miles a day each way to school in the Pyrenees, without a coat, as his parents could not afford one. The few pictures of the young Coppi show groups of children with the stick legs and big heads that speak of deprivation. Young Eddy has fat cheeks and is often dressed up for this or that celebration. The Merckxs could afford a car and seaside holidays. Eddy would be given his chance to 'move up' socially in the conventional way, by studying and getting a good job, but he chose cycling. Unlike Coppi, Bahamontes or Van Steenbergen, cycling was a life choice for Eddy Merckx. The alternative was not subsistence agriculture or industrial labouring, but something easier and probably nearly as lucrative: a comfortable middle-class life. Eddy clearly needed to race his bike but he didn't have to do it out of economic necessity.

Jules and Jenny Merckx were contrasting characters. 'My mother was very gentle, with beautiful manners, very concerned at the idea I might have an accident,' recalled Eddy. 'I inherited her kind nature, perhaps a bit too much of it.' As for Jules, 'nervous, introverted and permanently worried . . . and not given to talking much' were terms that Eddy used to describe him. They could also be used for Eddy himself. Jules had a short fuse, but was never angry for long. He was 'not a man for discussion. Most of the time, he preferred a slap to a long sermon,' said Eddy. Jules liked to use maxims such as 'the more you have, the more you want' and 'in life, you will always find someone who is superior'. The first applied to his elder son, the second clearly didn't.

Trained as a carpenter, turned grocer, Jules's life 'was work, work again, and always work,' said Eddy. Early in the morning,

Jules would go to the market to buy fresh vegetables for the shop: every day in summer, three or four times a week in winter, on foot because initially at least they did not have a car. His acute sensibility made him shy, partly because of the language barrier no doubt. It was Jenny who served behind the counter in the shop, while Jules put his carpentry skills to use in making the wooden boxes in which the goods were displayed, working through the night to do so. The picture painted of Jules is that of an economic migrant, working his fingers to the bone for fear that he might fail and have to return whence he came.

He was a despot, said Eddy's younger brother Michel, a patriarchal character. 'No one dared put their spoon in their soup before him.' Michel recalled him as an 'unhappy ascetic, a man skinned alive, a sensitive character who hid his feelings with a tyrant's image', a man who worried so much it made him ill, and who would then hide the resulting stomach pains. It was Eddy who was most often on the receiving end of his temper – so disruptive an influence that at times Jules had to soak his head in cold water to calm him down. And on occasion, it was Eddy who would intervene to ensure that he got punished rather than his siblings.

Like a good Catholic father, Jules was strict: plates had to be cleared at the dinner table, and clear moral lines were laid down, as Eddy found out at the age of seven when he sneaked a toy off one of his teachers' desks, then told his mother it was a present. There were occasional little acts of rebellion. The teenage Eddy would sometimes smoke illicit cigarettes and would be berated when his father realised what was going on. One day, Eddy insisted on the barber shaving his head like a convict's. Tellingly, the youth was so sure this was what he wanted that he refused to get out of the barber's chair unless the razor was used. That didn't go down well either.

Guillaume Michiels recalls the Merckx parents as being 'too kind, too generous', something that would later be said of their celebrated son. 'When he raced, Eddy had four or five local supporters. After the race on a Sunday, Mme Merckx would say "come and drink a glass". Then they would stay to eat – because Jenny had the shop, it was just a matter of cutting a few slices of ham from behind the counter. Eddy would say *ma mère invite tout le monde*' – my mum asks everyone round. Michiels describes Jules as 'a man who would get an idea and stick to it'.

As his son grew increasingly famous, Jules would immerse himself in his work, and stay away from bike races. 'He was an introvert, he would never show his feelings, which he drowned in litres of coffee. He could not express his pride,' Jenny Merckx told Thirion. Eddy described his father as 'hypersensitive', and put it down to his shyness, which Jules himself apparently viewed as a weakness. Merckx senior was naïve, lost money to merchants who were more cunning – and again, his son would later show similar traits. Jules was a worrier, who, when he took his son to his first bike race in Laeken, on the other side of Brussels, ordered a taxi to make sure they wouldn't get lost. And he was also a perfectionist, who would watch his son cleaning his racing bike in the evenings and would then clean it again himself, just to make sure.

Jules Merckx's only distraction from his work was his long-standing love of cycling. In 1935, at the age of fifteen, he had ridden his bike the fifty-five kilometres from Meensel-Kiezegem south to Floreffe, close to Namur, to watch Jean Aerts become world road race champion. Eddy Merckx and his father were both fans of Constant Ockers – Stan to the Walloons, Stanneke to the Flemish – the Antwerp champion whose career coincided with Merckx's childhood years. Eddy was only six when Ockers came second to Coppi in the 1952 Tour de France, only ten when he won the 1955 world road race championship. Racing around the neighbourhood, Merckx played the role of Ockers while his friends acted the parts of Rik Van Steenbergen or the Flandrian hero Brik Schotte. He was only eleven when Ockers died of head injuries sustained in a track race at Antwerp, on 29 September 1956. Jenny Merckx was aware of the death of her husband and son's hero, and it was one reason why she was initially against Eddy becoming a cyclist. She remained worried about her son racing for many years: when he eventually quit bike racing after seventeen years in the saddle, she said it was the biggest relief of her life.

Merckx senior and junior were by no means Ockers's only fans: briefly, in the mid-1950s, Ockers became massively popular throughout Belgium for his combative racing style and his funeral was close to being a state occasion. Given Merckx's future career, Ockers was an intriguing role model. He was not a beefy Flandrian in the Van Steenbergen mould, but a small man, aggressive in his racing style. He was not a pure Classics man but able to perform in the Tours and the hillier Classics such as Flèche Wallonne and Liège–Bastogne–Liège, a rider who had all-round talent as both sprinter and climber. But unlike Merckx, who would blossom from his early twenties, Ockers did not achieve greatness until well into his thirties.

Merckx's admiration for Ockers reflected the fact that his view of cycling as a child was subtly different from that of a pure Flandrian. 'People where I lived called me "Tour de France",' he told me, adding that he wasn't interested in the Classics – something which would have been unthinkable for a child brought up in Flanders. Another reason for this was the fact the great one-day races took place on a Sunday. On that day he would have been working in the shop or was perhaps en famille with his grandmother at Meensel-Kiezegem. 'I listened to the Tour on the radio and my father took me to see it two or three times, and a couple of times he took me to see the six-day at the Brussels Palais des Sports', he told me in 1997. Still more improbably for a young Belgian, another boyhood hero was Jacques Anquetil, whose best years coincided with Eddy's adolescence. Merckx's wife Claudine told the writer François Terbéen: 'You can repeat it and shout it loud, Eddy placed Anquetil above them all, he was his hero. He dreamed only of him and deeply admired him.'

Eddy had begun riding a bike at three or four and by the age of eight he was riding to school, climbing back up the steep Kouterstraat every day. Later he was given a more substantial machine to deliver packages for his father. The story went that he didn't get paid tips from customers because he was the boss's son, so he transferred his services to the local milkman, which meant that he could save up for a racing bike. He used his bicycle to brave trams and cars to visit a bakery where they sold a cake called 'the atomic bomb'. On one occasion when he was with his mother, he broke the pedal of his kid's bike trying to catch a *vélomoteur* on a cycle path: he fell off and hit his head.

Jenny Merckx was not particularly happy at the idea of her son racing his bike, particularly as he became more serious about it. In 1960, at the age of fifteen, Eddy watched the Olympic Games road race, televised from Rome. The event was won by the USSR's Viktor Kapitonov, and the youngster set himself a target: he would be selected to ride in the 1964 Games in Tokyo. He had already raced his bike, at the age of twelve, in an unofficial event at Meensel-Kiezegem, against a field mainly composed of older children, up to eighteen. Jenny, on the other hand, had looked into it and had been told

– correctly – that the dropout rate was high; that no matter how promising a young cyclist's talent might be, only a few ever made a living out of it. She felt that her son's health was not suitable, and that Eddy was intelligent enough to pass his exams. She probably also feared that disappointment would make him unhappy. Jules, on the other hand, was apparently more cold-blooded about it: 'let him go and fight in the peloton if he doesn't want to go to school. Maybe he'll come back in tears.'

In the summer of 1961, Eddy did not go on the usual seaside holiday but stayed at home to help his father in the shop. That enabled him to earn enough to take out his first racing licence, and he rode his first race a month after his sixteenth birthday. His mother, according to some versions, was kept in the dark. Eddy and his father had worked out that being a cyclist was not in her plans for her son. The race at Laeken was a comedy classic. Eddy was wearing shoes that were too tight for his feet. He couldn't stand the pain they gave him and had to pull in by the road and wait for his father to come along in his van with another pair. He was determined to finish the race anyway and took various shortcuts to reach the finish, coming in two minutes ahead of the front runners. He probably should have been disqualified but was awarded sixth place, but it would be five weeks before he again came in the top ten.

It was clearly his father who was the driving force in his bike racing, but the relationship between father and son was a largely unspoken one. Jules took Eddy to every race as a youth, sometimes taking a lift in a wholesaler's lorry, but they rarely talked much. 'He transmitted his emotion to me,' Eddy recalled for Stéphane Thirion in *Tout Eddy*. 'When I won he would have tears in his eyes. He would say, "Eddy, how on earth have you done it again?" When I married, one day he just stopped coming. He never explained why.' Perhaps Jules felt that he no longer had a place as his son's key supporter, and felt embarrassed to be in the wings. 'Maybe I just wanted to make my parents proud of me – my father was . . . very hard, very severe with us. I'm probably a bit like him.' Jules died young, in 1983, after a life of hard work, little sleep and many cigarettes. Eddy felt he had been 'satisfied' with what his son had achieved, although he never said it.

It was not just Jules. Both Merckx's parents were closer to him than might have been the case in other families. He left home at a relatively late age, twenty-two, and other riders noted the time he spent on the telephone to them at night early in his career. There was pressure from Jenny as well, but more subliminally. 'I think I wanted to show my mother that it was important in life to do what you loved. And also that I could make my way without going to university because to start with she wasn't keen on my riding the bike. She wanted me to study, to go to university and have a stable, permanent job.' There was no safety net, once the decision was taken to drop his studies: it was worth going through all the pain and the angst to avoid any sense that his mother might be thinking 'I told you so' or his father might think he had not tried enough. He was, in short, caught between a workaholic, perfectionist father and a worrying mother. He inherited the best of both, and would try to live up to both.

Victory in Petit-Enghien gave young Merckx confidence, and it prompted Félicien Vervaecke to take more of an interest. That winter, the craggy old professional took Merckx to the velodrome at Schaerbeek, in the centre of Brussels, conveniently between the Merckxs' grocery in Woluwe and his bike shop in Laeken. Track racing is the perfect entrée for young cyclists, developing their pedalling speed, racing skills and the ability to negotiate a fast-moving bunch. The year 1962 began with young Merckx's second victory, in the *kermis* race at Haacht on 11 March, with no flukish element to it: he escaped early on, and was never seen again. As they say in Belgium, there was 'no one else in the photograph'. It was in that year that Eddy Merckx decided to become a full-time cyclist, surprisingly soon for one who had less than a year's racing behind him.

ARRIVA MERCKX

Via Roma, San Remo, 19 March, 1966

Eleven cyclists sprint flat out along the straight, slightly down-hill street to contest the finish of Milan–San Remo, the opening one-day Classic of the cycling season. Looking down past the coffee bars and ice cream shops, the spectators see four men ahead of the rest, one pair on each side of the road as they fight out victory in the race the Italians call *La Primavera*, Spring. On the extreme left two Italians: Michele Dancelli in the green, white and red national champion's jersey, and just in front of him Adriano Durante, in the light grey of the Salvarani team. The far right-hand side of the road belongs to Belgium: close to the gutter is Herman Van Springel, wearing the white of Mann-Grundig, and also in white, for Peugeot-BP, a few feet to his left, Eddy Merckx.

He is still only twenty years old, with less than a year's professional racing behind him, and his body language exudes the enthusiasm of a teenager. His elbows are spread wide at a ludicrous angle as he pushes and pulls every last gram of power out of his thigh muscles. His chin is close to touching the handlebars. His shock of thick black hair is pushed back by the wind; intense desire shines from his eyes. At the line the victory is his by a wheel from Durante and half a bike from Van Springel.

Merckx will go on to win more than thirty Classics, and he will ride victorious up Via Roma a further six times in the next ten years. But the first one matters more than any of the others. Merckx will become synonymous with a particular style of racing, and will become the benchmark by which every cycling champion is judged. Those final metres on Via Roma mark the end of the beginning, the final seconds of an apprenticeship that had lasted only a few months and was a happier experience than formal education.

School was something that young Eddy endured rather than embraced, from the first day he went, when the teacher – a regular customer at the grocer's shop in Place des Bouvreuils – had to bring him home because he cried deafeningly. He changed his ways, however, after it was explained to him that his mother was tired, being pregnant with the twins, and he should go without complaint, to lighten the load. But he had trouble concentrating, and found looking out of the window more enticing than listening to the teacher.

He struggled with homework. There were too many distractions; he would rather help his father by delivering bread on his bike than do the work he was set. By his mid-teens, Eddy was suffering with written French, mainly because it was not his first language, as he had been brought up speaking Flemish at home. Jenny recalled writing letter after letter to explain why his work had not been done. At a meeting between the headmaster and the Merckx parents, it was agreed that Eddy would aim to qualify as a physical education teacher and, in the spring of 1961, his mother managed, briefly, to reconcile Eddy's ambition in cycling and her fears for his studies by reaching a compromise: he would be allowed to race during the holidays if he got good results in his end-of-year exams. He came sixth out of thirty-six: good enough, in other words.

The teachers struggled, but the two key men in young Eddy's amateur cycling career found him a willing, rapid learner. Both contacts came, directly and indirectly, via Jules Merckx. It was Guillaume Michiels who gave Merckx his first cycling jersey, in the colours of Faema, the team which had been made legendary by Rik Van Looy, and which was to be forever associated with Merckx. There can be no doubt about the youngster's commitment: before that first race in 1961, the sixteen-year-old unpicked the stitched Faema logos from the woollen jersey, as it was not permitted to wear the colours of a professional sponsor. Michiels later became confidant, driver, leg-rubber, the man who rode a motorbike in all weathers with Eddy's front wheel inches from the back bumper as he worked on his speed and endurance.

It was Michiels who introduced his young protégé to Félicien Vervaecke, scion of a great Flandrian cycling family and a legendary member of the pre-war Belgian Tour de France team. Vervaecke had once been a great rival of Gino Bartali and now owned a bike shop in Laeken, where Eddy rode his first race, on the opposite side of Brussels from Woluwe. In his mid-fifties, gap-toothed and craggy-faced, Vervaecke had ridden the Tour seven times, twice winning the best climber's prize and finishing on the podium three times. He was not a man who said much in public, being as quiet as Eddy and Jules, but he was to be a key influence, drawing up young Eddy's training plans. Most importantly of all, he restrained the young blood from expending too much energy in his amateur years. Eddy would eventually wear himself out racing, but Vervaecke's ministrations ensured that he came into professional cycling fresher than most.

Under Vervaecke's supervision, Eddy began racing in Schaarbeek at Brussels' old Palais des Sports track – just a few years away from being demolished – on Tuesdays during the winter of 1961–2. The story is told that Rik Van Steenbergen, no less, became a fan of the youngster. '"The Boss" would be seen running to the edge of the track in the Palais des Sports, shouting "no, this time he can't do it, they'll get him"; a few seconds later he would subside, catching his breath and muttering "Fantastic, he hung on. Fantastic . . ."' Rik I (as opposed to Rik II, Van Looy, The Emperor) admired the young Merckx's way of riding every track race. The youth would attack two or three laps from the end, gaining twenty to thirty metres, then try to hang on ahead of the pursuing bunch. He usually managed it, a tribute to his pedalling speed and his courage. The track brought a marked improvement to his road racing. Early in 1962, and by now a member of the local cycling club, based in Evere, Eddy won four of his first five races, although he was riding to a restricted programme – one race per weekend, training on Wednesday afternoons only.

In late spring, however, the conflict between his studies and his racing loomed again. Eddy had been made to repeat a year of school as his results were not up to scratch. That winter, he should have been at French lessons on Tuesday afternoons, but because he wasn't his marks had declined accordingly. On the other hand, he wanted to prove he could earn his living on a bike. The conflict would soon be resolved. Jenny had an operation. Help was needed in the shop. Eddy wanted out of school. It all added up.

The turning point came on 1 May 1962, the day before school resumed after the Easter holidays. Eddy won a race south-west of Brussels at Hal (where he had already raced and won in March). He finished alone, four minutes ahead of the next lad, a massive margin at junior level, where the races are relatively short. Beforehand, Jenny had said that if Eddy didn't win that day he would have to study and pass his exams. 'My husband phoned about 5 p.m.,' Jenny Merckx said. 'He didn't have to say much: I understood immediately from the tone of his voice. I knew I had lost.' Eddy came home with 850 Belgian francs in his pocket – 400 for first prize, 450 for intermediate *primes*. 'He held the money out to me, shouting so loud that he could be heard on the other side of the square, "I've won. Hurray! I don't have to go to school any more". It wasn't what we'd agreed the day before [her point, presumably, being that she had not said in as many words that he could give up his studies] but what was the use in keeping on fighting about it?' Two days later the headmaster of his school called Jenny to ask if Edouard was ill. Why else would he not have come back to school? Jenny didn't quite have the courage to say that Eddy had quit school to devote himself to cycling full-time (although the head knew it involved bike racing: he had seen Eddy's name in the papers, where the results of the Tuesday races at the Palais des Sports were printed).

With the full support of his family, the seventeen-year-old went from strength to strength. His father ran him around in the grocery van. His mother kept tabs on his diet. Vervaecke supervised his training and delivered nuggets of advice. Eddy won twenty-four races in 1962, impelled by the knowledge that he had made a deal with his parents and he had no option but to keep to his side of it. 'I didn't have the right to let anyone down,' Merckx recalled. 'I had to keep to the rules – never miss training, be self-disciplined, always give my best. I had taken responsibility so I had to live up to it.' Some of the amateur racers who had watched him win his first event at Petit-Enghien stopped travelling to races in the north of Brussels: there was usually only one winner.

The big objective of 1962 was the Belgian junior champion-ship at Libramont in the Ardennes in early September. Michiels told him before the start that he might struggle to make the top fifteen. Eddy's response was direct: 'If I can't make the first five, I might as well change professions right now.' He took the trouble to inspect the course beforehand and won, of course, after riding a perfect race: holding back when the early move went and attacking to join the leaders. The win was not as simple as many of the others that would follow, but it underlined Merckx's utter determination. He bridged first to the lead group, then to one lone rider, Daniel De Hertogh, who in turn could not stay with Merckx as he pushed hard around one corner. That left Merckx alone in the lead with a lap to go. On that final lap, a strong chase group of half a dozen came together, and closed to about a hundred metres just before the final kilometre. At the line, Merckx had only a few metres' lead: in the finish picture, it looks as if he is leading in the group in a sprint.

Merckx's amateur career was short, and it left him physically fresh and hungry for success when he turned professional, unlike many talented amateurs who were pushed hard in their formative years. Vervaecke and his father were in complete agreement: Eddy had to race a relatively light programme as an adolescent, in order to permit his body to recover and develop. He was steered away from stage races, prevented from racing on successive days so that his body could develop unhindered. This also meant he had little time to fall into bad habits. There was no chance to remain in a comfort zone, taking one straightforward win after another. Later, Merckx was to say that this was the most important thing Vervaecke did for him, but what is particularly impressive is that he actually followed the advice. Vervaecke also made him use a lower gear than might have been expected, to ensure that he developed a rapid pedalling style – *souplesse* as the French call it – rather than hammering on a big gear to gain early successes that would be meaningless in the long term.

Vervaecke was important in other ways. He also just happened to be an occasional mechanic to the Belgian national cycling team and understood something of the politics involved. He advised Merckx to build a relationship with Lucien Acou, the former top track racer who ran the team, and to that end Merckx would drop into Acou's café near the abattoirs in the Brussels locale of Cureghem. The smoke-filled café was not the place to talk bikes; he was invited into the living quarters above, where, inevitably, he encountered Acou's daughter, Claudine, who was a year younger than him, and had her eyes set on a teaching career. She had already heard his name, because when her father was asked who had won a given race, he tended to reply: 'Eddy Merckx, again'. When they finally met, she was struck by the fact that he was wearing shorts.

Claudine had no intention of becoming the wife of a cyclist, having seen her father covered in cuts after falling off on the track. That didn't deter Eddy, although when they first met he was 'flirting a bit' with the daughter of one of his supporters. As he said later, 'to start with I went to see Acou, then it was Claudine'. At one point, the national coach pointed this out to his daughter, to her great embarrassment. Claudine said that she knew as soon as they met that they would become husband and wife, but the courtship lasted four years; the marriage is now approaching forty-five years and counting.

There were other influences, among the group of twenty or twenty-five professional riders then living in the Brussels area. Guillaume Michiels and others would meet in the centre of the city, at the start of the main road to Leuven; the little training group also included the local star Emile Daems. As a winner of Paris–Roubaix, the Giro di Lombardia and Milan–San Remo and a multiple stage victor in the Giro d'Italia and Tour de France, Daems was probably the biggest *Bruxellois* star of the time. Another was Willy Vannitsen, equally talented, also a Classic winner, but not as devoted to his métier. The half-dozen or so regulars would cover up to two hundred kilometres depending on the weather, the wind and the numbers.

'One day Guillaume said *"tiens,* I've got a young rider I know, he's not bad," and that was Merckx. He didn't come regularly, he was still racing as an amateur, in fact he might have been at the *débutant* stage, but he was already strong.' As they rode, the pros would play at racing on their bikes, attacking each other, dropping a weaker element, chasing, working together. One day they left Merckx 150 metres behind. There were four of them in front, and they thought they would see what he was made of. They rode hard together for fifteen kilometres; at the end of it, they turned round, and the teenager was still 150 metres behind, having kept up with the four of them on his own.

Sometimes, they took in a cobbled climb at Reimy Pont, south of Brussels in the French-speaking part of Brabant. It was not long, 250 or 300 metres, Daems says, but steep – 15 per cent. The group would race up it, with a mock finish at the top. A tarmac path ran alongside the cobbles, and the riders would fight to use this smoother surface, which was far easier to ride on. Again, Merckx showed his strength: on one occasion – when he was only in his teens – he managed to match the pace of the older men, but he did so while riding on the cobbles as they took the smoother route up the tarmac. Already, Daems recalls, he was clearly more powerful than might have been expected for his age.

Also on some of those rides was Bob Lelangue, a former Belgian amateur champion, who would go on to be a *directeur sportif* at Merckx's Molteni team. And, at about this time, Merckx first got to know a young footballer with the Sporting Anderlecht club, when the pair of them were waiting for their respective parents in the same café in the Brussels suburb. The same youth, tall and blond, also turned up at the grocer's shop in Place des Bouvreuils to sell coffee in the mornings before he went to train. Later in life, Paul Van Himst and the cycling star would become firm friends, and shining lights in Belgian sport.

Another acquaintance from his teenage years was Patrick Sercu, a young sprint specialist from just outside Ghent who bore more than a passing resemblance to Eddy – high cheek-boned, solemn-faced, black-haired – and would go on to become the greatest six-day track racer of all time. The pair struck up a firm friendship from the day when they both needed a partner for a Madison race on the track in Brussels. Sercu's father and Vervaecke were old friends and put them together: they were regular winners over the winter. 'I went to their house often to eat when I was at the barracks in Brussels doing my military service,' Sercu told me. 'Eddy was timid, didn't talk much, but I was the same.' The sprinter described Jenny Merckx as being like an Italian mother, constantly filling his plate, while Jules was more reserved, darker in his moods. The pair were perfectly matched on the track – Sercu the sprinter, Merckx the stayer – and went on to win ten six-days together. Later, Merckx helped Sercu to the green points jersey in the 1974 Tour de France.

At Vervaecke's insistence, Merckx rode only one stage race as an amateur. The Tour of Limburg, in May 1963, was a fairly flat five-dayer, which he won by taking victory in the time trial stage. One journalist of the time recalled a thin, timid-looking youth with dark black eyes, who turned into a dominant force once he was on his bike. Merckx turned down invitations to race in the biggest amateur events of the day, the Warsaw–Berlin–Prague Peace Race and the Tour de l'Avenir – run by the Tour de France organisers to discover future Tour heroes – but did take a trip to race in East Germany in 1963. There, he beat Gustav Schur and other Eastern bloc greats; all men who had amateur licences but were professional in all but name.

By 1964, with fifty-five junior and amateur wins to his name, he was established as one of a number of rising Belgian stars in contention to ride the world road championships. It was not smooth progress, in spite of his efforts to forge links with Lucien Acou. The generation of Belgian cyclists born in the years around the end of the war was extraordinarily strong, so competition to get in the national team was even more intense than normal. A key selection race was the Belgian amateur championship, on a tricky course, and Merckx was one of many riders to fall off, crashing twice. He had already fallen the week before at a circuit race in Woluwe – while sprinting for a *prime*, an electric razor as it happened – and the selectors had found out because an arm injury had kept him off his bike for the previous week. Merckx had ripped a tendon in his arm, which had been operated on without anaesthetic. They were not keen to select a rider who seemed accident-prone.

A far bigger problem emerged, however, when he underwent the compulsory medical examination at the pre-world championship training camp. He had a minor heart problem, the doctor declared, and ironically in view of the restraint Vervaecke and his father had made him show, the diagnosis was that he had been racing too much. Not surprisingly, Eddy was devastated. 'It was like a hammer blow to the head. I thought my life was going to change just like that.' This was not the first time Merckx had been turned down. In 1963, he had also been in contention for the world championship team, but his form deserted him at a critical moment and he was dropped from the shortlist.

This time round, Mme Merckx intervened. First the family doctor was called on: there was no problem with Eddy, he said. Next up, Merckx's mother tackled the selectors. After a certain amount of bluster – Mrs Merckx was merely a proud mother, the trainer Oscar Daemers said, adding that her son couldn't climb a motorway bridge – the team manager conceded that they might find a place for him in the team time trial. Jenny

Merckx was no fool: if Eddy was physically capable of riding the team time trial, that surely meant he could ride the road race. A couple of phone calls later, the Belgian team doctor admitted he had been advised it might be a good idea to turn Eddy down. Soon enough, Eddy was invited in for a new test, which cleared him.

The only conclusion that can be drawn is that Merckx was being deliberately kept out of the team. According to his biographer Joël Godaert, the underlying problem was the national federation's need to juggle the various local interests in Belgium. 'Against all logical expectations, the best riders were not necessarily picked. The world championship selectors were partly guided by "interests" and by the strongest voices of provincial delegates. The selectors wouldn't hesitate to favour riders belonging to a province with a larger number of racing licence-holders or to respond to pressure from delegates who wanted to give a helping hand to favoured riders.'

Merckx was selected for the Belgian team alongside Walter Godefroot, Willy Planckaert, Jos Spruyt, Roger Swerts and Herman Van Loo. The race was at Sallanches, near Mont Blanc – later famous as the place where Bernard Hinault won the world title in 1980 – on a rainy day, over sodden, hilly roads. Merckx had been reminded over and over again by Acou and Vervaecke to hold back. He made his effort with thirty-five kilometres to go, after Swerts – later to be a solid second string in Merckx's professional teams – told him that he was not going to manage to bridge to the main escape of the day. Merckx responded to the four-man move including his teammate Van Loo by making a series of attacks with Felice Gimondi the only rider able to hold him, initially, as he rode across to the break.

'He fell on the quartet after a few kilometres of chasing,' reported Robert Pajot of l'Equipe. 'He had barely given himself time to breathe before he attacked again . . . one by one his erstwhile companions fell back. Accelerating again on the final climb of the road that climbed to Val d'Assy, Merckx forged a lead of a hundred metres in spite of the courage Luciano Armani showed in hanging on to his back wheel. It was enough of a lead to earn him the world title by a clear margin.' He was the youngest world amateur champion to that date: nineteen years old. Twenty-seven seconds after Merckx crossed the line, his teammate Willy Planckaert won the sprint for second place, unaware that Merckx had escaped and convinced that he was the world champion.

Merckx achieved his dream of racing at the Tokyo Olympics later that year, but while the ambition to ride the event had driven him since his early teens, the race itself was anything but a defining occasion. As the amateur world champion, he was no longer just another rider. He was heavily marked by the entire field as he attempted to split the race apart – not the last time he was to find this happening. He suffered from cramp. He rode a less restrained race than in Sallanches, and was chased down by Gimondi when he made his move three kilometres from the finish. Fate had stepped in. The night before, his wallet had been stolen from his room in the Olympic village; in it were the 12,000 Belgian Francs he had brought to pay his teammates. That was the best way to be absolutely certain that they would help him to win. Instead the Belgian team rode for themselves: the gold medal went to an Italian, Mario Zanin, with Godefroot winning the bronze medal and Merckx twelfth. His meteoric amateur career was all but over.

Merckx turned professional on 24 April 1965 for the Solo-Superia team led by Rik Van Looy. He had been keen to make the step the year before but Vervaecke felt it was too early: he had his military service to do, and his training time would be limited. By mid-April, however, Eddy had won four amateur races out of the five he had started, and clearly he had nothing to gain by remaining in the lower category. The deal was orchestrated by Jean Van Buggenhout, a former six-day rider from the 1930s, and sometime art collector. Van Buggenhout had become young Merckx's manager following the world championship at Sallanches, after trying to get Eddy on his books since his win in the Tour of Limburg the previous year. Inevitably, Van Buggenhout was one of the influential characters Jenny Merckx had phoned when she was trying to sort out the imbroglio of the 'failed' medical check the previous August: he had pulled strings to get Merckx into the team.

Van Buggenhout had far more clout than most: he virtually ran post-war Belgian cycling. He had been a member of a highly successful six-day team, the 'Brussels aeroplanes', whose jersey in the city colours of red and green incorporated an image of the Mannekin Pis statue. He was a talented rider, with the ability to break away at the moment in a race that he knew would cause the crowd to get to their feet. If you pleased the crowd, the fee went up proportionately.

He was also an accountant who brought his negotiating skills to his six-day career then moved into race promotion just before the war. In the first criterium he organised he raced as well, turning up in his kit to collect money and issue entrance tickets to the circuit. Later he would supply promoting towns with a complete service from contracts to race staff to riders.

As well as his various criteriums, he also ran the Brussels velodrome, and he had an office there. It was a good place to spot emerging talent such as Merckx in the youth events. He had branched out from promotion into managing six-day riders and moved seamlessly to running the careers of the two Riks, Van Steenbergen and Van Looy. 'Everyone was afraid of him,' recalls Patrick Sercu. 'He was a hard man, didn't say a lot, but was imposing. He really knew his cycling, he wasn't just a moneyman.' He had more riders on his books than the other great wheeler-dealer of the day, Daniel Dousset of France, whose biggest name was Jacques Anquetil. The pair seemed to have had an unspoken pact that each would keep off the other man's turf. Van Buggenhout also ran the Solo-Superia team, led by his brace of Riks, so it was the obvious place for his new protégé to go. Unfortunately it just happened to be completely the wrong team for an ambitious, talented young Belgian who didn't come from the Flandrian heartland.

Van Steenbergen was not the stumbling block. He had pretty much retired from the road and was riding criteriums and track races, scooping up one start purse after another before hanging up his wheels. Merckx was no threat to him, and he wasn't bothered about the new lad. He just wanted to make his money. Van Looy was another matter, however. He was the most dominant member of the little clique of a dozen or so stars, the *grands coureurs*, who effectively controlled professional racing across Europe. Those who crossed him tended to find that their careers were brief: the criterium contracts dried up and there would just happen to be a dozen riders on their coat tails when they attacked in a race, all of them keen to be seen doing what they felt The Emperor wanted. Rik II was probably the greatest Classics hunter cycling has ever seen, the only man ever to win all the major one-day races: the feat would elude even Merckx himself.

The team Van Looy had built for himself was legendary. It had taken him three years to pull together, and the riders were collectively nicknamed 'The Red Guard', as they wore the crimson jersey of Faema. The Red Guard is credited with inventing the lead-out train, in which the riders control the final kilometres of a race so that the team's sprinter can do the business at the very end. They were paid more than the norm and were more talented than average. Discipline was rigid: those who stepped out of line were sacked. They were big, fast men, and included such talents as the Dutchman Peter Post, winner of the Paris–Roubaix Classic in 1964 at the fastest average speed recorded for any one-day race at the time.

Solo was Van Looy's team. The squad was managed by his brother-in-law, and the two of them had already proved too much for the previous *directeur sportif*, Robert Naeye, the man who had persuaded the margarine company to back the team in the first place. Ominously for Merckx, Van Looy already had a protégé under his wing in Ward Sels, nearly four years older and already Belgian national professional champion. Merckx would eventually eclipse Sels by a massive margin and would be more celebrated than Van Looy, but that problem did not raise its head in his first season. Merckx was not yet that good. It came down to this: recruits to Solo had to fit into Van Looy's scheme of things, but Merckx was his own man.

To start with, the youngster was from Brussels, not the Flandrian heartland. It was not the first or the last time that this would be an issue. He was friendly with several of Van Looy's rivals from around the capital, riders such as Daems, who was one of the few to refuse to work for Van Looy in the Belgian national team at the world championships. Merckx was young, serious and sensitive, and had not been away from home a great deal. The team's banter was hard for him to take. Van Looy's domestiques nicknamed Merckx 'Jack Palance' – because of his black quiff perhaps – and teased him over his love of rice pudding with flavoured syrup.

This was trivia, but Merckx was sensitive, just turning twenty, and it hurt. According to one witness, Jos Huysmans, Van Looy was a character who liked to get under another man's skin, and quickly made him aware that he was taking the mickey. 'For

Merckx it must have been terribly humiliating and he never forgave him.' The only instance of Van Looy holding Merckx back in a race came in that year's Belgian national championship, when the Solo leader advised the youngster not to go after an early move, and he just happened to miss out on the win. The advice might have been well intentioned, but it was later interpreted as the old champion trying to restrain the upstart.

When I interviewed Van Looy about his career, he spoke about Merckx without being prompted, insisting he only wanted the best for him. 'He was only nineteen when he turned professional. It was normal that when he came into the team, the guys would have a bit of a laugh. They were all about thirty, they would say *"petit*, what are you doing here?" I didn't want him to leave. For me, it would have been better if he had stayed in the team. We would have been together, won races just like that.'

The Solo experience also underlined that Merckx had a relatively low key start to his professional career. It would have been astonishing if he had found it easy, as the jump in distance and speed from amateur racing is considerable. He turned professional before his twentieth birthday – young even by the standards of the 1960s – and his training had been curtailed by his military service, first in Ghent, then closer to home in Brussels. His first race was the Flèche Wallonne, a long, hilly one-day Classic, one of the hardest events on the calendar. It was run in horrendous weather that year and not surprisingly Merckx cracked with thirty kilometres to go. After that, the novice spent the bulk of the summer riding *kermis* races and track races. He took the first pro race of his career soon enough, at Vilvoorde in the Brussels suburbs – later to be the home of Ireland's Sean Kelly – on 11 May. The man he beat was none other than his erstwhile training partner Emile Daems: a significant scalp for a twenty-year-old, although Daems was close to ending his career. 'It was a hard circuit,' the older man told me. 'I escaped towards the end, but he caught me one kilometre from the finish and beat me in the sprint.' By the close of the season, Merckx had clocked up a more than respectable nine wins in *kermis* races.

Fortunately Merckx and Van Looy didn't race together a great deal, because the youngster wasn't yet at the level of the old champion, but clearly by the end of 1965 Merckx had worked out that he had no option but to leave. There was an approach from the Bic team at that year's world championships in San Sebastian, as the manager Raphael Geminiani recalled. Merckx was recommended by Van Looy, and, as Geminiani tells it: 'I thought "shit, this is Van Looy talking, I'll take two contracts' – presumably a copy for each party – 'and I'll go and see the Belgian team in their hotel".' Geminiani's offer was 2500 francs a month – a tenth of what a star such as Anquetil might earn – but Merckx accepted. 'I had my two contracts signed and I say to myself that's great, but Merckx was a minor, and when he gets back to Belgium and he talks to his manager Van Buggenhout, and he says "is it true that you've signed a contract with Gem?, it's not valid, it's your father who has to do that". And he signed for Peugeot!'

Permitting his protégé to move to the French team Peugeot was a masterstroke by Van Buggenhout. He kept his options open with both Merckx – the future, perhaps – and Van Looy, the best-paid star in the sport. France's oldest team might have seemed a curious choice for a Belgian, but the manager Gaston Plaud was an eclectic recruiter, given to signing Germans and Britons. Merckx spoke French, which obviously helped, the contract was worth 20,000 francs per month, and Peugeot was not run with the same rigid discipline as Van Looy's teams. If he wanted to race in his own way, Merckx would have the opportunity.

In March 1966, Paris–Nice was the first major stage race of the year, and the first stage race of his professional career. In fact it was only his second stage race ever, as in 1965 he had avoided multi-day events. He was not that keen to race, having just finished the Antwerp Six-Day. His initial goal was merely to race conservatively and get to know his new team-mates. There were immediate hints that he would have to fight for his place: towards the end of stage one, at Auxerre, he set off in pursuit of a three-man escape, his team leader Roger Pingeon, Michele Dancelli and Adriano Durante. With Merckx closing, Pingeon decided not to slow down a little to allow his teammate to catch up, so that the two of them could take on the Italians on equal terms, but pushed as hard as he could. Not surprisingly, when he caught up, Merckx was tired and could only finish third.

There was another key indicator for the twenty-year-old, on the stage to Montceau-les-Mines. Here he finished 'best of the rest' as the five times Tour winner Anquetil and his big rival Poulidor, no less, did battle on the toughest climb of the race, the four-kilometre, one-in-five Col d'Uchon. Merckx pulled on the white leader's jersey, and held it for a stage, but the key moment came in the time trial in Corsica, late on. He caught and overtook Van Looy, who had set off two minutes ahead of him. He didn't look at him as he sped past. It was only the second time trial of his career, and the longest. The time trial win went to Luciano Armani of Italy, while Anquetil triumphed in the overall standings, but fourth behind the Frenchman was a promising performance.

That led Merckx to San Remo, and that four-man sprint. Of the quartet, Merckx was not the most likely winner on paper. Van Springel was equally inexperienced, but he was almost two years older. Durante was a prolific winner of the big one-day races that made up the bulk of the Italian calendar, already a stage winner in both the Giro d'Italia and Tour de France, and had shown Merckx a clean pair of heels twice in the previous week's Paris–Nice. At twenty-three, Dancelli was coming off the back of a stupendous 1965: twelve major wins and the Italian title, decided on points over the season. That made him the overwhelming favourite for the final sprint. Merckx, on the other hand, had been racing as a professional for less than twelve months and he was not yet twenty-one.

Untested in the Classics, Merckx himself was worried about the length of the race: three hundred kilometres is a massive leap in the dark for a twenty-year-old. But he had the strength to follow a move by Raymond Poulidor on the Capo Berta, one of the series of small climbs that test the legs in the final phase of *La Primavera*. He had managed to split the field himself on the Poggio, the final ascent, with only the descent to that sprint finish remaining. Only eleven men remained with him at the top of the little hill; clearly Merckx was still fresh in spite of seven hours in the saddle. The group included Van Springel, Durante and Dancelli. The latter had responded rapidly when Merckx made his move, but he had not counter-attacked, a sign that he might be feeling the distance. Plaud had advised Merckx to leave his sprint as late as he could, so he opted to raise the pace eight hundred metres from the line: it was the last 150 metres before he truly went flat out. The finish epitomised the way Merckx would tackle sprints against men who were faster and more experienced on paper: time and again he would use his sustained power to temper their pure speed, opting for a long sprint rather than a sudden, late jump out of the blocks.

But the winner could have been any of the four. Van Springel, another debutant in the race, recalled that he was just behind Merckx as the sprint opened up three hundred metres from the line, and they both sprang out of the saddle at the same instant. As they did so, Merckx shifted his trajectory very slightly, not deliberately, and not so much that he actually impeded the other Belgian, but enough to make Van Springel check slightly and move to his left. In such split seconds, races are made and lost.

Merckx would go through his career a worried man and, for the previous eighteen months, he had been well aware that he needed to prove he was not just another talented amateur who had made it into the professional ranks and then stalled. He had won the world amateur road race championship in August 1964, but knew that there were plenty of world amateur champions who disappeared once they moved up to the highest level. He had looked at the results of others who triumphed as amateurs and noticed that they frequently went nowhere. At Solo-Superia he had competed almost seventy times but won only nine races. The move to Peugeot had been a courageous gamble; staying at Solo would have been the safe option. So the final metres that day on Via Roma vindicated his decision to quit Van Looy, and strike out on his own, and it meant his world title was not a mere flash in the pan.

With hindsight, something else would become clear. In 1946, Fausto Coppi of Italy had marked the rebirth of professional cycling after the war with a huge, decisive win in the 'Classic of Classics'. Coppi's win was the dawn of a new era in cycling. Merckx's victory twenty years later would be another turning point, after which the sport would be taken in a completely new direction by the greatest champion it has ever seen.

WORLD DOMINATION IN FIVE PHASES

The iconic status of Eddy Merckx is partly down to meteorology, for various reasons. Many of the most striking images of the great man were taken in rain and snow. The stories his rivals tell make Merckx seem superhuman in the face of brutal cold and wet. To take one example, Gianni Motta told of Merckx taking off his racing cape when it rained, so that he could go faster while everyone else shivered. Merckx raced hard in races susceptible to rain and snow – the Classics, spring stage races, the Giro d'Italia – whereas today's stars focus all their attention on one race held in July. And there is something else: because he won so much more than every cyclist before or since, the law of probability dictated that more of his wins would be in the worst weather the sky could throw at him and the peloton.

The list of races won by Merckx where he fought the elements as well as the usual opponents is a long one: the heavy rain in the Tour of Flanders of 1969 and 1975 and Paris–Roubaix 1970 and 1973, the snow, rain and cold of Liège–Bastogne–Liège in 1971. There are the legendary images of Merckx during the Tour of Belgium in 1970 and 1971, with half-melted snow blotching his shoulders and thick woolly gloves the only concession he is making to the conditions (he has no race cape, nothing on his head other than a thin cotton *casquette*, in the Namur–Helst stage of 1970 he has legwarmers, in 1971 not, and his nerves must be deadened with the cold). There is another from Paris–Nice in the early 1970s, when he has punctured and has snow all over him, again not even a covering on his shoes; the Tour of Flanders 1975 when the sleet can be seen slashing across his rainbow jersey. On the Stelvio in the 1972 Giro he chased the little Spanish climber José Manuel Fuente through a blinding mix of snow, sleet, rain, fog and high wind, so thick that he could hardly tell where the finish was.

One day in particular stands out. June snow in the Dolomites is not uncommon, but the snowstorm that hit the eastern end of the range on 1 June 1968 had ramifications that went far beyond the mountains. Things were never the same again after that blizzard, for Eddy Merckx in particular, but also for a whole generation of bike racers who tried to compete with him over the next nine years.

Of all the hostile forces that racing cyclists fear, wet snow in the mountains is dreaded the most. It melts on the road and the result is a constant spray of water, just above freezing temperature. It takes no time for a cyclist to be soaked through from below while from above the snow falls on bare arms and legs, the skin burning with the cold. As well as the usual challenges of racing up and down mountain passes – redoubtable enough in temperate weather – the descents are a freezing hell with numbed fingers pulling on unwilling brake levers, road spray and snowflakes lashing the eyes as they strain to see the next hairpin. Body and mind are tested to the limit as hypothermia sets in. This was what the cyclists of the Giro d'Italia faced as they raced towards Lavaredo on the twelfth stage of the three-week race on that June afternoon. The rain had begun that morning at the start in Gorizia, and drenched them all day: as the final climb approached, it turned to snow.

High above the town of Misurina, the Cima Piccola, Cima Grande and Cima Ovest di Lavaredo – the Tre Cime – rise up like three fingers, all close to three thousand metres high, up above the military road that climbs to the Auronzo refuge. From 1914 to 1917, the peaks marked the front line between Italian and Austrian forces; the climb to the refuge, 2333 metres above sea level, has been one of the classic Giro d'Italia ascents since 1967. That year, the riders, struggling on gears that were unsuitable, in a snowstorm, were pushed to the top by the *tifosi*, and the stage was ruled null and void; in 1968, to prevent any repetition of that, the organisers arranged for police to line the road. Like San Remo, Lavaredo was a key location in the progress of young Eddy Merckx into the record books. Here, in the most dramatic handicap race cycling had seen to that date, and in the teeth of that snowstorm, Merckx closed a ten-minute gap on a breakaway group to win the stage and seal the first Belgian victory in the Giro d'Italia.

By the time he arrived at the foot of the Tre Cime that day, ready to climb his way to world domination, Merckx had already found out a good deal about professional cycling. For a well-brought up Catholic boy from a small, relatively closed suburb where conformity was all and rules were rigidly enforced, the professional world must have been an eye-opener. Merckx had not actually raced that much internationally as an amateur. He didn't know about the pushing that was rife in Italian races. He tended not to get involved in combines, and didn't buy and sell races – although having won so many so early on he could have earned plenty of money doing so. There must have been occasions when he was offered cash to 'lose' a race, but no records that he ever did so.

The move to Peugeot had worked, to the extent that he had been given some liberty and had taken advantage of it. The French team was a different set-up from Solo, but was still not an easy environment for a young, talented rider. There were many different leaders all fighting for their place – Tom

Simpson, the reigning world champion, Roger Pingeon, Raymond Delisle, Charles Grosskost. While there were openings, the lack of structure meant that anyone with aspirations, no matter how senior they were, had to fight for dominance, like a mafia boss showing his strength to the other gangsters. Simpson appears to have been particularly jealous of his status.

Milan–San Remo was the young Belgian's only major win in 1966, although he took twenty victories in total, including his first professional stage race victory in the Tour of Morbihan. There was a stage win in the Midi Libre, a prestigious warm-up race before the Tour de France, and victories in one-day events that still have a certain ring to them: the Grand Prix Pino Cerami at Wasmuel, the Championship of Flanders, the Baracchi Trophy in Italy, the Montjuich hill-climb in Spain. All this was more than promising for a rider in his twenty-first year, but Merckx's first complete professional season is often unfairly judged by the standards of what he achieved later.

After San Remo, he had a series of setbacks that can be explained away by an understandable lack of physical and tactical maturity. A crash in the Tour of Flanders, a puncture in Paris–Roubaix, an alliance of stars who wanted Gimondi to win Paris–Brussels, where only he and Van Looy were interested in chasing the Italian. Merckx was in the mix in the world championships on the tough German motor-racing circuit at Nürburgring, but suffered cramp in the finale. Moreover, the big names in the peloton appeared to have worked together to ensure the win for one of their number, Rudi Altig. Afterwards the youth went through a moral crisis. He was in tears in his hotel room for two hours and later had to be virtually forced by Van Buggenhout to race again.

There was another near miss in the Giro di Lombardia, where he escaped with Vittorio Adorni – his future teammate – and Gimondi, but in the final sprint on the velodrome in

Como he tried to sneak past between Adorni and the hoardings at the top of the track. Adorni impeded him momentarily by sticking out an elbow, and his loss of impetus allowed Gimondi to win. It was the classic case of the older pros giving the talented, strong newcomer a hard time, but Merckx blamed himself. He had had the opportunity to look at the track in Como a few days earlier, but had not taken it. He had paid the price, as there was a bump at the entrance to the velodrome, he had not taken it smoothly, and had ended up in a poor position when the sprint began. It was the kind of detail he would attend to in future.

The youth hit the 1967 season running, winning two stages of the Tour of Sardinia, but the first major stage race of the year, Paris–Nice, was another learning experience. He went straight into the 'Race to the Sun' from Sardinia, won stage two – a dominant solo victory, with all the big names chasing behind him – and pulled on the leader's jersey. It should have been a simple matter of Peugeot defending the lead, but it didn't work out that way. Two days later, Tom Simpson attacked repeatedly, then made an early move with sixteen other riders on the climb up from the stage start at Saint-Etienne over the Col de la République, Merckx was left behind, and Anquetil in particular showed no interest in chasing. Simpson seized his chance, and it was probably no coincidence that Van Looy was in the move as well, combining with Merckx's teammate to put one over the young upstart. The *grands coureurs* were asserting themselves.

With a strong northwesterly on their backs, Van Looy, Simpson and company gained twenty minutes on the field, with The Emperor taking the stage and Simpson taking the lead. The fact that Simpson had attacked when Peugeot had the race leader in their team caused huge controversy. Simpson claimed that he had alerted Merckx to the danger of a split as they went up the climb, but Merckx didn't get in the move, so he decided there should be at least one Peugeot in there. J. B. Wadley visited the race for *Sporting Cyclist*: his description of Simpson's win makes no bones of the fact that Merckx was bitterly angry with Simpson and it is clear that Simpson – for all his embarrassment at annoying his teammate – felt he had no choice but to look after his own interests. The Briton was every bit as competitive as Merckx, and desperate for success after a catastrophic 1966.

Two days later, Merckx attacked in his turn, on the climb of the Col d'Ange, seventy kilometres into the stage from Marignane to Hyères – he was over eight minutes behind Simpson so had the right to make a move, but Simpson then attacked out of the bunch behind him. Under orders from Peugeot manager Gaston Plaud, Merckx played the devoted teammate, waiting for the Briton so that the pair could share the work all the way to the finish. Merckx crossed the line first, with Simpson respecting protocol by not contesting the sprint as he was guaranteed the overall title. The Briton thanked Merckx publicly, but Merckx said nothing: he had simply done the correct thing. 'I'm paid for this kind of thing as well,' he said. The young Belgian was certainly not bitter. A week later he agreed to race an Italian criterium on condition that the organiser invited Simpson (and his Peugeot teammate Ferdinand Bracke) as well. In late July that year, he was the only continental rider to go to Simpson's funeral after the Briton died on the Mont Ventoux climb in the Tour de France; he remains unhappy to this day that Simpson's name is so closely associated with doping

Few gave the young Merckx much chance of a repeat win in Milan–San Remo – odds of 120-1 were being given against him – but Simpson clearly felt he had no option but to get away from his young teammate early on. So he made sure he was in the early move just eight kilometres from the start, well before the Turchino Pass. It was a five-man escape that gained five minutes; it included Bob Lelangue, and Simpson's close friend Vin Denson. The race came back together sixty kilometres from the finish, largely because there wasn't a strong enough presence in the move from the Italian teams, something Simpson should have worked out.

So Merckx had his chance in the finale. He attacked on Capo Berta to create an initial selection in the bunch, then sprang clear on the Poggio accompanied by Gianni Motta. Merckx decided not to give it everything, held back a little, and the pair were joined by Gimondi and Franco Bitossi – the irony being that with three Italians in the lead it was highly likely that they would race against each other, and Merckx might then profit. Which was exactly what happened. Motta said later that both he and Bitossi were scrapping to get on Merckx's wheel as they knew – after the previous year's race – that he would be the fastest for the sprint; Motta lost a couple of metres, which was just enough to make the difference, helping Merckx land his second win in the 'Classic of Classics' in two years.

Merckx added Ghent–Wevelgem shortly afterwards. It was an event that carried far more prestige than it does now, it was his first 'northern Classic', and it was taken from the elite of Belgian hard men: Willy Planckaert, Noël Foré, Ward Sels, Herman Van Springel. Those two events marked another turning point: the beginning of nine years when Merckx was a factor in every race he started. His professional apprenticeship was clearly over. Already, riders and teams were basing their races around him. At the Tour of Flanders, Luciano Pezzi, the *directeur sportif* of Salvarani (former teammate of Fausto Coppi, future confidant of Marco Pantani), told Gimondi and his team that they had to work together to beat Merckx:

Gimondi would have to follow Merckx when he made his move, but he needed a teammate with him to have any chance of beating the Belgian. Pezzi was astute: Gimondi, indeed, got away with Merckx and he took with him his teammate Dino Zandegu, a guitar-playing, singing sprinter from Padua. The two Italians attacked Merckx turn and turn about, with the Belgian eventually letting Zandegu go, hoping that at a certain point he would be able to get clear of Gimondi and recapture him. It didn't happen.

Thus far, Merckx's career had been through three phases: a difficult initiation, an initial breakthrough and a struggle to confirm it was not a fluke. World domination was preceded by a fourth phase, when the 'heads' of the peloton didn't seem to care who won as long as it was not Merckx. That made perfect sense. This was a sport dominated by a small clique of established stars, who made a good living off appearance contracts for track and circuit races. It was in their interests to keep the magic circle small, so they would do everything they could either to keep the young champion out, or at least to subjugate him so they could integrate him into the system. In the Flèche Wallonne that April, Gimondi, Van Looy, Jean Stablinski, Foré and Victor Van Schil all seemed to be in league against Merckx to start with, with Peter Post particularly aggressive. There were attacks from the gun; Merckx missed an early group of favourites but bridged with Van Looy on his wheel, the older man giving no help. At one point Merckx was forced to pursue for forty-five kilometres after another group disappeared. He finally went on the attack himself seventeen kilometres from the finish, and after a quarter of an hour or so the rest gave up and left him to a victory that had a strong moral element to it. It was not to be the last time.

The double in Flèche Wallonne and its fellow 'Ardennes Classic', Liège–Bastogne–Liège, is one of cycling's most prestigious achievements, but Walter Godefroot got in Merckx's way that year. With Merckx piling on the pressure and his fellow Belgian clinging on, the pair escaped in the hilly final miles of the Classic. That year the *doyenne* finished on the athletics track in the middle of the velodrome in the suburb of Rocourt, because persistent rain had made the banked track too slippery and dangerous. They only had to complete half a lap: Godefroot attacked just before they arrived on the track, sprinting to the left as Merckx made the mistake of looking to the right. Like Gimondi, Godefroot would be a sparring partner for the rest of Merckx's career; he was one of the few stars of the time whose spirit never seemed to be broken by Merckx's domination.

The most important event of all that spring as far as Merckx's long-term future was concerned was not a race. It was a meeting in the Italian ski resort of Cervinia between the Belgian and a small delegation of Italians including Enrico Giacotto, briefly Fausto Coppi's manager at the Carpano team and now the manager at Faema, and the late Nino Defilippis, an ex-cyclist of some quality who had raced for Giacotto. 'He wanted my advice,' recalled Defilippis in his memoirs. 'The idea was to get Merckx riding for an Italian team. At that time all the critics considered that he was a new Van Looy, a great champion for the Classics, but an unknown quantity for stage races. Giacotto wanted to see him climbing, have a good look at him, see what he was worth.'

'He was stunning, the power he showed, the way he took the curves, the way he pedalled. Cervinia is not an easy climb, but I remember that as he got off his bike he looked at me and asked where it ranked among the great Alpine climbs. It was his way of showing how fresh he felt. I took Giacotto on one side and asked if they had a pen and a bit of card, anything, so that we could make this lad sign a contract for life, with no questions over figures, whatever he wanted. He was a prodigy. And as it turned out, Giacotto didn't let him get away.'

Giacotto was not the only manager looking for Merckx's services: Geminiani and Bic were again on the hunt. As Geminiani recalled it, he noticed after that Milan–San Remo that Merckx was not happy at Peugeot, and was aware that Bic were looking for a replacement for Anquetil. The biro company did not feel that Merckx was worth the 25,000 French francs' asking price, and opted to hire the Dutchman Jan Janssen, then a more established talent. Geminiani got a chance to manage Merckx towards the end of his career, but forty-five years later he was still livid about missing out on him at this formative stage.

Faema was not a run-of-the-mill team. They had a longer history than most, having been founded in the early 1950s, when the man behind the Faema coffee-machine company, Carlo Valente, began putting money into sport, initially boxing, then exclusively cycling, with the former *campionissimo* Learco Guerra as *direttore sportivo*. By the time Defilippis and Giacotto fixed their sights on Merckx, Faema's teams had been led by a series of greats: Federico Bahamontes, Charly Gaul – who raced in the distinctive diamond-logoed jersey of the Faema offshoot EMI – Hugo Koblet and, most famously, Van Looy, Merckx's old boss at Solo. Giacotto was legendary as well: his way of working was to profess no knowledge of cycling tactics, ask his riders for their thoughts, then do as he felt best. 'He was ahead of his time, a manager who believed in speaking to his riders as professional men, where in the past they had been treated like peasants,' one writer of the time told me. He sought out the best hotels for his team, although there was a condition: he was famed as a chainsmoker who would occasionally go to bed with a cigarette in his mouth, fall asleep and set the sheets alight, so he would scout out hotels that had insurance

for that eventuality. Lung cancer was to bring an early end to
his life.

Valente was a man of huge ambition, one of the first to
manufacture the espresso machines that are ubiquitous in
Italian bars, then branching out into white goods of every other
kind: fridges, ice cream makers, fans, toasters, fruit crushers.
Faema had an annual publicity budget of about fifty million
lire, of which two-thirds went on traditional advertising, with
some sixteen million going on the cycling team. As Valente's
son Paolo later explained, they didn't use Merckx and company
to sell coffee machines directly: it was pure PR. 'Cycling is
close to the people, close to our public, and we want to make
them feel good, all the time. Faema's cyclists build the prestige
of our company name through their exploits on the road. They
uphold an image, a wave of affection for the Faema name
throughout Italy, and abroad. Merckx is not a sandwich-board-
man. He is a standard-bearer.'

A possible employer from Italy with a colossal budget waiting
in the wings and a provisional contract in his pocket meant
there was an additional edge to the Giro d'Italia of 1967 for
Merckx. It was his first experience of a three-week stage race,
and it was also a showcase for his talent on the home territory
of his potential new bosses. For a twenty-two-year-old, who
was relatively immature, the race was promising enough. There
were two stage wins, one at the mountain-top finish at
Blockhaus de la Maiela, 2005 metres above sea level, where
he attacked to win from Italo Zilioli, the nearly man of 1960s
Italian cycling. Given that he had wanted to use the Giro as
a way of testing his ability in the mountains, that was encouraging. Another victory followed forty-eight hours later, in a
bunch sprint at Lido degli Estensi, which pleased him even
more. He rose as high as third overall, but faded towards the
end for ninth: this was more than excusable. That Giro was

contested amid rain and snow in the Dolomites. Having hung on to the front runners in the second Dolomite stage to Tirano, in heavy rain – a stage when all bar thirty-one of the field finished outside the time limit – Merckx struggled the next day en route to Trento, suffering from the beginnings of flu and the legacy of a heavy crash.

The Giro gave Merckx belief that he would win a major Tour 'someday'. It was also enough to spark off abortive attempts to get the Belgian starlet into the Tour de France. In mid-June there were reports that an agreement had been reached to enter a second Belgian squad in the Tour – contested that year by national teams – on condition that Merckx started. He would, it was said, only have to race the early stages through Belgium; the money was being found by a group of Belgian industrialists. The plan came as news to Merckx – who first knew about it when he picked up a paper in his local petrol station – and he wisely resisted. Instead, he raced. A lot. Between 7 August and 30 September 1967, for example, he was on the start line thirty-five times. Midway through that exhausting spell, however, there were two major developments.

On 2 September, Merckx set his course for the next ten years, signing a contract for 400,000 Belgian francs with Faema the night before the world road race championships in Heerlen, Holland. It was three times the salary he was earning at Peugeot and it set the tone: until the end of 1976 Merckx's sponsors were to be Italian and his teams would have a strong, if fluctuating, Italian element.

Merckx's move to Faema was not financial, however, but strategic. It appears that if there was a disagreement with Peugeot, it was over a fairly insignificant sum. The key issue was this: Merckx's experiences at Solo and Peugeot had persuaded him that he needed to be the undisputed leader of his team. At Peugeot, Gaston Plaud and the men above him in the cycle company were never going to let that happen. Peugeot was a team that dated back to the start of cycle racing and had a strict philosophy. There was no question that Merckx would receive team support when he needed it; it was just that Plaud and his bosses wanted freedom for others within the team. For Merckx, there was also the fear that in a French team any emerging French star would tend to be given precedence. As far as Peugeot were concerned, they had just won the Tour de France with Roger Pingeon, so why build a team around a Belgian, however talented he might be? Additionally, building the team around Merckx would mean hiring Belgians and firing French riders, which would be disastrous public relations.

In Italy, on the other hand, there was a tradition of having teams built around a single *campione* – of any nationality – with the best example Coppi's team, Bianchi, where outstandingly talented riders would be hired solely to help the leader. The Faema manager Giacotto had cut his teeth by setting up the Carpano–Coppi team in 1957, so he had seen the *campione* system first-hand. He was also used to working with foreign *campioni* within Italian teams, as by 1957 Coppi was fading and the Belgian Fred de Bruyne was actually the one who brought in the Carpano–Coppi team's results.

In the years after Coppi and Gino Bartali, Italy had become the place where professional cyclists were best rewarded and the best riders could obtain the best back-up. Peugeot, on the other hand, had its shambolic side as Simpson and Godefroot both observed, with claims that Plaud was more interested in glad-handing the company bigwigs than in running the team day-to-day. Merckx himself said: 'I bought everything myself at Peugeot: wheels, tyres . . . It was no coincidence that all the best riders of the time wanted to race in Italy. The teams were properly organised, had structure, and medical back-up.'

The contrast with Belgian teams was 'day and night,' sighs Godefroot. 'Travel, clothes, food, equipment. It goes back to the days of Coppi, when teams like Ignis, Faema, Carpano were set up with better finances, and that made the difference.' Belgian teams, even such outwardly imposing units as Flandria, were more worried about shaving off a few francs in travel expenses than saving time flying rather than driving, or spending time training in the warmth of the French Riviera.

With that contract in his pocket, Merckx moved seamlessly on towards supremacy. One of his biggest fears after taking the world amateur road race championship in 1964 had been that few cyclists won the amateur title and moved on to successful professional careers. The day after he settled his future, that fear was consigned to the past. To avoid conflict in the Belgian team at the world championships that year, the Belgian selectors had ruled out Van Looy and Godefroot on the grounds that they might ride against Merckx. Even so, hedging their bets, the selectors were unwilling to put the whole team at the youngster's service. The same rumours had surfaced about his 'heart problems' as in 1964, and a heavy crash at the Belgian championship (held that year on 31 July, five weeks before the world's) had left him concussed for several days.

Each of the team was invited to a pre-race meeting, to state openly what his form was and what his intentions were. The upshot was that the Belgians had four leaders, but only nominally: Guido Reybroeck, Daniel Van Ryckegehm and Josef Boons were not of Merckx's ability, although they were all older and Boons was the national champion. There were four domestiques – Merckx was allotted Willy Monty as his personal assistant with the rest dividing their attention between the other leaders – and a 25,000 Belgian francs' *prime* for each of the team if they won, which was less than in the days when

Van Looy led the world's team. Critically, each of the team agreed to work for whoever was in the best position, and not to race against each other.

The race itself was bizarre. Traditionally, the world championship builds to a climax. The opening laps see a waiting game, the pace increases lap by lap, and the final few circuits are decisive as the distance tells. In Heerlen, on the other hand, there was an early move from the Italian Gianni Motta, winner of the previous year's Giro d'Italia, who attacked on the first of the ten laps. The attack decided the race. Merckx, Ramón Sáez – a burly Spanish sprinter nicknamed 'Tarzan' – and two others went with Motta; Merckx had been warned to hold fire, but felt the Italian was worth taking seriously. Plus, being in front guaranteed him the support of his teammates, who would be forced to mark any chasers. The key moment in the race came when the Dutch team leader Jan Janssen bridged to the break with the help of his teammate Raymond Van der Vleuten. Merckx and Motta decided not to push on to keep Janssen at bay, after which the quintet were able to forge ahead with the Dutch team blocking along with the Belgians and Italians. In the final sprint Van der Vleuten led out, Merckx countered, then led in his turn, worrying about what Janssen had left in the tank – he turned twice to look at the Dutchman as he launched the sprint – but he had enough to hold on as Janssen and Sáez came back at him, with barely a wheel between the trio at the line. It was a little piece of history: only two cyclists before him had worn the rainbow stripes as world amateur and professional road champion, his fellow countryman Jean Aerts (1927 and 1935) and the Swiss Hans Knecht (1938 and 1946).

Merckx's world title and three Classic wins notwithstanding – at an age when most of the greats had barely begun winning – the Peugeot manager Gaston Plaud did not believe his rider had had the perfect season. The Frenchman felt his protégé had been too ready to compromise success on the road by accepting lucrative contracts to race on the track. At the end of the season, Plaud lamented that Merckx had not won the Giro di Lombardia and Tour of Flanders because he had compromised his preparation by track racing. 'It's as sure as two and two make four: he has missed out on the most amazing season imaginable. Add up what he has won and what he should have won, and tell me Eddy has not missed out on a unique chance to go far better than any of the greats managed at the height of their careers. I hope he has the chance to repeat the same combination of favourable circumstances that will enable him to have the glorious season that he didn't manage to have this year. But I doubt if it's possible. You can't have it twice in one lifetime.'

Merckx continued racing into early November, with the last victories of the year coming in the traditional Flandrian season closer at Putte-Kapellen, the motor-paced Criterium des As in Paris, and the Baracchi Trophy two-man time trial in Italy, where he was paired with his Peugeot teammate, the newly crowned Hour Record holder Ferdinand Bracke. After that there was more unfinished business to attend to. On 5 December, Merckx married Claudine Acou, daughter of the national trainer, Lucien. The relationship had taken a while to develop. Being a cyclist left little time for going out; and, as Claudine put it, her parents were strict and she was 'a serious daughter from a good family'.

Their relationship was, not surprisingly, measured out in bike races. They had begun going out around the time Eddy turned professional, in April 1965, and the marriage proposal – Eddy asked her father – was made at a track meeting, between races, so that there was little room for discussion. There was pressure from Jules Merckx to delay the marriage but Claudine insisted: now or never. After the marriage, she devoted her life to supporting her husband and bringing up their two children. Much of the organisation of The Cannibal's career would be down to this strong-minded, strong-faced lady. Claudine would answer fan mail, filter out the journalists, cook his meals and deal with his moods. She seemed capable of handling any situation, be it escorting her husband home after a brutal crash, or dressing up to meet the king of Belgium, all of which would happen within two years of their marriage. She was far better at public relations than her husband, who could be painfully shy or withdrawn, and she was a better judge of character. Merckx was fortunate to encounter her early in his career, in the same way that he was lucky to find Michiels, Vervaecke and Van Buggenhout at the right time. Giacotto was another key influence and not just in cycling: it was the *direttore sportivo* who found a secluded hotel where Eddy and Claudine could stay for their honeymoon.

As the winter ended, Merckx began to tap into the reservoir of knowledge at Giacotto's Faema, which could be traced back to the experiments that Fausto Coppi had made with diet and training and team structure in the 1940s and 1950s, and which had in turn filtered out to Louison Bobet, Raphael Geminiani and Jacques Anquetil. The team boasted a co-leader: the experienced Vittorio Adorni, eight years older than Merckx, his chosen roommate, and the man Giacotto intended to mentor the starlet as he turned from a Classics specialist into an all-rounder who could dominate stage races as well.

'We spoke Italian and French,' recalls Adorni, whom Merckx called – and still calls – *professore*. His task was to channel Merckx's talent and physical strength. 'There were things he had not thought about. They had a different approach in Belgium. They hardly ever thought about stage races, only Classics. Eddy was really strong, but didn't have the tactical ability for a twenty-day stage race. Experience matters there: I had lost two Giri because of juvenile errors I'd made. I think he learned pretty much all he needed in one year, knowledge that had taken me eight years to pick up. He was *esuberante*, uninhibited, youthful, he wanted to get away, constantly: but in a stage race you have to choose your moment. He had such a massive engine inside him, however, that he was easy to teach.'

With Faema, for the first time in his career, Merckx followed the custom that went back to Coppi, and attended the first pre-season training camp of his career. He changed his diet and his weight dropped to seventy-two kilos – the principal reason why suddenly he turned into a great climber. 'We Belgian riders, the Flandrians, had a habit of eating *en bon bourgeois*, I'd say, perhaps too much [after the race], then in our [hotel] rooms we'd have biscuits, chocolate and so on. That means your body has to work too hard. And the Italians, especially Adorni, helped a lot in this area.' The Faema squad for 1968 was half Italian, half Belgian, with the massively experienced and highly intelligent Adorni alongside the core of the great Merckx teams: Jos Spruyt, Roger Swerts, Martin Van den Bossche.

At the start of the 1968 season, Merckx made an immediate impression by winning a stage of the Tour of Sardinia by more than six minutes, after Adorni had told him to wait for the toughest day, a stage lashed by rain and snow. Seasoned followers of the sport felt he couldn't possibly go on like this. 'We found out later that this was Eddy Merckx's way of racing and that he had the wherewithal to sustain such a prodigal use of energy, but at the time we had the right to think: he's doing too much and will break his neck,' recalled the French journalist Roger Bastide. Lack of restraint, followed by lack of results: the world champion abandoned Paris–Nice because of a knee injury, lost Milan–San Remo to Rudi Altig, was unable to match Walter Godefroot in the Tour of Flanders. Van Looy, who always had a weather eye on his apparent successor, began saying to the press that it was time Merckx started to act like a leader.

Merckx, on the other hand, claimed that the rainbow jersey was making him an easy target. The fact was that all the Belgians, led by Van Looy, were racing against him, partly because he was riding for an Italian team and sponsor and it was obviously better for Belgian sponsors if any Belgian won, but also because it was the only way for anyone other than Merckx to win. But the twenty-two-year-old could afford to be patient. Paris–Roubaix turned Merckx's early season around: no one could match him in a memorable race of elimination through punctures and crashes, with only forty-four riders making it to the finish. Merckx ended up with only Herman Van Springel for company and took the sprint.

Still only in his twenty-third year, Merckx could not risk racing both the Giro d'Italia and Tour de France in 1968. He might have wanted to tackle the French race, but in his first year representing an Italian sponsor the Giro was obligatory. The stage race lessons had begun before the start, when he turned up with three suitcases of kit and Adorni asked him 'are you going on holiday to the Bahamas?' Organising personal effects is a skill that helps save energy on a stage race: 'you're in small hotel rooms, two of you, only need personal stuff and two or three days' kit – he had everything for three weeks. Most of it could go in the team van. We had a discussion about it, then we emptied the cases, and got them down to one.' With his kit safely stowed in the team van, he landed two early stage wins: in Novara, where he embarrassed the sprinters by breaking away alone to win, and the next day in Aosta where he was asked by an RAI television reporter: 'did you have it in mind to go for the win today?' His answer was classic Merckx: 'Why do you ask me that? Why do you think I'm here? To watch the others win?' The man from Italian television was clearly unaware that Merckx 'had it in mind' to go for the win every time he raced.

As a result, Adorni had to rein him in. 'In Novara, the *gruppo* was all together, he attacked with a kilometre to go, won the stage, and took the *maglia rosa*. I said to him "but didn't we agree we would hold back?" He said he wanted to test the field a bit, so I then said we would have to let someone else take the jersey, to take the pressure off. I said "if you want to win the Giro, you have to be *tranquillo*." He was all youthful exuberance: it wasn't easy to hold him back. On every climb he wanted to attack, he was constantly asking if it was a good moment to go for it.'

At the start of the stage to Lavaredo, eleven days in, the race was still open. The pink jersey was on the shoulders of Michele Dancelli, who had finished fourth to Merckx in the 1966 Milan–San Remo. He was a strong one-day racer, but an average climber who would clearly struggle once the race hit the Dolomites. Merckx was lying second, two minutes behind Dancelli, and no one had yet emerged from among the favourites – Merckx, Gimondi, Adorni, Gianni Motta, Italo Zilioli – so the time was ripe for one of the little group to make a statement of intent. 'It was raining at the start, it was a long stage, two hundred and fifty kilometres if I remember rightly,' says Adorni. '*Una tappa mitica*'. A stage of legend.

By the penultimate climb, the Passo Tre Croce, a six-strong group looked set to fight out the stage, as they had a ten-minute lead. Merckx was chafing at the bit, as usual. The general feeling was that Gimondi would order his team to race hard from the off, in order to pre-empt an attack from the Belgian. Merckx wanted to get his response in first but Adorni warned him to wait. 'He kept saying, "we will never get that move back", but I would say "wait, it's not the moment to declare war". He attacked, two climbs from the finish, and got away. I asked the *direttore sportivo* to go and stop him, and he said to me "what if he says no?" I answered "if need be, run him off the road. Just stop him!"' There was a difference of opinion, and eventually Merckx stopped, pretending to change a wheel so that it did not seem he had slowed down deliberately. 'On the Tre Croce, he looked at me, I said "attack", Gimondi was on his wheel and cracked.' Then Adorni escaped in his turn, to link up with the Belgian. Not long afterwards, as the effort of catching Merckx told on him, the Italian said his leader should ride his own race. 'I am a cyclist, not a motorbike,' he said after the finish.

What took place that afternoon high above Cortina d'Ampezzo was essentially a handicap race, with Merckx carving his way through the riders spread out in front of him up the climb, passing the lesser lights as if they were standing. Both the groups, break and bunch, were in pieces. Giancarlo Polidori was the last man to fall, two kilometres from the finish line.

The images from Lavaredo are iconic: Merckx, bare-armed, barely visible through the driving snowflakes, several centimetres of snow on the roadsides, the people at the finish wrapped in macs and capes. He crossed the line, pushed away a few of the people attempting to help him stay upright, then was wrapped in blankets, still strapped to his bike. Motta and Zilioli finished more than four minutes behind, Gimondi at six minutes – incredible gaps for a single mountain top finish. Gimondi, the defending champion, and the race favourite after his win that spring in the Tour of Spain, was seen later on Italian television in tears, apologising for having let down the public.

The parallels with Coppi, on Italian roads, were obvious and were duly made. The headlines the next day included 'SUA

MAJESTIA MERCKX'. Jean Bobet wrote: 'He has revived and brought new honour to the concept of the all-round champion, which is refreshing for all of us. The last generation of champions was a generation of specialists. Van Looy in the Classics, Anquetil in stage races and time trials, Gaul in the mountains. Merckx is a champion on winter indoor tracks, in Paris–Roubaix and the Tour de France.' Bobet praised Merckx's wisdom, characterising him as 'mature, grounded, thought through, and owing a large part of his success to his organisational sense. He is not running a season but a career.' Lest we forget, he was not yet twenty-three.

The rest of the Giro was a formality, as might have been expected after a killer blow of that kind. It was Belgium's first victory in the Italian Tour, but that little piece of history was insignificant compared to the importance of the win for Merckx himself. Since turning professional he had won Milan–San Remo, the world championship and Paris–Roubaix. He had made a high-profile, big-money move to take sole leadership of one of the biggest teams in cycling, and had then delivered victory in the Giro d'Italia. Lavaredo was the moment of confirmation. 'It was a logical win given how he had ridden, given his physical strength, but there he truly understood what he could do,' says Adorni. 'Before, in stage races he didn't know what he was physically capable of. He didn't know what would happen, what strength he had. Afterwards in the Giro and Tour he did what he wanted.'

It was a critical turning point for Merckx in another way: he lost his fear of the mountains. He realised that none of the climbers were strong enough to threaten him if he could ride at a sustained, high speed – they might gain a little bit of ground, but then he was sure to catch up. It was a rule that Coppi had followed, so too Anquetil, and one which Hinault and Indurain would follow in their time. Merckx also became aware that the effort of chasing down a climber on a mountain was no more demanding than chasing down a rival on the flat – and he recovered just as quickly. He now felt he could look after himself on all terrains. He was ready for the Tour de France.

At the world championships in Imola in northern Italy that summer, however, the team leadership issue came to the fore yet again. Unlike in 1967, Van Looy was allowed to ride for the Belgian team and he was determined to ride his own race, Merckx or no Merckx, defending champion or not. He felt excluded, he told me, when the Belgian team set off for the start without him, leaving him on his own in the hotel. The only option left to The Emperor was that chosen by Tom Simpson in Milan–San Remo the year before: an early, speculative escape. Van Looy took with him Adorni, who had a dual role: protecting both Italian team interests and those of Merckx, his trade team leader. The lead was around ten minutes with about sixty miles to cover to the finish when Adorni got rid of Van Looy. Merckx had no intention of setting the Belgian team to chase his trade teammate, so Adorni enjoyed a triumphant procession to victory, the high point of his career. The victory brought nothing to Faema, however, as Adorni transferred over the winter, to cash in on his rainbow jersey at another team.

Stage five of Merckx's rapid progress to world domination was completed at the end of 1968, when he overcame Gimondi yet again, this time to win the Tour of Catalonia. Gimondi had been the precocious new star of Italian cycling: handsome and urbane, son of a postwoman and a lorry driver who initially could not even afford to buy him a bicycle. He was three years older than Merckx and, at twenty-six, approaching full physical maturity. On the bike, he was a stylist: spinning the pedals far more smoothly and with less impression of effort than the brutally physical Merckx. Watching him ride, the purists purred.

Their careers had run parallel since he won the Brussels–Alsemberg amateur classic ahead of Merckx in 1963. In 1964 Merckx won the world amateur road race championship with Gimondi fifth. At the Olympic Games, Gimondi had been responsible for Merckx being caught after a late attack. Unlike Merckx, the Italian had broken through immediately he turned professional in 1965. That year, he became one of the youngest ever Tour de France winners, and he added the Tour of Spain and Tour of Italy in the following two seasons, plus Paris–Roubaix and the Giro di Lombardia. It was all enough for the Italian media to crown him as the obvious successor to their late lamented darling Fausto Coppi.

Suddenly, however, Gimondi was confronted with a rival who was faster in every area, and who was considerably younger. After Merckx defeated him in the time trial in Catalonia the Italian lay awake that night in a state of torment, wondering what he had got wrong: had he made a poor tyre choice? Had he selected the wrong gears?

He said later he felt that his fate was sealed. 'I had had a vertiginous rise and suddenly I had to be happy winning far less. I can't say I hated him. It was tough. I had trouble adapting to the problem he set me because all he wanted to do was win. That was all. I had to change my mindset. There were a couple of years when it was very hard to get used to. I had to begin again from nothing, take the initiative less in a race because when he was there it was hard to get a grip on things.' While Godefroot, and later Roger De Vlaeminck at least managed to cling on to the idea that they might stand a chance against Merckx in the Classics, Gimondi seemed broken. Between 1968 and 1972 he would not beat Merckx in any head-to-head confrontation in a major race.

The year 1968 had marked the point when Merckx gained such a psychological hold that most of his rivals had no option but to wait for him to make his move and then see if they could hang on, and if so, for how long. COMINCIA IL CICLISMO – cycling starts here – ran one headline after Lavaredo, and it was true. A new era had begun. The Cannibal had been unleashed.

OUI OR YA?

The Eddy Merckx metro station lies on the outer reaches of the Brussels underground, the *Bruxellois* equivalent of Cockfosters or Alperton. Line five crosses the Belgian capital from east to west, a modern, airy mass-transit system. The Merckx station, penultimate stop on the south-western branch, is bizarrely understated given that it is named after the country's leading sportsman. You can leave by the north exit without even noticing the tiny display that commemorates the great cyclist, although when you come back through the south exit you can't miss it: the small glass case on the platform, with a track bike, a section of the wooden boards from a cycling track and a handful of photographs. And that's it. Other than the Merckx display, there is a very fine Magritte-style surrealist mural – which holds the attention for far longer than the Merckx artefacts – and, outside, a large stand for supermarket trolleys.

Forty miles away in Oudenaarde the travelling cycling fan gets a very different experience indeed. The Tour of Flanders museum stands in a brand new building opposite the vast church just outside the main square. Up top is a fine café and a shop crammed with memorabilia, while the basement is devoted to a huge display that celebrates the great race that has criss-crossed the area since 1913 and the men who have forged its history. There are the obligatory woollen jerseys, vintage bikes and fading race programmes, a glitzy film that underlines the connection between Flandrian cycling and the area's strong Catholic tradition, but most amusing is the exposition of what it means to be a Flandrian cyclist. *Homo flandriensis* is epitomised by Briek Schotte, a professional for twenty seasons and a double winner of the Ronde van Vlaanderen. It is Schotte who is the model for the statue *De Flandrien*, in his hometown of Kanegem, a statue unveiled by the Flemish minister of culture. The picture of Schotte bent over his bike on the museum wall is accompanied by a list of attributes of the Flandrian cyclist. It is only partly tongue in cheek: races best in foul weather, rides his bike until he can't remember the name of his parish, silent and never complains, physically strong and persevering, inexhaustible, best as an underdog. Plus, most critically: comes from East or West Flanders.

Regional identity lies at the core of this race and the entire cycling culture that is built around it. They are so closely entwined that it is impossible to say whether the race stems from the culture or the identity comes from the race. The founder of *de Ronde*, Karel Van Wijnendaele, 'linked the sporting battle of "his" Flandrians to the quest for a more self-aware Flanders' says the museum literature. He also wrote a best-selling book that underpinned this cycling subculture: *Het Rijke Vlaamse Wielerleven* (The Realm of Flemish Cycling Life). Hidden among the panels on the walls is a rather smug one which underlines that this whole race and the cycling culture that goes with it is about separateness, the sense of difference. The panel deals with how cyclists from Wallonia, Belgium's French-speaking region, have fared over the years in the *Ronde*. It describes a single victory and a few podium places, and points out that Van Wijnendaele was not above Flandrianising the names of the rare Walloons who made it on to the podium, so that they fitted better into the race's identity – Karel for Charles, for example. Elsewhere, there is little about the hat-trick scored by the Italian Fiorenzo Magni between 1949 and 1951. This is a happily chauvinist, inward-looking institution.

One parallel for Flanders' place in cycling would be rugby and South Wales. In both sports and regions, wrote Geoffrey Nicholson, 'a people who feel themselves exploited and outsmarted have come to use sport as a means of demanding recognition of their worth and separate identity'. In a region of 'industrial grime and domestic spit and polish,' as Nicholson wrote, Flandrian cycling culture is one of stern tradition, handed down through generations. There are many cases of brothers being professional cyclists, of fathers, sons, grandsons. It is a world of Catholicism, big families, unswerving loyalty to one's birthplace and the language. Writing about Roger De Vlaeminck, the English humorist Harry Pearson was only partly joking when he said: 'He speaks Italian, a bit of English, a smattering of Spanish, but he regards French as the language of the enemy.'

Outsiders can be co-opted as Flandrians if they come here and live and breathe cycling – the Australians Scott Sunderland and Phil Anderson, the Russian Andrei Tchmil, Ireland's Sean Kelly and the Americans Joe Parkin and Tyler Farrar are all examples – but cycling here is about localism. The Tour of Flanders itself is based in one small area: the hills between the rivers Schelde to the west and Dender to the east. Known as the Flemish Ardennes (as if to underline that hills are not restricted to the Ardennes of Wallonia) the hills are peppered with cobbled lanes with legendary names: *de Oude Kwaremont*, Patersberg, Koppenberg and, on the east side of the Dender valley, the *Kapelmuur* at Geraardsbergen. Each Flandrian cycling hero has his own supporters club, based in a local bar that in turn is likely to be run by a former professional.

The linguistic divide cannot be understated in cycling terms. Over the years, relatively few Belgian cyclists racing at the highest level have come from outside the Flandrian heartland. Merckx is one of those few, along with his henchman Jos Bruyère, a Walloon from the French-speaking area between

Liège and the Dutch border. (Ferdinand Bracke, winner of the Tour of Spain in 1971, was brought up in Wallonia, but came from a Flandrian family.) Bruyère actually spoke Dutch as well, because he had a Dutch mother and that was what they spoke at home. 'Eddy spoke both languages but the team spoke Flemish. There might be ten riders, one Walloon – me – eight Flemish riders and Eddy talking both [languages],' he says. The Flemish riders did tend to look down on the Walloons – 'they would say we weren't courageous, because we were used to riding on hilly roads where the bunch would split, and it was said that the Walloons would race three years then quit.'

As for where Merckx fits into the linguistic and cultural divide, the answer is simple: he is on neither side, in the same way that the metro station that bears his name seems a slightly awkward add-on. Merckx was born into a Flemish-speaking family and has won *de Ronde* twice, both in epic circumstances, but that doesn't make him a Flandrian. One great Flandrian snorted derisively when the question was put to him. Merckx merits respect as a double winner of *de Ronde*, and receives his due in the museum displays, but he still does not have the credentials of, say, Johan Museeuw – born Varsenare, near Brugge; a triple winner, the third time on a route that had been modified to take in his home village; the man who said winning *de Ronde* was more important than taking the yellow jersey in the Tour de France.

'In Flanders, though personal style is much admired, local patriotism is the dominant passion,' wrote Geoffrey Nicholson. 'The rage for success breeds strong attachments and deep jealousies. To respect Merckx is to despise [Freddy] Maertens. Every man who fights his way to the top is avidly searched for the flaw in his character.' So it was with Merckx, with elements of the Flandrian media at least. The importance of the linguistic identity is shown by the bizarre story of Merckx's marriage vows, which became, briefly, a major national issue after the newly crowned world professional champion married in December 1967. The question concerned the choice of language for the ceremony. It became a matter of national debate, because the implication was – erroneously – that Merckx must have a preference for one Belgian language over the other. In fact he speaks neither perfectly, most probably because he spoke Flemish at home as a child, but was educated in French. Sometimes he mixed the two: he is most at his ease in *Bruxellois* dialect, which is primarily French, with its own adjuncts from Flemish. The Merckx marriage ceremony was in French, so the Flemish newspapers took that as a statement. In fact, Claudine happened to pick up a marriage certificate which was in French, and the custom at the time was that this meant the ceremony would be in French as well. The curé asked Merckx's mother if she wanted anything said in Flemish, and she said it wasn't worth it. It probably wasn't but Flandrian sensitivities meant that it was taken the wrong way.

As one writer put it, the marriage 'fixed the linguistic impression of Merckxism for good. Because he said "oui" instead of "ya" the Brabançon would never be totally accepted by the Flandrians.' Merckx received aggressive letters after the news was revealed; the question did not go away: when he met the King in 1970, rather than what he said to the monarch he was asked in what language they had been talking. Similarly, there were calls from the Flandrian media, when he won the 1969 Tour, for Flemish fans to cheer him on in Flemish rather than French. 'The most astonishing example of the linguistic worry came with the birth of Sabrina. She should not have been called Sabrina. Claudine had chosen Laurence for a girl, Didier for a boy. But it was too French,' wrote Marc Jeuniau. Both the Merckx children, Axel and Sabrina, have names which are neither Flemish nor French. The issue also arose – again through the papers – when Merckx's children grew up: was he bringing up his daughter Sabrina to talk Flemish or French, asked journalists. Every time Eddy donated to charity, Claudine said, he had to do it in equal parts, one for Flanders, one for Wallonia.

Regional identity within cycling was stronger in the time of Merckx than it is now, not merely in Belgium, although there it was particularly pronounced. The extensive calendar meant that cyclists could race largely in their home areas, and the teams would have strong local identities, because there were so many cyclists of talent coming out of the various bits of Flanders that managers could pick riders from their region rather than a little further away. For example, one great with whom I discussed Flandrian identity felt that even he was not really accepted, although Flemish was his first language, merely because he came from East rather than West Flanders. In this world of clearly delineated identities, Merckx could not be pigeonholed, in the same way that his region was linguistically ambiguous, neither Wallonia nor Flanders. Asked at the age of twenty by an Italian journalist which of the two he was, his answer was emphatic: 'Belgian. Belgian and nothing else.'

Merckx's status as a non-Flandrian had always mattered, from the day he began to race a bike. Here, his parents' move from the country to the city immediately after the war ended played a role. The area where he was raised was not as cycling mad as the working-class villages of Flanders were, each of them boasting at least one former champion within the population, with Meensel-Kiezegem being no exception. In contrast, the more middle-class population of the Chant d'Oiseau locale in Woluwe was interested in tennis, hockey, fencing – one suspects because cycling was seen as socially inferior – and perhaps this was another reason why Merckx's mother was

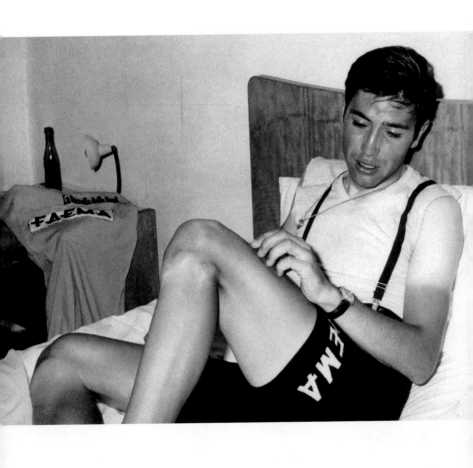

initially against him racing. In the long term it was probably better for him. As he said early on, only a handful of people outside his family followed his racing. There were no outpourings when he won a race. Instead, he clearly felt he had to fight to prove his right to be a cyclist in the face of his mother's doubts.

Merckx has said that not having a supporters' club such as those found across Flanders helped as well: no one ever told him he was doing well when he wasn't. There was a small party for his win in the Belgian amateur championship in 1962, but nothing more. He received little unconditional praise. 'Morally, I had to work things out for myself and that was an advantage in the end.' He also lacked the financial support a supporters' club might have given him in his early years – that in turn meant his only obligation was to his parents, and there was less need to repay debts. Merckx could concentrate on what he wanted to do: race, and win.

Moreover, his attitude to cycling was not parochial in the slightest. It did not begin and end with the Tour of Flanders: Merckx was taken to watch the Tour de France by his father as a child and his earliest goal was a gold medal in the Olympic Games. As a youth, he was not interested in the Classics, only the Tour de France. His early heroes, Stan Ockers and Jacques Anquetil, never won *de Ronde*. The Tour de France was his dream, and not the Tour of Flanders.

Throughout his career Merckx simultaneously embraced and endured the status of a *Bruxellois*. He was on the edge of Flandrian cycling but participated wholeheartedly in its greatest races and pulled cycling in Flanders upwards as he rose to world domination and others tried to match him. He earned respect, won many hearts and minds but was never completely integrated. He was within it but was not of it. 'Brussels is both the capital of the kingdom and the capital of bilingualism,' wrote Léon Zitrone. 'A *Bruxellois* can become the symbol of the whole nation, not so much because he comes from the capital but because he can use both languages. Being from Brussels means you gain the favour of the entire nation.'

When Merckx began making a name for himself nationally, he had to fight for his place in the face of the Flandrians, for example when he struggled to get his place in the 1964 world amateur championship. Later, he had to overcome a pro-Flandrian bias in the papers of the time. 'If you didn't come from East or West Flanders you had to have a serious case if you wanted people to believe you were a star. There was a sort of "Flandrian reflex",' said one journalist. Belgian cycling was not short of stars, and Flandrian stars at that: a young lad from French-speaking Brussels didn't get the media that excited. Having seen how the press dropped Van Looy at the end of his career, Merckx learned to be restrained in what he said and vigorous in what he did on the bike. The best response he could provide was to be seen on days such as 30 March 1969.

It was raining heavily in Ghent that day, but this was entirely in the order of things. The Tour of Flanders is not always rained on but it is an event that needs wet and cold to be truly epic and so it was for Merckx's first victory in *de Ronde*. The rain poured, a wind howled out of the west. The race remains legendary. The day's events hinged on a change in the course direction after a hundred kilometres, when the race reached Torhout after heading west from Ghent: there the gale changed from a pure headwind into a crosswind, favouring action at the head of the bunch. The hostilities were started by Frans Verbeeck, who epitomised the Flandrian professionals who lived for and through the April Classics. Merckx then took charge and the bunch split to bits with over 160 kilometres still to race. Only twenty-three riders survived the wind-lashed selection to make it into the front group, including four Italians – Gimondi, Franco Bitossi, Dancelli and Marino Basso. Merckx made his first move on the *Oude Kwaremont*, a narrow strip of windswept cobbles running through the fields above the town of Kluisbergen, up a hill that ran parallel with the newer main road. A puncture held him up, but he attacked again on the *Kapelmuur* – a one-in-four brute out of the town of Geraardsbergen to a hilltop chapel – where Gimondi and his countrymen kept him on the leash.

He kept on attacking and with about seventy kilometres remaining – before the race returned into the wind to finish in Gentbrugge, close to the start – he got clear, simply by pressing a little harder on the pedals. Rather than making an intentional, dramatic attack, he ratcheted up the pressure. The journalist Théo Mathy described the scene: 'Going through the village of Tollembeek, after doing his turn at the front of the group, he gained a few bike lengths on the others. He moved across to the side of the road, turned round and assessed the situation. Then he went on. There were 70km left to the finish. It was raining and the gusts of wind were bending the trees. No matter.' Merckx's thinking was simple but typical of him: riding back to the finish into the headwind, it would be far easier for the other riders to hang on in his slipstream. That meant they had to be eliminated beforehand. In this version of the course – which has changed several times since then – there were no major climbs in the run-in to the finish. If the lead group remained together, it was by no means certain that he could beat Basso, who was particularly rapid in a sprint. During the slog to Gentbrugge, the time gaps stretched out to a ridiculous extent. Gimondi came in second, five minutes thirty-six seconds behind. The lead group was eight minutes back. Van Looy, now definitively yesterday's Emperor, was a quarter of an hour off the pace.

Merckx's status had changed since his world title and his Giro d'Italia win. He was now expected to win everywhere he raced but the paper that sponsored the Tour of Flanders, *Het Niewsblad*, had speculated that maybe Merckx lacked that little something special it takes to win their race. There has always been a strong element of nostalgia to Flemish cycling, best expressed in the fact that 'the Last of the Flandrians' is an honorary title that has been bestowed several times, notably on Schotte and Museeuw. With this implicit concern about how the present matches up to the past, the question was clear: could the new, *Bruxellois*, champion match the Flandrian legends of yesteryear? Merckx said to Guillaume Michiels that he could answer his critics if the weather cooperated, and so he did, leaving the strongest cyclists of his generation floundering in his wake.

There were other statements that spring: Merckx had won Milan–San Remo for the third time in four years. That *classicissima* victory came at the end of a seventeen-day winning spree in which he took nine victories – the overall and three stages in both the Tour of the Levant in Spain and Paris–Nice – which would have been a more than satisfactory season for most professionals. He won in San Remo after a descent of the Poggio which was so insanely fast that no television or stills motorbike could keep pace with him: at the summit his advantage was a mere ten metres over a chase group; at the foot it was thirty seconds. 'I thought he was going to kill himself,' said Vincenzo Giacotto. Going downhill fast on a bike sounds simple to the outsider, but to do so that much faster than a chase group in the final miles of a major Classic is only possible if a cyclist is physically in the finest shape, so that he can sprint out of each hairpin in the biggest gear possible, and mentally has pitch-perfect reactions, to calculate each corner faultlessly. Merckx backed up victory in Flanders with another hugely dominant Classic win, in Liège–Bastogne–Liège, taken with a seventy-kilometre escape in pouring rain together with his teammate Vic Van Schil. The margin was eight minutes. There may have been shock at the emphatic nature of the win, but there can have been little surprise.

That Tour of Flanders was marked by one particularly celebrated episode, which marked another little step in Merckx's emergence as a champion in his own right. Faema's biggest signing over the winter of 1968–9 was not a cyclist, but a new team manager, Lomme Driessens. That completed the transformation of Faema from a mixed Italian–Belgian team to a largely Belgian squad. Vittorio Adorni left, and the number of Italian *gregari* dropped from thirteen out of twenty-six to seven out of twenty-four. That had effectively sealed the squad as being completely focused on Merckx, with one proviso: relations with the new manager were never easy. Driessens was unsurpassed as a self-publicist. His fame was based on his claims that he had managed Fausto Coppi, whereas in fact he just looked after Coppi's Bianchi team only when they raced in Belgium. 'Lomme' was also nicknamed 'Guillaume the liar', 'not a perjorative term in cycling, just a tribute to his ability to play his cards close to his chest,' wrote Roger Bastide. Not long after Merckx had made his escape in the Tour of Flanders, Driessens drove up alongside in his Peugeot and asked him the question: what was he doing, had he gone mad? Merckx's answer was short and to the point: 'kiss my ass'.

Driessens' appointment had been Van Buggenhout's idea. It was his way of sorting out undercurrents of conflict between the Italian and Belgian elements within Faema, and, some claim, also a way of 'selling' Merckx to Flandrian cycling fans through Driessens' big personality. Lomme had close links to the Flemish press, the idea being that he would smooth Merckx's path with them. That had a side effect, however:

Driessens tended to exclude the francophone media while sweet-talking the Flandrian writers. Driessens had made friends with Merckx during the 1967 Giro, when he was managing the delightfully named Romeo-Smiths team. None of their riders were up to the job, so he offered advice to Merckx on a daily basis, whether Merckx wanted it or not one suspects. But Merckx had little time for actors and he soon found out that Driessens was all mouth and no trousers.

Driessens' rigid notion that his riders should race to a plan was at odds with Merckx's view of competition as guerrilla warfare. In a race, Merckx was constantly ready to improvise, always looking for a chance to surprise his rivals. Merckx tended to attack, then ask Driessens if he should go on. Driessens usually had no option but to agree, telling Merckx what he wanted to hear, but – so it is now said – with trepidation at the thought that if Merckx cracked he would be held accountable.

This was the background to the now legendary incident at that Tour of Flanders: a new manager, not yet quite sure what his protégé was capable of, and well aware of the press opprobrium that would follow if he failed. Merckx broke away, opened a gap, but there were still over an hour and twenty minutes' racing until he reached the finish. For most cyclists, this would have been a pure suicide move. On paper, nobody was capable of staying away alone for such a distance, into a powerful headwind, with a strong group chasing behind. The little exchange with Driessens followed, and the relationship never really worked out. In the summer of 1971 Driessens was looking for another job. Freddy Maertens would be his next protégé. The point was this: Merckx would run his teams in his own way, bringing in his own man, Bob Lelangue. In future, his team managers would never question his way of racing.

After San Remo in 1966 and Lavaredo in 1968, that day in Flanders was another landmark. Merckx's identity as a

Bruxellois was the more pronounced, and his struggle for acceptance among the Flandrian media all the harder, because he raced against an incredibly strong generation of Flandrian cyclists born at or just after the end of the Second World War: Van Looy, Eric Leman, Godefroot, Van Springel, Sercu, Maertens, De Vlaeminck, Johan De Muynck, Michel Pollentier, Ferdinand Bracke, Lucien Van Impe, along with a host of strong second stringers such as Verbeeck, André Dierickx, Ward Sels, Willy Planckaert and Marc De Meyer. The late 1960s and early 1970s were the high-water mark of Belgian cycling, which is still hankering after those golden years.

After Merckx had beaten the Flandrians on their home roads in the only race that truly mattered to them, and done it in such emphatic style, his dominance was no longer under discussion. The matter had been settled because of the huge number of world-class adversaries who had been left trailing over the last two years, with no idea how to respond. 'Merckx is Van Looy plus Coppi', said one team manager.

March the thirtieth 1969 also marked the end of Van Looy's struggle to assert himself against the *Bruxellois* upstart, which had continued in Milan–San Remo a few weeks earlier when The Emperor initiated an early break to get away from Merckx. The rivalry with Van Looy has to be seen in the Flandrian context of incestuous enmity: this was a tightly knit little world composed of rival clans and teams and personal interests. 'It was an eye for an eye, tooth for a tooth,' as Godefroot recalled. 'We would fight fit to burst for a win or an insignificant *prime*.' It was only partly about money, more a battle for prestige and bragging rights in that milieu; within the borders of Flanders it all mattered intensely, while outside it was perhaps not accorded major significance.

A profile in *Time* magazine painted an evocative portrait of The Emperor, a man who lived only for his bike: 'On those rare occasions when he is home, Van Looy is all work: before dawn each morning, he struggles out of bed, climbs on his bike and does his "daily 50" – a fifty-kilometre grind over the quiet roads around Herentals. He has little time for friends, even less for his fans. He smiles only under duress, refuses to sign autographs, pose for pictures or answer questions before a race. His vocation has deformed his body, leaving him with a bony chest and shoulders, arms that are stumpy and weak. He runs only with difficulty, and he cannot even walk very far without agonizing cramps.'

The rivalry between Van Looy and Merckx was not the stuff of Corinthian romance. Merckx would tell the story of how Van Looy would chase him down in a criterium when he attacked to take a *prime*, and then would sit on his wheel, saying, 'you're the greatest, you'll have to do it all yourself you know'. He would then sprint past young Eddy for the *prime* with a comment along the lines of 'so, you only win when you've got ten teammates alongside you, is that it?' Merckx's explanation was that Van Looy had never got over the fact that he, Merckx, had left his team. 'I've tried at least ten times to calm things down between us but each time he provokes a new argument. I've reached the end of my tether. I don't talk to him any more.' Van Looy is aware of this, and told me that if he clung to Merckx's wheel it was because it was the obvious thing to do, the sensible tactic. 'When I was the best guy, it was the same for me,' he said.

In 1970 Merckx said of Van Looy, 'I admire the champion, I like the man a lot less. The relations I've had with Rik leave me few good memories.' Merckx cited a criterium, in 1968, on his home turf at Woluwe-Saint-Lambert, when Van Looy 'played dead' then outsprinted him. 'A champion of his dimension should have stopped earlier, with more panache.' The pair received an eight-day suspended ban (a slap on the wrist in essence) for negative racing after a criterium in 1969 when Van Looy held Merckx's back wheel as if glued to it, and Merckx responded by slowing up so drastically that they were both lapped by the field. That evening, in another race, Merckx attacked out of every corner until Van Looy was dropped and humiliated.

Van Looy, at the same time, was not charitable about his young rival, producing lines such as these: 'he's vulnerable, he's been lucky, I wonder if he'll bounce back when he is beaten head-to-head, he's morally fragile and can't take defeat, half his team left him this year, I wonder why, he's not an easy guy to get along with, he will never be the greatest, Anquetil made me suffer more, and then I was at my best, when I took over from Van Steenbergen he was only twenty-nine, I wish it was the same with me and Merckx' (Van Looy was now thirty-two). That last phrase was key: he sounded like an old champion who was unhappy at the arrival of the young pretender. For Van Looy, the rivalry was about more than prestige: at issue was the contract money from the national criterium circuit. It was a huge proportion of a cyclist's annual income. Van Looy was declining physically but was hugely popular because of his racing style and public image; Merckx gave less to the public but won more.

The eclipse of Van Looy was total now, and that marked the birth of a new hierarchy within cycling. During the late 1950s and through the 1960s, after the decline and death of Fausto Coppi, the top end of professional cycling had settled into a fairly rigid structure, with the arrival of Rik II and Jacques Anquetil at the top of the sport. The Emperor dominated the Classics. Master Jacques ruled the stage races. Around them there was a clique of leaders who formed a little magic circle, the *grands coureurs*. They creamed off the bulk of the start money in the criteriums and track meetings and didn't exactly fix the major races as such but did their utmost to ensure that the circle of big winners was kept small. That way, their appearance fees remained high. It wasn't formal: a rider could break in, and quite a few did, but they had to abide by the unwritten rules and not rock the boat. Everyone at the top benefited, because they were guaranteed a relatively straightforward existence in a super-tough milieu.

Anquetil and Van Looy were in decline when Merckx arrived, but his emergence put an end to their manner of doing things, because he raced in ways that the elite weren't used to. He would attack many miles from the finish and would defy tactical logic by having the strength to hang on. He could sprint, he could climb, he could win three-week stage races, and he was forming a strong team around him. They simply didn't know how to respond: the bitterness Van Looy showed was largely because he could see change happening and he could do nothing about it. Merckx could be beaten but it took a bludgeon, or, rather, several bludgeons, rather than the waving of a purse. The only solution was for a team to be present in numbers at the key moment of a race – as the Flandria team were in Paris–Roubaix the week after that Tour of Flanders in 1969. There, they had four men in the front group: Roger and Eric De Vlaeminck, Eric Leman and Godefroot, who attacked three times and got clean away the third time.

Physically, Merckx as champion did not fit the Flandrian mould either. 'A miner and built like one. Billiard-table legs and a chest like the front of a coal barge' was one British writer's description of the average Flandrian. The Flandrians tended to be stocky, gritty, bulldog riders in the style of Walter Godefroot, Rik Van Looy, Frans Verbeeck or Eric Leman, and later on Marc De Meyer and Michel Pollentier. Stylish grey-hounds such as Roger De Vlaeminck or Freddy Maertens were the exception rather than the rule.

Merckx was emphatic rather than aesthetic in his style. The Giro d'Italia stage to the Tre Cime di Lavaredo had first revealed to the cycling world the sheer strength of the man who was now its master. Merckx's way of riding was only partly dependent on pedalling speed and suppleness. Mostly, he relied on pure power, 'hardly aesthetic but admirable for its intensity and its efficiency', as one writer observed. Flat out on his bike, Merckx had a style that was unique and lacked the effortless grace that was the hallmark of Anquetil, Coppi or Hugo Koblet, the legendary *pedaleur de charme*. 'He wobbles his shoulders, grapples with the bars, stands on the pedals, moves his hips like a madman,' wrote one journalist. 'He doesn't fight like a stylist but like a thug. It's like the difference between a boxer sparring and a whirling Apache horde.'

That had first been noted when he won his amateur world title back in 1964, when *l'Equipe*'s correspondent described him 'moving his head from one side to the other to the rhythm of his pedal strokes . . .' although when he rode the break off his wheel it noted he was 'still nodding at the head but in a more accentuated manner'. 'He may be a pleasure to watch but he's not elegant,' said the Frenchman Albert Bouvet. 'He's extremely efficient and he gives an impression of extraordinary power. He sits back in the saddle and gets the entire weight of his body on each pedal as he presses it down. He moves his body from side to side, there is a certain stiffness, a bit of heaviness. It's all power.'

Watch footage of Merckx racing flat out, be it up a mountain pass or trying to escape the pack in the finale of a Classic, and the left–right movement of the shoulders with each pedal stroke is always there, varying with the effort between mild and extreme, to the point where at times it looks as if he's going to dive off his bike, particularly when he is attacking on a mountain. It is the same throughout his career, be it the stage victory at the Blockhaus in the 1967 Giro d'Italia, training sessions behind the motorbike of Guillaume Michiels or the mountains of the Giro and Tour in the mid-1970s. At times it is as if he is diving forward over the bike with his arms bent on the brake levers. The mouth is half open beneath the slicked back Elvis Presley hair, the high cheekbones and long sideburns. The effort is there for all to see, and that went down well.

'When Anquetil made an effort you couldn't see him making it, even when he was dropping everyone, but with Eddy, you could always see him working on the bike,' Patrick Sercu told me. 'You could see the rage on his face, his shoulders moving. That impressed the public as well.' Merckx differed from the archetypal Flandria champions in one vital respect: he was – just – slender enough to get over a mountain pass with the best climbers. Climbing was an area in which the traditional Flandrian champion such as Van Looy or Van Steenbergen did not excel, hence the rarity of victories by Belgians in the Tour de France, last taken by a Belgian in 1939.

Most importantly of all, Merckx differed from the Flandrians in his focus. There were Flandrians such as Leman who built a career around winning the Tour of Flanders – which he managed three times – and those like Verbeeck who spent an entire career trying to win it and narrowly failing. For Merckx, the Flandrian Classics mattered only in that they were races, prestigious races, but there to be won among a raft of other great events rather than the crowning glory of a season or a career.

Ironically, however, although he never fitted the Flandrian cycling template, and spent all of his career apart from the first and last years in the service of French and Italian sponsors, Merckx would raise his sport to a level never seen before in his home country, precisely because his lack of linguistic identity meant he could attain universal popularity. Asked a week after his first Tour win what he stood for, he said 'a symbol of unity'. Another Belgian described him as 'our uncrowned King'.

'Merckx elevated the status of cycling in Belgium' believes Walter Godefroot. In this, Merckx's status as a *Bruxellois* was critical. 'His personality meant there was more respect accorded to the sport as a whole, and his victories felt good whether you were Flemish or Walloon. He was invited by the King and his son into the castle because they were supporters of him like everyone else.' Indeed, the Belgian royal family were so keen on Merckx that you suspect they were hoping some of his lustre would rub off on them. They travelled to see him race, and watched the Giro when they were on holiday in Italy. They were photographed with him informally, at tables strewn with bottles that suggested they had been drinking happily together.

With the royal seal of approval and a cyclist from the capital to admire, cycling in Belgium changed over the Merckx years. It ceased to be seen as a purely working-class Flemish sport and became one with broader appeal, one which the middle classes could watch without the feeling they were lowering themselves. In France, in contrast, the educated middle classes remained prejudiced against the peasants' sport for many years, because they could not identify with sons of the soil such as Anquetil and Bernard Thévenet. 'Here in Belgium we have a third generation of prime ministers who ride bikes,' says Godefroot. 'Having the prime minister ride a bike was unthinkable fifty years ago. It's Merckx who made the sport respectable, universal. There was no discussion of whether he was a

Flamand or a Walloon. He was one of us.' Gripings about language in the Flandrian media apart, Merckx transcended nationalism in a way that made him akin to royalty, and in fact he transcended royalty. He had gained his heroic status through his own efforts rather than through birth. His near-daily appearances at one race or another made him more accessible and better known than the King. It was summed up in the cartoon that depicted him shaking hands with the King, with the caption: who's this man next to Merckx?

All the Belgian riders – and that meant the Flandrians – raced in Merckx's shadow henceforth: they were all compared to him, continually. The process started when he quit Rik Van Looy's Solo team and goes on to this day. When a promising amateur went up into the professional peloton, the same questions would arise. Could he beat Merckx? Was he a possible successor to Merckx? For the established stars, from now on racing centred on Merckx. If he was absent from a race or under the weather, they would have a chance. If he was present and in form or merely motivated, their only option was to base their race around him. They reacted in different ways. Lucien Van Impe opted merely to be the best climber – this was a domain where he knew he could hold his own because it was outside Merckx's dominion. Herman Van Springel made a speciality of the Bordeaux–Paris Classic, a race that Merckx never entered. Roger De Vlaeminck simply didn't worry about pushing for the overall win in the Vuelta, Tour de France or Giro after contesting a single Tour with Merckx.

In the 1976 Tour, it was noted that Freddy Maertens was constantly reproached because he did not ride like Merckx. 'It's true that I'm not very popular because of Eddy Merckx,' said Maertens, tipped, like many, as the next Cannibal. 'Those who like him, and they are numerous, can't like anyone else. It's normal. He's a great champion. Still, I'm used to it.' When he reached his peak in the mid-1970s, Maertens clearly felt that he had no option but to race like Merckx, attacking alone rather than using his sprint – which was more than good enough to win most races – and pushing himself to feats such as a quartet of Classic wins in 1976, and a victory in the 1977 Tour of Spain with thirteen stage wins along the way. There was massive controversy between Merckx and Maertens at the world championship in Barcelona in 1973, largely because the Flandrian media were discovering a new hero and that hero had to be a rival for Merckx. In the process of attempting to become Merckx's equal, Maertens burned himself out, psychologically, physically and financially, and the man who acts, occasionally, as guide at the Tour of Flanders museum in Oudenaarde seems like a shadow of a great cycling champion.

SAVONA

The Italian writer Gian-Paolo Ormezzano had always had a soft spot for Eddy Merckx, since the day in March 1966 when his editor at the Torinese newspaper *Tuttosport* had asked him to write his prediction for Milan–San Remo. He chose Merckx purely on a hunch, having seen him racing the previous week, and because he felt like living dangerously. Ormezzano was also close to Merckx's manager, Vincenzo Giacotto, and accompanied Faema's *direttore sportivo* when he travelled to Brussels to sign the Belgian in September 1967.

That explained why, on 2 June 1969, he found himself being given a flask of Merckx's urine, with a walk-on part in one of cycling's greatest whodunits. 'Pure Agatha Christie,' he recalls when asked about the episode that is now known as the '*scandalo di Savona*'. It remains one of the great unexplained cycling stories, the centre of claim and counter-claim, one theory after another over the years. But it is more than a mere controversy: the greatest moments of Merckx's career can be traced back to this one day in the small, dingy resort of Albisola Marina on the Ligurian coast, thirty-five kilometres from Genoa.

As June began, Merckx was in complete control of his own destiny, or so he thought. The year had gone seamlessly with victories in the Tour of the Levant, Paris–Nice and three Classics, each a masterpiece in its own right: Milan–San Remo, the Tour of Flanders and Liège–Bastogne–Liège. The Giro d'Italia of that year had started in Garda on 16 May. Merckx was planning to ride more defensively than the previous year, as he was set to compete in the Tour de France as well, but he began to shake the race up as early as stage three over the Abetone Pass to Montecatini, which he won. He added the next day's time trial – his hundredth win as a professional in a mere four years – then landed stage seven to Terracina and took the pink race leader's jersey on stage nine to Potenza. After the stage to San Marino, stage fifteen, he was leading his old rival Gimondi by one minute forty-one seconds. The Giro was not over by any means but with the toughest stages still to come he had a strong chance of repeating his victory of 1968. According to journalists who spoke to him during the rest day at Parma, he was totally confident he would win. As Ormezzano recalls, there was little doubt among any observers that the race would belong to Merckx, and that he would dominate as completely as he had done in the previous year.

However, there were reminders that events might intervene: Merckx came close to crashing in the finish of the stage in Savona when his back wheel was hit by the front wheel of a television camera motorbike as he cornered during the build-up to the sprint. But by then he had won four stages out of sixteen. At 10.15 on the morning of 2 June, in room eleven of the Hotel Excelsior in Albisola Marina, Merckx and his teammate Martin Van Den Bossche were killing time for the last quarter of an hour before setting off for the start of stage seventeen. Merckx was lying on his bed with the pink jersey he would wear that day spread out alongside him; Van Den Bossche was crunching into an apple when the door opened, and the Faema *direttore sportivo*, Vincenzo Giacotto, entered with the race director, Vincenzo Torriani, a television camera crew and two journalists: the Belgian Théo Mathy and the Italian Bruno Raschi.

The message was brief and devastating: Merckx had been found positive from the previous day's stage, for the stimulant fencamfamine, which was similar to amphetamine but about half the strength: it was found in a commonly used appetite suppressant called Reactivan, which was available over the counter in pharmacies. Merckx had no right of appeal and must leave the race forthwith. It was a *fait accompli* to which there was no answer. To complete his humiliation, he was interviewed shortly afterwards by RAI television, with other riders and journalists crowding into his hotel room. The pictures show Merckx in a state of collapse, holding his head in his hands in despair as he lies on the bed. When interviewed, he was in tears, wiping his eyes with a handkerchief, his voice cracking, a little high-pitched, as he said in French. 'It's shameful. I don't know what to say. I am sure I took nothing. I'm sure of it. I don't understand anything.' It was the first time a race leader had been found positive and thrown off a major professional Tour.

As the tears flowed in the hotel room, Giacotto drew Ormezzano aside, and passed him the little bottle of urine. The idea was that, perhaps, it might be possible to use the sample to carry out a private, unofficial analysis, which might at least prove that Merckx did not have the substance in his system. The test would have absolutely no legal value – it's unclear as well how it would have been proven that the urine in the flask even belonged to the Belgian – but in such moments any straw is worth clutching. The analysis was never done: the urine was not used. Ormezzano does not remember what he did with it: he assumes it was thrown away.*

Merckx drove home through the night with his wife Claudine in the knowledge that he was banned for a month, which

---

* There are reports that a private test was carried out that day, in the presence of Ormezzano and two other journalists. The Italian's version of events clearly suggests such a test never happened.

meant he would not be able to start the Tour de France. He returned, contemplating putting an end to his career. There was speculation that Faema might sack him. The letters of support started flooding in and moves were begun to have the ban overturned.

The 'Savona affair' has to be seen in the context of the time. The anti-doping process – it wasn't yet sustained enough to call it a campaign – was still in its formative years. It was less than two years since Tom Simpson's death had led to the re-examination of the way doping was policed, it was less than twelve months since the *Tour de Santé* of 1968 which had seen the first regular urine tests, and the authorities were still trying to work out what approach was best. The notion that tests should happen at all was still relatively new. The tide had turned in favour of the pro-testing lobby, but such absolute basics as the list of banned substances, the methodology of testing – how often tests should be done, what counter-analyses to apply – and the scale of sanctions were still embryonic. The background issue, that in terms of racing and travelling the riders' workloads were insanely heavy, remained the same as before Simpson's death.

In 1968 ten riders had been found positive in the Giro, including some of the biggest stars such as Franco Balmamion, Gimondi and Motta. The scandal implicated the Giro winners of 1962, 1963, 1966 and 1967, while Gimondi's positive test was most damaging of all because of his status as the heir apparent to Bartali and Coppi. The episode led to Gimondi and Motta being dropped from the *azzurri* for the 1968 Tour, although Gimondi and Balmamion were subsequently cleared on technical grounds. The substance found in Gimondi's and Van Schil's samples was none other than fencamfamine, the suspected source Reactivan, naturally.

The 1968 test results were announced only after the Giro, and, with so many of the top riders implicated, that left the race with a sense of anticlimax. To avoid a repeat of this, the Giro organisers began using a mobile dope-testing laboratory sponsored by Hewlett-Packard to speed up the process of dope-testing in the 1969 event. It was a system that had not been validated, but the process had been accepted by all the team managers, apart from Merckx's boss, Vincenzo Giacotto. Merckx's sample was tested in that lab, which had been set up in the car park of the local police station. The first positive was apparently found at 4 a.m., the second test completed at 8 a.m. in the presence of a toxicologist, but, critically, without the Belgian being informed of the positive on the first sample.

The process was so full of holes that today it would not be contemplated for a second. The regulations stipulated that the rider should be informed of the first positive, then permitted to watch the second test with his lawyer, who could double check that the sample was sealed correctly before it was opened and tested. The second sample usually contained a small capsule holding a form that had been signed by the rider when he gave the sample. That meant that if he requested a second analysis, he could be certain it was his sample that was being tested in front of him and his lawyers. But to enable the 'accelerated process', the control sample at that year's Giro didn't contain that capsule and form. Without that safeguard, the process was just that little bit more open to abuse. Other objections were raised to the use of the mobile lab. There were questions over whether transporting the dope-testing equipment every day might affect its integrity, and whether it was appropriate for the personnel carrying out the dope-testing to be in daily contact with members of the race caravan due to the obvious risks of corruption and threats.

There was more than enough there for the conspiracy theorists, who felt that the sample had been tampered with or switched. In addition, it was likely that Merckx's samples could be identified, although the testing process should have ensured complete anonymity. All the riders had to sign a register when they were tested, and the sample numbers were added to this. Merckx usually registered first, so his number could be identified by riders who signed after him, and by anyone who might be accompanying them. There are various theories about what actually happened. The most common is that Merckx was asked to let an Italian star win but, being Merckx, he simply didn't take the question on board and kept on as usual. Not winning was alien to him. Merckx himself said, 'they certainly didn't want me to win in 1969. I was offered money which I refused and two days later I was positive.' The person who offered him the money was not Gimondi, who went on to win the Giro, but another rider. Merckx was certain it was a set-up. 'I think the money that they wanted to give to me ended up being given to someone else [to set up the test]. I can't see any other explanation.'

The obvious implication is that Merckx's sample was spiked to avoid a repetition of Faema's dominance of the previous year. There were other theories: a water bottle swap while Merckx and other riders were attending mass; a dope-control officer who was befuddled and confused Merckx's sample with that of another rider. In truth, all bets were off, but the one consistent fact is that whether Merckx was set up or not, the whole affair appeared to him and much of the public to be seriously unjust, because Gimondi had been let off for an identical offence the year before. Hence the graffiti reading 'Gimondi the thief' which appeared on the roadside, hence the Italian writer Indro Montanelli writing in *Il Corriere della Sera* that he felt more Belgian than Italian amid hints at a conspiracy. Hence also Gimondi's embarrassment when he was interviewed about the affair, and his refusal to wear the pink jersey the following morning. Ormezzano notes, however, that Merckx's big rival – the man who had most to profit from the leader's 'positive' – did not take advantage. 'I felt he behaved well, he didn't try to profit from the incident by saying that Merckx was a cheat or anything of that kind.'

The resulting media storm was almost on the scale of a diplomatic incident between Italy and Belgium. Merckx had the support of the Belgian government which issued a statement saying that the accusations 'were without foundation' and that Merckx was the 'sacrificial victim of a criminal plot'. After the scandal Claudine Merckx estimated that her husband received 10,000 letters of support. It took until the end of the Tour de France to answer them all, and she had to call on the help of her sister, a neighbour and her five children, with some opening the letters, others writing the addresses, and the rest sticking on the stamps.

The rules stipulated Merckx should be banned for a month, which would have made it impossible for him to start the Tour, which began on 2 July, but on 14 June an extraordinary meeting in Brussels of professional cycling's governing body, the FICP, cleared him on the basis of 'benefit of doubt'. That was a double-edged sword: the statement was ambiguous, as it simultaneously backed the work of the doctors and accepted that the Italian Federation had the right to suspend Merckx, but at the same time said the chances were he was innocent 'because of his irreproachable past and the dozens of controls he has been through'. Cynics might speculate that the fact that the Tour de France was due to visit Merckx's home town of Woluwe-Saint-Pierre could have focused minds as well. Had the Belgian remained banned, the race would have been like the feast in *Macbeth* without Banquo.

The decision to clear him was not universally popular. Some professional riders threatened to strike. There were attacks in the press, with the French paper *La Voix du Nord* criticising the inconsistency. Adding to the confusion, the International Cycling Union – whose president was the Italian Adriano Rodoni – issued one statement supporting the dope-testing process, then another saying it was not valid under the rules. The fact is that at that time there were three accredited laboratories which were allowed to carry out drug tests within cycling: Paris, Ghent and Rome. Any test outside those three was irregular, making the entire Merckx ruling invalid. However, the FICP did not unambiguously clear Merckx on the grounds of incorrect procedure – as it should have done – probably because he might then have sued the Giro organisers. Merckx himself was not happy about the 'benefit of the doubt', on the grounds that it was ambiguous. 'I didn't take drugs, so there should be no doubt. They should have simply stated I was innocent,' he said. More significantly, the FICP called for a complete overhaul of anti-doping measures and the upshot was the adoption of a suspended ban for a first drug offence.

The Giro went on, although it had little interest for most onlookers, who knew that Merckx would probably have won. 'No one in Italy believed that Merckx was guilty, absolutely no one. Ninety per cent of people believed it was a trap,' says Ormezzano. 'Everyone was sure it was either a mistake or a set-up. The impression was that Merckx was the moral winner, but the race continued, and two days later, everything was forgotten.' In Italy maybe. At his home in Belgium, Merckx cut himself off from the world. He did not touch his bike for fourteen days after the positive test, and he told Guillaume Michiels that he was going to give up cycling. His conviction today is that he was framed, because someone, somewhere, felt uncomfortable with his domination. Ormezzano feels the same. 'I'm convinced it was sabotage. Many years afterwards, he told me he knew who put the substance in his bottle.'

The only person he talked to was the racing driver Jacky Ickx – the day after Ickx visited him he was seen to nip out on his bike for an hour. That evening he went down into his cellar-cum-workshop for the first time since the test to look at his bikes. He began ferocious sessions of motor-paced training with Michiels. He dragged his teammates out for 240-kilometre rides in the pouring rain. He started racing again on 18 June at the Criterium de Caen. On 23 June, Merckx won the *kermis* race in Ottignies, south of Brussels, where one group of fans spat at him, whistled at him and shouted that he was a drug-taker.

'Savona' was the moment when Merckx lost his innocence, when the sport that gave him fulfilment and deep joy revealed a darker and more sinister side. The blow was all the more cruel because of that curiously innocent side to his cycling. In many ways he had not changed a great deal from the teenager who woke up after taking his first victory and said to his mother 'isn't winning fun!' For Jean Van Buggenhout he remained the small boy who couldn't believe how good it felt to win. 'He has some love of money, because you have to count your pennies in this day and age, but the way he talks each day is like an amateur. A winner's bouquet makes him euphoric even if he doesn't show it and defeat makes him grind his teeth. This juvenility in his feelings leads him to maintain the discipline of an athlete, day to day, without any great effort. He can train winter and summer and keep his mind on the task in hand without ever feeling mentally tired.'

Merckx said once that what drove him was 'dreaming. It was stronger than me. I was a slave to it. There was no reasoning involved.' All kids dream of winning. What set Merckx apart from his contemporaries was the totality of his involvement, a childlike quality – his ability to focus on one thing to the exclusion of all else. 'He always kept a beginner's mentality,' noted one contemporary, the 1977 Giro winner Johan De Muynck. 'On the bike, he had the enthusiasm of a child, which used to surprise most of his colleagues, who saw things in a more routine way. He's like a boy who is suddenly discovering the pleasure of tobogganing. Merckx just kept playing.' Merckx never grew up in the sense that, over his career, he never thought about the long-term consequences of his actions, something his wife Claudine observed. 'He would do something simply because he felt he should. He's always had a spontaneity to him which defies logic.'

Savona was the moment when the big kids in the playground ruined the dream. 'Eddy is still the same man with the same faults and the same qualities but this scandal made him realise what life was,' said Jean Van Buggenhout. 'He was made brutally aware that life is not a bed of roses. Up to then, everything had worked for him. The episode made him more sceptical, less trusting, harder.' As Marc Jeuniau wrote, 'what was most beautiful and most pure in Eddy – his naiveté – had disappeared for good'. Savona was in a different, harsher register to the shenanigans before the 1964 world's, or the machinations of senior pros such as Van Looy and Simpson: this was public humiliation, daylight robbery. Merckx was a man who liked things to be fair and the biggest injustice of that June was that he could not be formally proven guilty or innocent. There was no closure. It was not something he could forget. Inevitably, he became less trusting. Equally inevitably, he wanted to prove himself again. It was a potent mix.

'The career of Eddy Merckx is divided,' wrote Théo Mathy, 'between the joy of winning for the pleasure of being the best, and the drive to dominate, to mete out a kind of personal justice, like the ancient law of *talion* [the Babylonian notion that the punishment for a crime should be equal to the offence] adapted to modern sport.' But between the two extremes came something else: the desire for flight preceding the need to fight. Panic followed by regrouping and vengeance.

Merckx was not phlegmatic. He did not have a peasant's fatalism. Compared to the tough upbringings of Coppi, Anquetil, or Van Steenbergen – who was rolling cigars at the age of ten to bring in a few francs to the family – he had been spoilt. He had had the support of his parents, of Vervaecke and Michiels. He had been given the option of school or cycling, with his mother there to cross swords with the Belgian Federation when he was excluded from the world champion-ships. As a result, in adversity, he would always initially have the urge to flee, to give up cycling, to go home. Then he would react.

Savona coloured the whole of the 1969 Tour, which Merckx rode as if brimful of confidence, although actually the opposite was the case. He felt obliged to win everything in his way, to carve out the biggest possible advantage, to make absolutely certain that nothing could happen to rob him of the win he had wanted for so long. But he made no bones about having another reason to show his strength: he wanted to show he was clean by being tested every day, and to erase the Giro from people's minds.

Ironically, however, Savona may have helped in another sense, one which would never have occurred to Merckx at the time. With his form already close to a peak, Merckx was forced to have an unaccustomed rest, taking two weeks out of training and sixteen days away from racing. He raced only five times in the twenty-six days before the Tour started. For him this was, briefly, an incredibly light programme: it looks similar to the 'tapering' a modern-day cyclist would do before a major competition. For once in his career, Merckx was actually rested at the start of a major Tour, with no travelling or racing for a decent period during the heart of the season. The result was to be a display of pure strength, in a register that cycling had never seen before and has not seen since.

REVOLUTIONARY MERCKXISM

In late July 1969, a new joke began to do the rounds in cycling circles. It ran like this: Felice Gimondi and Raymond Poulidor were fined fifty francs for taking a tow from a lorry up the Col du Tourmalet. But what about Eddy Merckx? He was towing the lorry.

The point where Merckx went from being merely super-human to borderline supernatural came close to the top of the Tourmalet on 15 July 1969, and there was no lorry involved. The mystery started when Merckx was seen fiddling with his gears. Initially his rivals thought he had a problem but actually he was preparing to change gear. On a mountain such as the Tourmalet, the cyclist will use a low gear, with a chainring of 39 or 41 teeth, a sprocket on the back wheel of 21 or 23. Merckx was shifting to 53x17. That is a massive gear for a mountain-top sprint. For a motor vehicle, it would be like first gear versus fourth.

His teammate Martin Van Den Bossche, a classic climber with lanky build, long legs and slight shoulders, moved a little way ahead: he had asked his leader if he could be permitted to take the prestigious prize on the summit, but Merckx was not having it. Two days before, Van Den Bossche had let it be known that he would be leaving the team to ride for Molteni and Merckx was in no mood to do him favours. He sprinted past his teammate for the summit and began the descent on his own, with the rest of the field initially a few seconds behind. He admitted that the notion of catching Van Den Bossche, nipping past him at the top, then dropping him on the descent, was too much to resist. There was a tactical consideration as well; descending on his own would reduce the risk of a crash or a mechanical problem. Merckx was, however, 'certain that once I hit the flat I would be caught'.

He had a forty-five-second lead – relatively insubstantial – at the foot of the steep descent which ends with a dead straight section to the town of Luz-Saint-Sauveur, which he would have hit at one hundred kilometres per hour. On the valley road afterwards, he eased up and ate as he rode through the *ravitaillement* (feeding station) at Argelès-Gazost. His *directeur sportif*, Lomme Driessens, told him to keep something in reserve, so he slowed down, but the lead group still had not caught up. 'Turning round, he felt how ridiculous waiting would be, what a loss of dignity,' wrote Jacques Goddet. 'He began riding hard, so that at the very least there would be no stain on this Tour de France. The others would surely join him but at least it would feel like a race.'

He had a minute's lead at the foot of the Col du Soulor, a ten-mile series of twists and turns that leads on to the still higher Col de l'Aubisque: after that he upped the ante, and extended his lead to five minutes at the summit. 'On this torrid day, Merckx was fresh, not just physically, but mentally,' wrote Léon Zitrone in *Merckx, La Rage de Vaincre*. 'He took, out of the front pocket of his yellow jersey, a small piece of card on which he had stuck the *"stage profile"* from the morning's newspaper. He studied it closely and read a kilometre post on the left of the road. A smile crossed his lips briefly: it was obvious to him: soon he would tackle the foot of the Aubisque.'

After the Aubisque – which follows the Soulor, on the opposite side of the plateau – seventy-five kilometres remained to the finish in the 'new town' of Mourenx and Merckx had eight minutes' lead. From then on, the stage might have seemed like a procession, but it was not that simple. His team car broke down, which meant that Driessens had to hitch a lift in a press car, taking a couple of spare wheels with him (this is why in some accounts Driessens is said not to have been there to watch Merckx doing the ride – he was there, but the highly visible Faema car was not). What sounds like one of the most straightforward stage wins in the Tour was anything but: Merckx got hypoglycaemia at Laruns, fifty-six kilometres from the finish, losing two minutes in just sixteen kilometres. Suddenly, his strength ran out. His style was no longer smooth. He was sweating heavily. He did not panic, however, merely steadying his pace so that he could eat, before going on. Later he described being in pain, all over his body, during the last twenty kilometres.

It was an epic that called for absolute commitment over more than four hours. During escapes like the one to Mourenx, he told me, he felt something of what the Irish star Stephen Roche described as 'the joy of the exploit' – the feeling of euphoria at the knowledge he was putting something special into the history books – but tempered with the need to keep his head, 'concentration on the race, giving yourself utterly, thinking that your adversaries mustn't catch up, thinking about getting to the line first. You get pleasure because you have proof that you have worked well. All the effort and sacrifice has been rewarded. You suffer but at the same time there is a sort of joy.'

'I hope I have done enough now for you to consider me a worthy winner,' he said afterwards to the journalists. They were as hyperbolic as might have been expected. 'MERCKXISSIMO' was the celebrated headline over Goddet's story the next morning, while the French writer Antoine Blondin described Mourenx as 'one of the most convincing attempts at world domination that I've ever seen imposed on cycling'. Merckx, he wrote, 'is going to sleep in the purple cradle where living

Gods are born'. For the also-rans such as Herman Van Springel, getting to Mourenx was merely about 'hanging on as best I could'. The film-maker Jørgen Leth, who would immortalise Merckx in *Stars and Watercarriers*, described the stage as 'extraordinary. He outclassed the others but was testing himself to an enormous degree as well. Pride was his dominant characteristic, so he was doing far more than he needed to do to win.'

That joke about the lorry has a serious side to it. The reaction the next day showed that the world of cycling simply did not know how to react. The length of the escape was colossal: about four hours' constant effort on a hot afternoon, with no let-up, no assistance, no companions to shelter behind. Even before he got to the top of the Tourmalet – one of the longest and highest passes in the Pyrenees – he had conquered two lesser climbs, the Peyresourde and Aspin passes. These were not roads to be taken lightly.

He doubled his lead in the overall standings to sixteen minutes. It is this final fact that explains why Mourenx was so remarkable. Merckx had an eight-minute lead anyway. He had no need to do anything other than monitor the rest and progress to Paris. That set this afternoon apart from what he had already achieved: the epic escape to the Tre Cime di Lavaredo and the seventy-kilometre race into a headwind to win the Tour of Flanders had a logic to them. If he wanted to win on those days, that was what needed to be done. But at Mourenx, he could have sat tight and watched his rivals.

Road racing is a sport where calculation of physical effort matters immensely, and nowhere more so than in the Tour de France, cycling's ultimate endurance event. The colossal physical demands of the race mean that the Tour lends itself to defensive riding. The classic way of riding it is to conserve energy as much as possible while not losing time, then make killer efforts when it matters. Once an advantage is gained, it is defended, and it is extended only if that can be done without incurring risk. Only the greatest champions of the sport – Fausto Coppi, Bernard Hinault – go outside that tactical framework, and only on very limited occasions. For a debutant in the Tour to do so with six days' racing remaining was tactical madness.

The race was won, so the risks far outweighed the potential gains. This was not a straightforward ride to the finish over easy roads and there was a very real danger that Merckx would push himself too far and pay the price. The attack of hypoglycaemia showed what was at stake. He got over it, but even so he was not exactly 'pottering along in the style of a superhero, which came naturally to a supernatural talent' was how Antoine Blondin described it. In fact, he was teetering on the tightrope between glory and failure. Had he weakened and perhaps lost a little time, with a summit finish in the Massif Central and a time trial still to decide the race, that Tour could have been lost.

Mourenx was such an outlandish event that parallels in other sports are hard to suggest. Imagine George Best putting Manchester United 4-0 up in the Champions League final, then sending half the team off the field, and popping in another two on his own. Or Juan Manuel Fangio lapping the field at Monaco twice by half distance then opting to repeat the feat twice more rather than controlling the pace. Boxing's reliance on the knockout means no equivalent can be suggested for Muhammad Ali, unless you imagine him offering a repeat of the Rumble in the Jungle with one arm tied behind his back.

Jacques Goddet for one realised that this was a unique occasion, in the Tour and quite possibly in the whole of sport. He wrote 'one of the mysteries of human creation is the way that we can add lustre to shining light' – think of great artists who feel compelled to produce one more masterpiece – and compared Mourenx to the 'gratuitous acts' of Jean-Paul Sartre's existentialist heroes. Mourenx happened simply because Merckx felt he could do it and because he wanted to do it. There was no intrinsic need for it. 'The feat achieved by this sublime athlete is different from anything written thus far in the annals of road racing, because Merckx accomplished a gratuitous act. His latest achievement was spontaneous and it has reduced all around him to rubble, including the minds of the opposition and the very concept of competition.'

The stage win in Mourenx can be said to be the ultimate expression of Merckx's cycling career. The Belgian spent his cycling years surprising the world, in various ways. That was, after all, his fundamental goal at the start of his career, when he said he wanted to 'give my fans new exploits every season. The ideal thing for me would be to go a bit higher each year. Do something better than the year before, every year up to 1974 or 1975.' It was the most outlandish act of a career spent defying the norms and nostrums of professional cycling. Across his professional career, Merckx rarely saved his strength. He tried to win everything he could, no matter how big or how small the race, rarely ever recognising the politics of professional sport. He accepted, even embraced, the risks involved in not making friends, not calculating the value of every effort. Mourenx was the ultimate expression of the way he did things. To understand Mourenx is probably to understand Merckx.

Given that the 1969 Tour de France now epitomises complete and utter dominance, Merckx began the campaign with a rare mistake. It was Lomme Driessens' idea that he should start the prologue time trial in Roubaix first of the 130 starters, the notion being that Merckx would be resting in his hotel room by the time the other favourites started. As with other teams which have tried something similar more recently, it backfired: a wind got up while he was riding but died down and didn't affect the others. The organisers took longer than expected to clear the publicity caravan off the circuit and put the start back by five minutes, disrupting Merckx's warm-up. Finally, affected by nerves, he started too fast. The upshot was that he came second by seven seconds to Rudi Altig, the German who won the 1966 world title. Merckx was not happy about it and he did not repeat the experiment. Presumably it did nothing for his relationship with Driessens.

The following afternoon, however, in his home town of Woluwe-Saint-Pierre – close to the White Star football club's stadium where he used to play – Faema won the team time trial and he took the yellow jersey. The next morning the route began with a detour through Tervuren, the Brussels suburb where Merckx and Claudine lived: in the best tradition, he escaped as soon as the start flag dropped and rode alone in yellow in front of his home crowd. After that it mattered little that the yellow jersey ended up on the shoulders of his Faema teammate Julien Stevens.

That was the stuff of schoolboy dreams, but the atmosphere around Merckx outside the race was particularly tense: after Savona, he and his team were afraid of sabotage. He accepted not a single bottle from the hundreds held up by supporters in the mountains. His hotel room was declared out of bounds (something which was not normal at the time), and Faema appointed bodyguards to restrict access to the hotel each evening. One writer described the atmosphere as 'akin to a bad cops and robbers drama'. Another complained 'we were not permitted to cross the threshold of the hotel, in the same way that we were kept out of his room by Faema's gorillas. There would be a fifteen-minute wait, with radios holding on for live broadcasts and photographers with their fingers on the shutters.' By the standards of the twenty-first century it was mild stuff, but for a sport in which journalists took for granted their right to interview the stars when and where they wanted it was new territory. There were banners by the roadside: 'The Italians stole the Giro from Eddy Merckx, take revenge in the Tour, Eddy!' and 'Rodoni is a Judas!' One rider was designated to collect Merckx's bottles from the team car, and he was only permitted to bring bottles with his leader's initials on, which had been prepared either by Merckx himself or by Driessens.

There was an amusing episode later in the race when Merckx himself tried to go back up to his hotel room after dinner only to find he couldn't open the door. His soigneur had locked it but because he didn't use the right key he had damaged the lock. The race favourite ended up sitting in the corridor with two Belgian journalists waiting for a locksmith, and had to take his evening call from his wife in reception. Similarly frivolous, in the view of the press, was the brief spell Stevens spent in the yellow jersey, compared by Antoine Blondin to Beau Brummel getting his valet to 'wear in' his clothes. By day six in Mulhouse, with the first mountain stage through the Vosges looming large, Merckx was just nine seconds behind the race leader Desiré Letort of France. The first big climb of the Tour that year was the Ballon d'Alsace, with the finish at the summit, and it set the tone for the Merckx years in the Tour.

Faema were the pacemakers and Merckx escaped well before the climb, along with Altig, the Dutchman Rinus Wagtmans, the Spanish climber Joaquim Galera and De Vlaeminck. At the foot of the Ballon they had a two minute forty second lead. Relentlessly, Merckx rode the quartet off his wheel as the climb progressed. Wagtmans and De Vlaeminck were the first to go – and De Vlaeminck would never again start a major Tour thinking he might get the better of his fellow Belgian – while Galera cracked seven kilometres from the top. That made Altig the last survivor, but all Merckx had to do to dislodge the German was to cut through a couple of hairpins four kilometres from the top, raising the pace as he did so, and Altig blew up, rivulets of sweat running down his forehead. So complete was his collapse that he lost two minutes in four kilometres and by the summit only Galera was within reach of the Belgian. Ten per cent of the field finished outside the time limit due to the high speed set by Merckx and the organisers had to extend it. Even so, those men eliminated included Rik Van Looy, a symbolic moment if ever there was one.

The consensus was that the race was already over. *L'Equipe*'s correspondent described it as 'one of the most remarkable spectacles I've ever seen in sport', while Merckx himself was surprised by how simple it had all been. Like a card sharp upping the ante to weed out the weaker hands, his goal had been to get rid of as many of the field as possible before the climb so that his task would be easier. There would be fewer men to watch and follow. He was defying convention by doing more work than anyone else and still remaining fresh. He would do it again and again. Among the other favourites, only Roger Pingeon of France remained defiant, stating that he and the rest of the favourites simply failed to realise how hard the finish at the Ballon would be – because they had not taken into account how hard Merckx would make it.

Pingeon was clutching at straws. With the Alps beckoning, the next stage was the 8.8-kilometre time trial at Divonne-les-Bains: Merckx won, at an average speed of over 49.6 kilometres per hour, with Altig – still a possible rival at this point – only two seconds behind. The very next day, he left the entire field apart from Pingeon behind en route to Chamonix although, for some bizarre reason, he had decided to fit longer cranks on his bike and was not entirely at ease. Gimondi was over two minutes back, while Altig was seventy-sixth, and now completely out of the picture. The next day the Tour climbed the Col de la Madeleine for the first time, then the Col du Galibier. Here there was another reckoning: De Vlaeminck was one of fourteen riders who abandoned. The margins were surreal: Janssen, the 1968 winner, was more than twenty-five minutes back, Altig was at forty minutes, and Lucien Aimar, the 1966 victor, was three-quarters of an hour behind.

The only remaining opposition seemed to come from Pingeon, who attacked the next day on the Col d'Allos, as the race headed south through the Alps to Digne – Merckx responded with a counter-attack of his own, with the Frenchman and Gimondi chasing a couple of hairpins below him. He overhauled two Spaniards, Mascaro and Santamaria, who had broken away earlier in the stage, waited for Gimondi and his group, then attacked again on the descent from the Col de Corobin, ten miles from the finish, to win the stage. The next day it was a similar story. Fifty kilometres from the finish in Aubagne as the race passed through the Massif de l'Espigoulier in the Marseilles *arrière-pays*, Merckx went after an attack from the rider lying fifty-fourth overall – the little-known Jacques de Boever – and although Gimondi won the stage, this time Pingeon was the one who was caught out and lost time. Overall, colossal time gaps were already opening up, with the tenth rider in the standings twenty-five minutes back. And this was only stage twelve.

Merckx was showing the Tour de France something that had not been seen on *la Grande Boucle* since the days of Coppi, Hugo Koblet and Louison Bobet in the early 1950s. The Tours after Anquetil's fifth victory in 1964 had been 'interim' races, each taken by a rider who had come from left field and would win only once: Gimondi, Aimar, Pingeon, Janssen. Anquetil's 1964 win had been a tight affair taken by a whisker from

Raymond Poulidor; he had dominated the previous three Tours but in a way that was more calculating and tactical, based on his supremacy in the time trial stages. Of Anquetil's 1963 victory, Jacques Goddet wrote: 'For the entire three weeks, Jacques was the master of the race, in the sense that he gauged the capacity of his principal adversaries, he strictly controlled their movements, he limited the dangers that arose whenever they showed any aggressive intent.' Goddet compared Anquetil to Fangio, 'taking only necessary risks, contenting himself with total clarity of mind, with giving each adversary the response that sufficed to keep him quiet'.

Merckx's style, clearly, was as different as 'total football' compared to *catenaccio*. Any calculation was based on what he felt he could do rather than what he needed to do. One comparison was with a gaoler who plays with the prisoners' minds – every day the fellow cyclists expected some bizarre new punishment so when Merckx attacked they just let him get on with it. There were jokes among the riders that they could do with some Faema coffee themselves, and the inevitable allegations that Merckx had a superdrug of some kind, but Doctor Dumas (the man who tried to revive Tom Simpson and led the fight against drug-taking at the end of the 1960s) had this to say: 'Merckx is the cleanest rider I know.'

And so onwards, implacably, Merckx proceeded towards Mourenx. The third time trial stage, at Revel, underlined his superiority: over a distance of only eighteen kilometres, Pingeon was a minute behind, Gimondi one minute thirty-three seconds, losing five seconds per kilometre. These were immense gaps in a time trial this short, and Merckx's race was effectively won, a week before the finish in Paris. In the overall standings he had 8 minutes 21 seconds on Pingeon, 9 minutes 29 seconds on Gimondi, 12 minutes 46 seconds on Poulidor. Thirty-six hours later came the great Pyrenean set-piece stage, 214.5

kilometres long, over the classic quartet of cols: Peyresourde, Aspin, Tourmalet and Aubisque. After staying close to the front on the Peyresourde and Aspin, Merckx changed gear on the Tourmalet and the next 145 kilometres went into the history books.

Not surprisingly, the stage to Mourenx ended the Tour as a contest. The final mountain-top finish at the Puy-de-Dôme was an anticlimax, won by the *lanterne rouge*, a window cleaner named Pierre Matignon. The final day belonged to Faema, with Jos Spruyt winning the morning stage to Creteil, and Merckx, in the natural order of things, taking the afternoon time trial to the velodrome at Vincennes for his sixth stage win. In spite of his massive lead, he was so het up that he nearly fell off close to the start when he hit a barrier, and he misjudged a bend just before the entry to the velodrome, almost turning right rather than left. That sealed a total triumph, with Pingeon seventeen minutes fifty-four seconds behind, Poulidor at twenty-two minutes thirteen seconds, margins that compared with those opened by Anquetil and Coppi in their greatest days. As well as the overall standings, Merckx added the mountains, points, team, combine and most aggressive rider awards, a whitewash of every prize on offer. No cyclist has ever matched this.

It was, he said a few years later, the highlight of his career. 'The win overwhelmed me. When I was a child I went into every tiny detail, with a passion that consumed me. Jacques Anquetil was my idol. Of all the champions in sport, he was the one that I most wanted to resemble one day. So you can imagine how I felt when I raced the Tour for the first time. Since winning the world professional road title I had been convinced that my mission was to be the first Belgian to win the Tour since 1939.'

Special trains had been laid on from Brussels to Paris to take the fans, who thronged the metro; the Cipale velodrome in Vincennes became '*un vélodrome Belge*' for *l'Equipe*'s man on the spot. Among the onlookers was Sylvère Maes, fifty-seven years old, who had cut short his seaside holiday to be there to applaud the man who succeeded him as Belgium's first winner since 1939. That night the Belgian Prime Minister Gaston Eyskens dined with Faema. It was the day that Neil Armstrong walked on the moon, and Merckx was rushed from his celebration dinner to a Belgian television studio where he talked live as they broadcast the moon landing. 'Merckx's win had as much impact in Belgium as events in space,' wrote René Jacobs in *Gotha*. The victory was probably amplified by the bitter defeat of the previous year when two Belgians, Ferdinand Bracke and Herman Van Springel, were in contention for victory on the final day, only to be defeated by, of all people, a Dutchman, Jan Janssen. The morning after his win, Merckx and Claudine rode through Brussels in an open-top Mercedes, hailed by crowds that completely filled the main square. The King, Baudouin, made a point of being the first to receive Merckx officially before the country's national summer holiday and was duly presented with a yellow jersey.

It is hard to conceive that Merckx might have lacked confidence. His racing style is so dominant, based as it is on showing the opposition precisely what physical reserves he has, that the notion that it is born of insecurity is difficult to take on board. But when I asked Merckx to explain Mourenx he said simply: 'You're never certain of winning. You can always have a bad day, no matter how much of a lead you have. The bigger the lead you have, the more time you have to play with. You can lose ten minutes on a bad day. It can always happen.'

Events in Merckx's other Tour wins show that he was actually not far from the edge on occasion, in spite of his utter dominance. In the 1970 Tour, he had a lead of nearly ten minutes over Joop Zoetemelk and had only to control the race for the seven days remaining until Paris when a small stone was thrown into the air from the road and hit him in the eye, about five miles from the end of the stage in Toulouse. He pulled into the side of the road and tried to clear his watering eyes as he could barely see. He regained contact with the bunch *in extremis*, his team unable to perform at his level as they tried to catch the speeding field. The 1971 Tour saw him short of form, and fighting off a brutal challenge from Luis Ocaña. The year after that he wound up with a saddle boil, and an upset stomach from drinking an over strong coffee. There were no issues in 1973, but the win in 1974, as we shall see, was achieved when circumstances were particularly tough. Merckx, seemingly so invulnerable, was actually not far at times from overload and collapse, as is normal for most athletes at this level.

There are echoes of another seemingly dominant racer, Fausto Coppi, who famously believed that something might go wrong even when he was half an hour in front of the next man with two days to go in the 1952 Tour. Mourenx was born of the need to seize every opportunity to build that lead. If Merckx had not taken the opportunity, then afterwards something had gone wrong, and he had lost by a few seconds – what then? And, indeed, such were his nerves that on the final time trial to the Parc des Princes he twice came close to crashing.

Not long after that 1969 Tour, Merckx's manager Jean Van Buggenhout said that his protégé was actually no more ambitious than previous greats of the sport such as Rik Van Steenbergen and Fausto Coppi. All champions were super-humanly ambitious, believed the manager, but they were all different in the attention they paid to their profession. Coppi was fixated with detail and would never change his mind. Van

Looy was equally obsessive, continually changing his bars and saddle during a stage race for example, examining every contract to the last phrase. Van Steenbergen, on the other hand, simply took life as it came. Merckx, in that context, was somewhere in the middle, 'a worrier'. 'He is permanently preoccupied with some problem or other. There is always something on his mind. He asks questions continually, and because he isn't able to obtain closed, precise answers, he keeps on vacillating. He thinks, studies, examines, and weighs each problem.'

Van Buggenhout describes Merckx's preoccupation with the details of his bike (compared with Jacques Anquetil who would simply get on the machine and race) but his punctiliousness went further than worrying about his position. 'Eddy thinks about the future a great deal and already, even though he isn't yet twenty-five years old, he is concerned with what he will do after he has finished racing. He is continually asking himself the question: what will I do with my life after my sporting career?' One Belgian paper asked Merckx if he was a worrier and if it was a weakness. He answered yes to both, adding that he had trouble sleeping before a race, as 'I wouldn't want to disappoint myself or the team or the supporters'. In his eyes, worrying was a virtue, because 'in cycling, being sure of yourself is an almost inevitable guarantee of not winning'. Insecurity meant minding every detail and never underestimating the opposition.

Merckx had, he said in other interviews, always been nervous, 'almost irritable'. 'I used to feel taken over by doubt, by fear. There were times when I wouldn't be able to sleep. Sometimes my stomach wouldn't keep my food down.' It was a patronising parallel, but there was something in the assertion of a rival team manager who said Merckx was 'like a little third category amateur who isn't sure what the result will be'. The opposition might have been sure; he wasn't.

As well as Mourenx, those emphatic solo wins in one-day races come down to insecurity. Merckx was a strong sprinter, but there were no guarantees if there were any other men present at the finish. 'My sprint wasn't strong. I was strong after a long distance but in a shorter race a lot of riders could beat me. Someone who's faster in the sprint will attack less, but I was insecure about my sprint. You're never certain of winning a sprint. You could puncture with a kilometre to go. Riders like Godefroot and De Vlaeminck weren't easy to beat in a sprint. I could beat them, but I was never sure of doing it. The lone victories came from a need to win, rather than a need to show that I was stronger or the best. When you are alone you are always certain to win.'

The Tour victory, emphatic and ecstatic as it was, would never entirely erase the memory of the 1969 Giro from Merckx's mind. 'Savona is not forgotten. It is the nightmare that haunts his sleep,' recalled the journalist Théo Mathy. He added that Merckx 'dissected every defeat with cold anger to better prepare for the next win'. I suspect that whatever anger Merckx felt was not 'cold' in the sense of controlled, but it was certainly directed. Mourenx was the act of an angry man. Merckx was powered by inner rage, he said. It made him 'fight against journalists who said bad things about me, against the rivals I imagined wanted to beat me, against people who didn't believe me. That aggression gave me the power to overcome the pain. I wanted to leave people with their mouths wide open.' And after the injustice of his expulsion from the Giro d'Italia a few weeks earlier, he had reason to be angry.

Merckx felt a continual need to prove himself, to show his worth to the world. This is seen in his early fear that his amateur world championship would be as good as it got, and in the way he saw the 1967 Giro, where, astonishing as it might seem, he had been happier with the bunch sprint at Lido degli Estense rather than the prestigious mountain stage at Blockhaus. His explanation was as follows: 'Up to now, everyone has underestimated me in the sprints. Everyone takes for granted that riders like Jo Planckaert [three-time stage winner in that Giro] and Dino Zandegu are instrinsically superior to me and if I can beat them at the end of a Classic, it's more due to my pure power than speed. In other words, people believe that I only win sprints when the real sprinters are tired from the race distance. Perhaps I believed it myself. But at Lido degli Estensi, I beat pure sprinters on their favoured ground. That's why it's more significant for me. At the Blockhaus, I wasn't turning over any established ideas: it was my first race in the mountains. It may be normal. Time will tell. But I am certain you wouldn't have found anyone willing to bet on me in a bunch sprint against Planckaert and Zandegu after a flat stage of 160 kilometres.' In other words, it was the challenge *per se* that counted. He wanted to turn people's ideas about him on their heads. The 1969 Tour offered him the ultimate test: reversing the injustice of his expulsion from the Giro, and his designation as a cheat in some quarters.

His response to the challenge did not end once he had arrived in Brussels to a hero's welcome. Eyebrows were also raised after Paris–Luxembourg, a few weeks after the Tour. The race no longer exists, but it was prestigious enough in its day for the best riders of the time to take part: Gimondi took the first of the two stages, and seemed to have a conclusive enough fifty-four-second lead in the overall standings.

Merckx saw it differently, and seized his chance in the final eight kilometres, attacking on the steep hill at Bereldange, getting rid of the field, and gaining a minute by the finish on Gimondi, who had Roger Pingeon, Michele Dancelli and Roger De Vlaeminck to help him in the chase. Up front, Jacques

Anquetil, no less, had taken a forty-five-second lead with Guido Reybrouck before the hill was reached: Merckx overtook the duo in the final kilometre and flew past to take the stage win. No one, said Anquetil, had ever dropped him so close to the finish of any race. Merckx rode like a man possessed, and there was speculation that he was making Gimondi pay for the events of that June.

Mourenx had been a key moment in the Merckx story, the moment where it became clear that cycling now had to deal with a phenomenon that was completely new to it. The sport was in unknown territory. Fausto Coppi and Louison Bobet had made epic escapes that had devastated their rivals. Jacques Anquetil had ridden Tours de France that married physical courage and tactical calculation. Charly Gaul had produced stupendous feats in the mountains. But none of these stars had looked to dominate when it was no longer necessary. As Goddet wrote, Mourenx was an *acte gratuit*. It was not even done to impress. Merckx was winning this way simply because he could. Driven by his insecurity, he was racing as if there was no tomorrow to revenge himself on his rivals. The Savona affair had made him believe, like the chief in Goscinny's *Asterix*, that tomorrow the sky might fall on his head. Events later that year were to prove him right.

PART TWO

THE 1970s

DESCENT OF A GOD

'In the 1970s, wherever a bike race went, the word God was spelt MERCKX', *Eric Fottorino*

The oval concrete velodrome in the central France town of Blois was like dozens of others in communities across the country, used for local track meetings and the occasional professional event. Most came to life only for the traditional 'after-Tour' meeting, when a mix of celebrities and journeymen riding for appearance fees would draw in the local fans. The meeting on 9 September 1969 was typical: the Tour de France winner Eddy Merckx topped the bill along with Jean 'Popov' Graczyk, a Tour points winner in 1958 and 1960, of Polish extraction, now in the final weeks of a lengthy professional career. Others present included Raymond Riotte, Tour stage winner and yellow jersey, as well as the only Czech in the professional peloton, Jiří Daler.

The evening had been drizzly, leading to doubts that the meeting would go ahead – an eternal bugbear for promoters on outdoor tracks – and the uncertainty meant the crowd was correspondingly sparse. For Merckx, the evening was just another in the lengthy round of 'after-Tour' events, when, like most professionals of the time, he raked in most of his annual income from start money. The previous afternoon he had won a prestigious Breton criterium, the Circuit de l'Aulne at Chateaulin, after which he had enjoyed a lengthy, alcohol-fuelled evening with Jacques Anquetil and the other stars.

The 1967 Tour winner Roger Pingeon recounted the evening to the historian Jean-Paul Ollivier. The session had begun at a post-race reception where Anquetil decided to see how much champagne Merckx could put away. Afterwards, Anquetil, Merckx and Pingeon headed for a nightclub where the five-times Tour winner and the new king of cycling held a whisky-drinking contest, won clearly by the younger man once they had moved on to doubles. They moved on from the nightclub after the somewhat unstable Anquetil had an altercation with a photographer. 'Master Jacques' was taken back to his hotel by his wife Janine, while Merckx suggested dinner and was joined by Pingeon, Lucien Aimar and Jan Janssen. The three of them were a little the worse for wear and they could not believe their eyes when Merckx devoured onion soup with grated cheese, a chicken breast, and a large steak on top of the alcohol. His appetite, clearly, was not limited to winning bike races.

The evening in Blois, sadly, would have a different, tragic ending. The meeting comprised a three-round omnium, each of the rounds contested behind Dernys, little custom-made motorbikes which could take the riders to a speed of about forty miles per hour. They were pedal-assisted, partly to boost the small engine, but also because the gyroscopic motion of the pedals provided stability on a banked track. Racing behind the machines was far more common then than it is now. The end-of-season Derny-paced Criterium des As over one hundred kilometres in Paris was a fixture on the calendar and *de rigueur* for stars of the time. The Blois meeting came a couple of days after the Bordeaux–Paris one-day and included several of the star Derny drivers who had featured in the 360-mile, fourteen-hour 'Derby of the Road'. Merckx was paced by Fernand Wambst, at fifty-six probably the best *pilote* on the circuit, with twenty-three years' experience behind him.

Wambst earned his living from Derny racing, and had paced Merckx's erstwhile teammate Tom Simpson to victory in the 'Derby' in 1964. Jiří Daler was paced by the Frenchman Bruno Reverdy, in whose house he had stayed after finishing eighth in the 'Derby'.

Derny racing was not regarded as particularly dangerous, not compared to racing behind the 'big motors', full-sized motorbikes which could reach speeds of up to sixty-five miles per hour. Head protection for the riders was minimal – they all wore 'hair nets' made of slender leather strips, while the drivers wore more substantial, cumbersome-looking 'pacers' hats' with large bands made of boiled leather. Ever the perfectionist, even for a race of this insignificance, Merckx dithered over whether to wear his usual hat or his spare and opted for the spare. Whether or not it was more robust cannot be proven, but it probably saved his life.

In the opening race, Merckx and Wambst won the first intermediate sprint, then the duo began to accelerate a couple of laps before the second. It was not yet a flat-out effort, but they were travelling at almost forty miles per hour. Merckx's factotum – he was not yet his soigneur – Guillaume Michiels was watching, having driven Merckx up from Chateaulin. 'During the first round, Eddy felt the race was dangerous, and shouted to Wambst "ahead, ahead", meaning that he wanted to stay in front.' Merckx wanted to avoid potential trouble, but the driver's reply was 'spectacle, spectacle' – in other words, they should hold back then surge forward to please the crowd. 'They came from behind, passing everyone, and as they came past the first Derny' – driven by Reverdy, with Daler in his slipstream – 'we never knew whether the pedal came unscrewed, or if it broke, but that Derny lost control, went up the banking, and hit the publicity hoarding at the top of the track. It left a twelve-metre long scorch mark.'

According to Michiels, Wambst made a split-second decision to avoid the skidding motorbike by going below it, although the usual wisdom on a banked track is that a rider should try to go above a fallen colleague, because if they land higher up the banking, they will slide down into your path. 'Eddy shouted "go up, go up", because Reverdy's Derny was always going to come back down.' The two motorbikes collided, and Merckx's pedal touched one of the motorbikes – as Michiels pointed out, twenty centimetres the other way, and he would have stayed upright. Both Merckx and Wambst landed head-first on the cement track. The impact was so great that the front wheel of the cyclist's track bike was bent into a banana-shape, the tightly fixed handlebars turned through ninety degrees.

Daler, who raced with the Frimatic–De Gribaldy team, has not spoken about the crash for over forty years, and is surprised when the phone rings with an English journalist quizzing him about it. The surface of the track was good, he recalls, the evening dry, the field only six or seven riders. He had been given the contract by his manager, a Dutch former track racer named Jan Derksen. 'Reverdy crashed on the banking at very high speed, I didn't fall, because he fell in front of me, and I went up the track as he went down. Wambst and Merckx were below, and hit him. They both fell together. It was such a bad crash that they called an end to the racing and I went back to my home in Besançon. I didn't find out what had happened to Wambst until later. It is a terrible memory. I have seen Merckx since then, but we have never spoken about it.'

Wambst died, while he was being taken to hospital, of a fractured skull; he was buried a few days later at Bagneux, close to Paris. Merckx hit his head on the concrete at the foot of the track, just fifty centimetres from the grass in the track centre, and only just avoided the same fate as his driver: he remained unconscious for three-quarters of an hour and woke up on the operating table in the local hospital. He had narrowly avoided serious head injuries. Guillaume Michiels found his crash hat broken in two, the leather bar that came over the rider's upper forehead held together only by the membrane. Merckx had injured his left leg, was concussed and had stitches in his scalp – the scar would cover half the left side of his forehead. The rest of his injuries were down to whiplash from the impact with the concrete: he had displaced his pelvis, trapped nerves in his back and bruised a vertebra. He spent a week in hospital before being repatriated to Belgium in a military plane.

'I was never the same again,' he told me. 'Back then, there was no rehabilitation if you were an athlete. I spent six weeks in bed in a clinic and at home. My pelvis was completely twisted. Later I visited osteopaths and physiotherapists but the damage was done.' He was advised to rest for two months but was racing eight days later; in mid-October he won a criterium at Scorzè, near Venice. Nowadays a cyclist would spend the entire winter recuperating from a crash of this severity but Merckx came back to top-level racing at the Baracchi Trophy two-man time trial in Italy in early October barely a month later. After finishing third with the Italian Davide Boifava, he was hardly able to walk when he got down from his bike.

It was not the first or the last time that Merckx would return to competition after accident or illness far sooner than was good for him, but Blois was the occasion that mattered most. It was one of a handful of truly serious crashes among the estimated seventy or eighty that he had during his career – the next worst being in Paris–Nice in 1972 when he cracked a vertebra, and in the 1975 Tour de France, when he broke his cheekbone. A quarter of a century later, Merckx was still being treated weekly by a physiotherapist for the after-effects. His left leg and his lower back were where the trouble was concentrated. The compression from the crash had aggravated the stiffness in the lower spine that is common to most cyclists, and the sciatica it induced in the long term obliged him to change his position on the bike constantly. Sometimes, a massive wooden board would be placed under the mattress of his hotel bed during a stage race to ease his discomfort.

There are two sequences in the film *A Sunday in Hell* which illustrate Merckx's obsession with his position on the bike. Early in the film, which centres on the 1976 Paris–Roubaix, Merckx is shown on the eve of the race in the team's hotel spending several minutes checking and double-checking the position of his saddle and brake levers. Fastidiously, he employs a spirit level, long metal ruler and tape measure. The following morning, when the race is stopped close to the start by a demonstration, his first instinct is to head for a rival team car and borrow a spanner so he can tinker with his saddle again. After Blois he tweaked his position time after time, always experimenting in a constant search for improvement. He even had two large mirrors set up next to the rollers in his cellar so that he could observe his position as he rode, from both front and back.

Merckx said later that Blois was the most traumatic event of his career, because of the death of Wambst rather than the actual crash. His nerves suffered and he insisted he was never able to climb as well after Blois. '[without the crash] I could have won races far more easily and performed greater exploits in the mountains. Before, they felt like demonstrations – the stage in the Pyrenees when I won by eight minutes, and the Tre Cime di Lavaredo stage in the Giro. I was a level above then; afterwards it wasn't so easy. There was less sparkle.' The upshot was that he tended to sit too low in the saddle and couldn't use the gears he was used to when he was climbing in the mountains. Normal physical progression meant he should have got better in the mountains as he matured up to about 1973 – instead he didn't improve but managed because he was stronger and more determined than everyone else. 'Before the accident, I didn't feel pain on the bike in the same way. After the crash, you could see the worry on my face. I was always afraid the pain would strike me again. I didn't feel I could dominate in the mountains.'

Merckx had always had a hypochondriac side to him – the result, possibly, of the health issues he had had in his youth, but also due to his anxious nature. 'He's a decent man but who believes a word he says?' asked Gimondi in the spring of 1969. 'Last year at the Giro he had a headache and . . . he won, and you know how. In Paris–Nice this year he thought he was coming down with an ear infection and waltzed in first. The night before Milan–San Remo he was worrying about his knee. You know what happened. He may feel pain before a race, I don't deny it, but once the start comes, the pain just disappears.' Now there were more serious problems to be dealt with, and they would get worse as his career progressed. The spring after Blois, he suffered from the first of a long series of injuries to his crutch – the obvious result of trying to get comfortable on the bike and pedalling with one leg putting out more power than the other. On occasions he would race with one crank slightly shorter than the other, to compensate for the fact that his legs were not precisely the same length.

The demands Merckx made on himself can be seen in one single winter, the one after the crash in Blois. He should have taken time off to recover from his injuries, but was racing again eight days later, and put in another eleven days of competition before calling it a day on 26 October. He decided to accept a number of track contracts over the winter and emerged with decent form but was nursing a minor knee injury. Winning Paris–Nice in spite of the mild tendonitis was vitally important, he felt, to show himself and the opposition that he was back to his old level, but perhaps he should miss Milan–San Remo to save his knee? No chance with an Italian sponsor – the same company as before, but with the team rebranded Faemino to publicise a new coffee machine from the Valenti stable. Additionally, he had missed the team training camp in Alassio in January because Claudine was not in perfect health as she awaited the birth of their first child, Sabrina, who was born on Valentine's day.

The only day in the whole of 1970 that Merckx felt like his pre-Blois self was 12 April, the day of Paris–Roubaix. That was a victory which set new standards for the 'Queen of Classics': a solo attack thirty-one kilometres from the finish to open a winning margin of five minutes twenty-one seconds, the biggest winning margin in the 'Hell of the North' since the war. As so often, however, early in the race Merckx didn't think he was going to get to the finish. On this occasion it was because he had had a cold. Ultimately, he produced a devastating victory in a race so tough that only forty-three of the 155 starters made it to the finish through heavy rain that teemed down for the final three hours. It was a win taken against the odds, with an early puncture costing him time and forcing him into a brutal chase. There were five riders from the Flandria team at the front that day, including Godefroot and De Vlaeminck, but they were powerless. The last to survive was Eric Leman, who had just won the Tour of Flanders, and lasted until thirty-seven kilometres from the finish.

Roubaix was one of six major victories in eighteen days that April, which began with Ghent–Wevelgem, taken after a late attack, four kilometres from the finish. The Tour of Belgium of that year is legendary for the particularly wintry stage to

Heist, in which Merckx, Roger De Vlaeminck and Godefroot left the bunch twelve minutes behind amid hail, snow showers and half a gale, with two-thirds of the field abandoning; the afternoon after that epic, Merckx took the time trial which guaranteed him overall victory. That led into the Roubaix spectacular. A week after that, Merckx tried to engineer a win for his new teammate Jos Bruyère in Flèche Wallonne – something he tried from time to time, as we will see later – but the domestique cracked close to the finish leaving his leader with no option other than to take the victory himself.

Not surprisingly, Merckx was not keen to return to the Giro d'Italia after events the previous year at Savona but Van Buggenhout and Faema's boss, Paolo Valente, proved too persuasive. Merckx was at the heart of the publicity campaign for Faema's new coffee machine: there were 50,000 posters with his picture on them waiting to be put up all over Italy to coincide with the race. A figure of 80,000 Belgian francs per day was quoted as his start money. The Faema leader would only return if the methods of doping control were changed, and samples were sent to a laboratory in Rome that year rather than being tested on the spot. That 1970 Giro was a controlled win, the first time Merckx had won a major stage race when he was not at his best. Ironically, his adversaries were so struck with the idea that Merckx was unbeatable that they let him keep the psychological whip hand although he was nothing like the star of the 1969 Tour.

On the third stage of the race he felt shooting pains in his left leg similar to those he had noticed in Paris–Nice. Three days later, his chain jumped as he was responding to an attack from Martin Van Den Bossche, his former Faema teammate, now riding for Molteni, and his left leg was deadened with pain. As a result he was dropped on the climb of Croce Domini and left behind again later in the stage. The Italian newspapers speculated that there might be a new fragility about him, making him vulnerable to pressure, but Gimondi and company were unable to respond. Merckx was riding in a new style, more watchful, less willing to expend his formidable strength, partly because he had half an eye on the Tour de France, partly because of his physical problems. He was keen to keep the race in a firm stranglehold. It was not a popular win in Italy, where the press derided his rivals as Lilliputian puppets.

There were similar feelings in France five weeks later after the Tour de France win that put him among the true legends of the sport: at that time, only Jacques Anquetil and Fausto Coppi had managed the double of Giro d'Italia and Tour de France in the same summer. Merckx's dominance was clear early on. The lack of suspense about who was going to win the Tour prompted Jacques Goddet to open one editorial meeting at *l'Equipe* a week into the race with the words: *'Messieurs, c'est le catastrophe.'* Even if Merckx was not in the same stunning condition as before, the fact that it was clear he was heading for victory was a nightmare for the promoting newspapers *l'Equipe* and *Le Parisien Libéré*, which needed high drama, if possible featuring a home rider, in order to boost sales. A Belgian crushing all before him was not going to send French readers rushing to newsstands.

Merckx began by winning the prologue at Limoges by substantial margins, given that the course was only 7.4 kilometres. After that, tactical niceties set in. On the stage to Angers, Driessens attempted to create a diversion by sending Faemino riders Italo Zilioli and Georges Vandenberghe away in an early escape. In a bizarre scenario, which probably contributed to Driessens' departure a year later, Faemino ended up chasing – with Merckx in the vanguard – as their own riders worked in the break in front. Zilioli earned the yellow jersey by four seconds, but Merckx was disgruntled at the team wasting energy in this way on behalf of the Italian, who was not the most robust of riders and might be needed later in the race. It had also made him and his team look foolish.

The next morning Faemino won a short team time trial – 10.7 kilometres – by a massive forty-seven seconds from Bic, and five days later their leader retrieved the yellow jersey at Valenciennes in curious circumstances. Zilioli punctured and none of the team waited for him, again raising questions in the press about the running of the team. Driessens explained, against all logic, that no one had seen the Italian, and it was Zilioli's own fault because all the team had to stay at the front with Merckx and the Italian had been in the middle of the bunch. Goddet's consternation was understandable, as the Tour was effectively over even before it reached the mountains. Merckx and the young climber Lucien Van Impe escaped on the stage to Forest, on Merckx's home turf near Brussels, then Merckx narrowly lost the afternoon's solo time trial to the Spaniard José-Antonio González Linares, but ended up two minutes clear in the standings.

The organisers were distraught at the notion that the Tour had no interest remaining, but in the first mountain stage, through the Jura to Divonne-les-Bains, it was the same picture: Merckx won and extended his lead to five minutes, having covered the 243 hilly kilometres at forty-three kilometres per hour. He was almost apologetic in his explanations: it was hot, his team was weak, he wanted to control the race. Two more stage wins followed in the next three days: first the time trial at Divonne, where he was three seconds faster than in 1969 over the same course, then, the day after that, a solo effort at Grenoble. The day after that came a body blow: after the stage finish in Gap, Merckx and Zilioli were taken to one side by the Italian journalist Gian Paolo Ormezzano – he of the Savona urine sample – and told that their manager, Enrico Giacotto, had succumbed to lung cancer. As well as the two riders,

Ormezzano was close to the *direttore sportivo* – which was why
he had received the news first – and all three men were in
tears.

Perhaps the impact of this devastating news was behind the
signs of weakness Merckx showed on Mont Ventoux, the bleak
'Giant of Provence', which the Tour cyclists had not tackled
since Tom Simpson had collapsed and died there in 1967. This
time, famously, the Belgian collapsed in his turn and had to
be given oxygen at the summit. Goddet's account in *l'Equipe*
has obvious echoes of the Simpson catastrophe: Merckx 'arrived
at the summit in a comatose state, collapsing on the finish
line. Lengthy attempts at reanimation using an oxygen mask
were required before the Tour's medical men made the champion breathe again.' It was not quite that simple, however.

By the Ventoux stage he was six minutes clear, with victory
assured and no real challengers, but when the Portuguese
Joaquim Agostinho threw down the gauntlet on the mountain
he responded. He had already reconnoitred the climb and had
chosen the spot where he would lift the pace: just before the
road leaves the trees after Chalet Renard and enters the bare
moonscape close to the summit, where the gradient is still
steep and there is just a little shade. He was ninety seconds
clear as he passed the Simpson memorial a few hundred yards
from the summit, but he slowed down as he approached the
finish. He took his hat off in honour of his former teammate
and crossed himself, then forged on to win by seventy-one
seconds from Martin Van Den Bossche. At the line, in the
freezing cold, he quickly answered questions from Belgian
television.

As other television cameras approached, the race leader's
legs buckled and he needed assistance as he crossed the road
to join Van Den Bossche in the race ambulance. Around him
was what the writer Roger Bastide described as 'a demented

throng which has lost any sense of sympathy for his suffering and has thrown decency to the winds in the urge to see and know everything, no matter the price'. He was given oxygen, but as a precaution. He was then driven to Avignon in the race ambulance, but not because there was any emergency: it was simply the fastest way for him to get to his hotel. He was given an ECG by the race doctors and the feeling was that his moment of weakness was a temporary blood pressure issue, due to his not taking any time to recover after the stage.

The picture drawn by Théo Mathy and others diverges from Goddet's account suggesting that his overwrought writing was probably down to subliminal memories of the Simpson catastrophe, and a wish – conscious or otherwise – to create drama by looking for possible chinks in Merckx's armour. Merckx himself blamed the gases from the race vehicles all around him, and the fact that no one allowed him to sit down for as much as a moment when he had crossed the line. 'It was bad, but it only lasted a short time,' said the Danish film director Jørgen Leth, who was on the spot. 'There was a shock effect among the journalists. It was a sign that he was not invulnerable. It was a moment of weakness.'

Collapse or no collapse, Merckx had extended his lead to nine minutes twenty-six seconds and, apart from a blip at La Mongie in the Pyrenees where the newcomer Bernard Thévenet landed the stage ahead of Van Den Bossche and Van Impe, his progress through the rest of the race looked straightforward. Victories in the last two time trials of the Tour left him twelve minutes forty-one seconds ahead of Zoetemelk when the race reached Paris. It was not that straightforward, however. Luis Ocaña's biographer François Terbéen wrote 'there were times when Eddy Merckx was vulnerable, after too many repeated efforts'. Hence his inability to match Thévenet when he escaped at La Mongie. The familiar pain in his left leg had troubled him on the Ventoux, and before his stage win in the final Paris time trial he changed first his frame, then his forks, because he was so unsure of his position on the bike. Even so, he won the *contre la montre* one minute forty-seven seconds ahead of his future great rival Luis Ocaña, another huge margin. It was his eighth stage win, a record for a single Tour which has only ever been equalled, never bettered.

Relations between Merckx and the Tour organisers became a little tense that year after an incident at Saint Gaudens in the Pyrenees. Faemino and other riders were lodged in a school in the town but the sleeping accommodation was in dormitories which had not been partitioned. They booked into a nearby hotel and were preparing to sleep there until the organisers turned up brandishing the rule book, which stipulated that the riders had to sleep in the accommodation provided for them. As far as they were concerned the riders had to abide by the rules and the leader of the race had to set an example. It was the night of 14 July, Bastille Day, so Merckx and company didn't sleep due to the fireworks. At the start the next morning, on top of the complaints about accommodation, Merckx showed the journalists the contents of the *musette*, the official race food provided by the organisers. He tipped the inedible apricots and hard rice cakes on to the tarmac, then ground them under the heel of his racing shoe. He was beaten that evening at La Mongie by Thévenet, and Goddet produced an editorial entitled 'the moods of the affronted king', stating that Merckx's complaints were an excuse for his defeat – ignoring the fact that they had preceded it.

'Since the Ventoux any interest in the Tour hinges on Eddy Merckx's health . . . we can't see anything that will hinder his progress towards Paris apart from an *extra-sportif* virus, a cursed fever or bubonic plague', wrote Antoine Blondin wryly. 'Has Merckx got the beginnings of a headache? Will he get a stone in his eye?' The only illness Merckx had, joked Blondin, was *jaune*-dice, due to the colour of the jersey. As in 1969, the opposition did not seem to know how to respond. This was partly because it was a year of transition. There was a marked decline among the old guard such as Lucien Aimar, Jan Janssen and Roger Pingeon, all Tour winners in the 1960s. There was a wave of new, younger rivals, who were not yet mature but would dog Merckx to the end of his career: Van Impe, Ocaña, Agostinho, Thévenet and Zoetemelk. The Dutchman, in his first year as a professional, followed the leader for most of the race: later he was, rather unfairly, nicknamed the 'wheelsucker', and the 'rat'. A rather clumsy joke began to do the rounds: why does Zoetemelk end the Tour as pale-skinned as when it started? Because he spends the race in Merckx's shadow.

Images of Merckx from the 1970 Tour make up part of the experimental film *Eddy Merckx in the Vicinity of a Cup of Coffee*, a blend of poetry and images by Jørgen Leth, better known for the documentaries *Stars and Watercarriers* and *A Sunday in Hell*. Leth told me he was fascinated by Merckx's face. 'I shot the material myself in 8mm, because I was close to Merckx at various times, in the start village, at the starts and finishes. The images are close up because that was how I observed him. I was fascinated by him as a man. He has this Asiatic face, high cheekbones, very central eyes – "bedroom eyes", with long eyelashes. He is handsome in a very unorthodox way. The close-ups were almost sensual.'

Leth's fascination with Merckx is at odds with the public view of the Belgian at the start of the 1970s. The common feeling was that he was an implacable, almost inhuman, machine. That view began to circulate during 1969 and 1970 and would be prevalent until Merckx's decline began during 1975 and 1976. The tone was set by the French writer Lucien

Bodard in 1970, in this celebrated passage. 'Merckx, a super-winner in unprecedented style, walks away, without a hint of fatigue, with nothing to say, just a hint of boredom. He has robotised himself. There are no aspirations, no sense of destiny, just an awareness that he is set apart, unique. So he has transformed himself into a machine with the utmost meticulousness. He is half-man, half-bike.'

Bodard, in turn, was echoing the Breton writer Georges Perros, who saw Merckx at the Circuit de l'Aulne in Chateaulin the day before Blois, and portrayed him as 'the man with no shadow', a reference to the inhuman yet supernaturally powerful vampire Count Dracula created by Bram Stoker. 'With an absence of nerves he pedals as if in a dream, in I don't know what kind of a secondary state, with fatigue banished, eyes fixed on the tarmac, fishlike mouth half-open. We will learn nothing. There will be no sign of complicity, no connivance, nothing but bloodless hyperactivity. He seems to feel no pleasure, no difficulty. He pedals, that's all. Where is Eddy Merckx? Who is he? What's he thinking of? Of whom? Of nothing, obviously. Of no one. He is indifferent to everything apart from the act of dominance, inexorable, monotonous . . . He suggests a rather unhappy god who descends to earth here and there. He is a man with no shadow who can look straight into the sun without a quiver of his beautiful eyelids, and his destiny is one from which weakness and any joy at merely existing seem to have been excluded.'

Another description came from Marc Jeuniau in *Qui Êtes-Vous, Eddy Merckx?* 'Merckx is not a joyful champion. His look is dark, his face closed, his smile rare. He's calm, pleasant, polite but distant and cold. He is certainly neither exuberant nor warm. He speaks little and never confides, even in his closest friends. No one ever knows what his next plan is. He's secretive, worrying and discreet . . . Cycling is not a joyous adventure for him. It's a hard, demanding, pitiless profession in which he needs to make a small fortune as quickly as possible.' Watch any extended footage of Merckx off the bike and he rarely seems calm: he is variously closed, mistrustful, worrying, a little animated. But never at peace.

It was the essential paradox of any sporting great: Merckx was winning so often and so brilliantly that it was expected of him; it had become banal. As a result the press and fans looked intently for cracks in the carapace. As Blondin wrote: 'May the best man lose, but not too often.' Merckx's defeats became a better story than his victories. Like other dominant figures since, Merckx did not understand and was hurt by that. Some of it was wishful thinking: journalists hoping for a Merckx defeat in the same way that writers like me would optimistically watch for Miguel Indurain or Lance Armstrong cracking in the 1990s and 2000s. For example, during the 1970 Tour one journalist recalled listening to commercial radio as the commentator excitedly proclaimed that Merckx was struggling. The dramatic news was eagerly picked up by the radio commentator's colleague, the only problem being that, as he did so, the writer who related the story was watching Merckx stamping out his rhythm at the front of the bunch.

The year 1970 saw the first hints of hostility towards Merckx, which would become more marked throughout his reign and would culminate in the incident at the Puy-de-Dôme in 1975 when he was punched by a spectator. Spectators spat in his face as he ascended the Col de Porte and there were whistles at some of that year's stage finishes. *France-Soir* explains: 'There is more applause than there are whistles, but it's true that Merckx's apparent coldness and his haughty attitude do not make for a sympathetic reception. And the French feel uneasy about his dominance.' Part of the lack of sympathy stemmed from the fact that Merckx himself was unable to play to the crowd. His mother had noted when he was a boy that he didn't really manage to 'sell himself' to customers in their shop. Spontaneous public gestures of joy did not come naturally to him: he was too worried for that.

Publicly, Merckx was restrained in what he said and did. As Geoffrey Nicholson wrote: 'Merckx is a good-looking man but he has the high-cheeked, graven features of a totem pole and they break into laughter about as often. So much so that it has become a kind of game with the press to record instances of him smiling.' He was nicknamed *il mostro* – the monster – in Italy. According to Ocaña, many riders referred to him as 'the crocodile'. Presumably this was for the same reason that he was given his most famous nickname, The Cannibal, because he devoured the opposition. But describing Merckx as sphinx, despot or vampire was simplistic. There was a resounding dissonance between the Belgian's public and private personae. 'Are you an introvert?' asks one television interviewer. 'I suppose so' is the muttered answer, with a shrug.

Like his father, Merckx was 'shut in on himself', he said. 'I was a fairly secretive person. I didn't have a big mouth, because I wasn't like that, and I was brought up in a different way. You can be charismatic, but keep quiet. There were moments when I felt far better than everyone else, but I never said so. I didn't care about my image.' The parallel he always drew was Rik Van Looy: adored in his pomp, abandoned when the new star – Merckx himself – came along. He had worked out early on that the emotions of press and public were transient and fickle. Behind the dominance on the road, the picture that emerges of Merckx is of a shy man who became public property and responded by putting up a barrier between himself and the more extreme elements.

It was Antoine Blondin who noted 'a certain nervousness' in Merckx and concluded that, contrary to the image of him as a two-wheeled robot, he was 'not a cold-blooded being'. Blondin got it right, and not just the nerves. Those close to Merckx recorded his good humour. Mario Milesi, one of his mechanics, said: 'Unlike most of the champions I worked with, Merckx didn't treat his mechanics with disdain. He never asked me to do anything without first using the word "please". It seems like only a little thing but it's still nice working with someone as friendly as he was.' Others such as his close friend Jacky Ickx, the racing driver, would note his sensitivity. Imperious he may have been on the bike, but he was the opposite away from it and after retirement.

Those close to Merckx – Jos Bruyère, Guillaume Michiels, his *directeur sportif* Bob Lelangue – clearly enjoyed the experience of being in his orbit, as I shall explore later. It was not just his intimates who saw his humorous side. Once, when a Tour de France stage was en route to Catalunya, Merckx – having had the political situation in the Basque country explained to him – told the Spanish climber Santiago Lazcano that he would shout 'Long Live a Free Basque Country', in Basque, when the race entered Spain, at a time when speaking the language was forbidden by Franco. 'We were absolutely panic-stricken because if he had done it we'd all have gone to prison,' recalled one of Lazcano's teammates.

The most intimate picture of Merckx is drawn by his manager and confidant Jan Van Buggenhout, quoted at length in *Qui Êtes-Vous, Eddy Merckx?* 'He never discusses the figures in his contracts. He has blind confidence in me. But when it comes to business he is less trusting. He examines every detail and does nothing lightly. He can hesitate a long time before signing up for a lucrative deal.' Van Buggenhout added that Merckx needed to be guided rather than led or driven. 'When it's something delicate or unpleasant you have to use a lot of psychology. The key thing is never to tackle the issue head-on but take him there by a roundabout way.' Merckx, he said, would 'listen, but wouldn't hear. Sometimes he seems as if he is open to being influenced; in fact he's not that interested in what those around him have to suggest. He has his opinion and sticks to it. If he hesitates, it's due to the questions that he himself is asking rather than what is being asked by those around him.'

The king of cycling was certainly not mechanical or robotic in his diet and lifestyle. He did not follow the lines drawn up by Fausto Coppi and Louison Bobet, who were legendarily strict in their diets and lifestyles. He was not an ascetic semi-monk like Gimondi. He was fond of a beer. Smoking was actually recommended by some team doctors to wind down after a race; the Faema doctor advised Merckx to have the odd one so he would occasionally nip into Roger Swerts's room to get a cigarette, Swerts being the team's smoker. If anything, he veered more towards the *bon vivant* lifestyle of Jacques Anquetil, although without the excess of Master Jacques, said Van Buggenhout. Vittorio Adorni came across Merckx and his teammates knocking back beers in his hotel room one evening during the 1968 Giro.

The evening before the fatal track meeting in Blois he had shown he was no ascetic. Jørgen Leth recalls a similar episode when Merckx visited Copenhagen for a criterium. Naturally Merckx won the race, and he and the Danish time trial specialist Ole Ritter then spent much of the night in a famously louche nightclub knocking back whisky, after which the great man flew on to his next appointment in Spain, where he won again. 'It made a huge impression on Ritter, the fact that, like Anquetil, Merckx could let his hair down,' says Leth. Over the winter he would tend to put on five kilos, getting down to seventy-five at the start of the season and seventy-two by the start of the Tour. A cycling god he may have been, but he had human frailties.

For cycling, the next three or four years were those of what Antoine Blondin termed, with no apparent sense of irony, 'the glorious certainty of sport'. The irony was, of course, that the certainty among fans and media that Merckx would win stemmed largely from Merckx's personal fear of losing. Théo Mathy summed it up: 'Bike races live through Merckx. He gives them meaning, logic and lustre.' It was not merely that Merckx would be expected to win, he would dominate every area. The only parallel for this in recent years in cycling has been Lance Armstrong's ascendancy over the Tour de France from 2003 onwards. The difference is clear, however: Armstrong did it only in one three-week race, once a year.

Merckx achieved dominance in spite of the after-effects of Blois, but paradoxically also because of the crash. Put together, the fatal accident in central France and the doping scandal at Savona brought an abrupt and brutal end to Merckx's precocious youth. After 1969, he knew that nothing could be taken for granted. His innate tendency towards insecurity was firmly established. The death of Fernand Wambst scarred him, and his own serious injury at Blois showed that everything he had could evaporate in an instant. The 'positive but not positive' episode at the Giro proved that human duplicity could rob him of any victory. Before those two events, he was by far the strongest cyclist in the world both physically and mentally; afterwards it was hardly surprising that he would consume everything his sport had to offer, amid complaints that he was leaving too little for the rest.

In the early 1970s, Merckx seemed to have no limits, but the other side of the coin was that racing Merckx-style implied complete domination. This did not make the Belgian popular in France. The equivocal feelings among the French towards Merckx were best summed up by Jacques Goddet, who had been similarly undecided twenty years earlier about Fausto Coppi. For all his stature in French sport, Goddet clearly could not reconcile his triple role as race organiser, *l'Equipe* head and enthusiastic sports writer. In fairness to the Frenchman, no one could have steered an even course through this set of conflicting interests.

'Merckx arrived in Paris to seal an imperial feat, admired but surrounded by a rather indefinable halo of embarrassment,' wrote the great man at the end of the 1970 Tour, responding to his own criticisms of Merckx forty-eight hours earlier. 'We have ended up with a disconcerting paradox, because we get tired rapidly of watching a super-athlete winning every day and imposing himself on an event merely by the fact that he is there. We almost resent the fact that such a phenomenon exists. Power wears us down, dictatorship leads to rebellion.'

As early as the end of the 1970 Tour, Goddet was almost pleading for Merckx to show signs of weakness: 'In order to idolise a sportsman we have to see the object of our affections occasionally struggle and show fear, go through dangers without necessarily being able to overcome them. At the end of this Tour, all those who follow the race are asking the same question: what do we have to do to avoid Merckx gagging cycling thanks to his permanent supremacy? What particular formula must the Tour adopt – assuming we consider it the main event in cycling – to escape the effects of Merckxism?' Goddet didn't know the answer, but it was actually simple: call in the Spanish.

SCORCHED BY THE SUN KING

'The finish of today's stage of the Giro will be transmitted at 3.30 for Merckx, 4 p.m. for Gimondi'.
Italian joke of the 1970s

There was a talented cyclist who happened to be born at the
same time as Eddy Merckx. Like so many others, the cyclist
spent the best years of his career trying to beat Merckx but was
constantly frustrated. Time and again he knew he was in perfect
form, time and again The Cannibal defeated him. When he
died, the pro went to Heaven and was greeted by St Peter. The
saint put him on the start line of a race on the smoothest velodrome he had ever seen, on the finest handbuilt Italian frame.

All the greats who had predeceased him were on the start
line: Fausto Coppi, Maurice Garin, Ottavio Bottecchia and so
on, but, even so, our cyclist knew he could win. He rode the
perfect race, timed his effort just right, and had victory in the
bag on the final lap. As the line approached, however, he sensed
a wheel coming past, glanced to the side and saw the face of
The Cannibal.

Afterwards, in a state of some distress, the cyclist went up
to St Peter and said, 'Eddy isn't dead yet, what's he doing here?'
St Peter replied gravely: 'That wasn't Merckx. It was God. He
likes to pretend he's Merckx.'

*

Merckx's rivals are rarely given the respect they deserve. It's not just the jokes. In his 2011 history of Italian cycling, *Pedalare! Pedalare!*, John Foot describes the pop songs that were written in Italy about Gimondi's constant defeats by Merckx. 'I am even more alone than before, and The Cannibal is already at the mountain top and I have to press on to catch him,' sang Enrico Ruggieri. In the song 'Sono Felice' (I am Felice or I am happy) Elio e le Storie Tese wrote, 'Sometimes he [Merckx] rides off, he doesn't wait for me, he leaves me with Bitossi, it drives me crazy'. The press – who wanted to see epic battles and nothing else – derided Merckx's rivals as dwarves and Lilliputians. Jacques Goddet's report in *l'Equipe* the day after his epic ride to Mourenx set the tone: 'For 120 kilometres they proceeded in a sad, desolate retreat, men resigned to their fate, soldiers who seemed almost demobilised. It was not a glorious attitude but you can understand how heartbreaking it must be faced with such a basic inequality in opposing forces and relative strength.' The same newspaper described Merckx's opponents in the 1970 Paris–Roubaix as 'reduced to bit-part players, poor creatures covered in mud, flattened, dazed, incapable of understanding why they had such contrasting status'.

One thing cannot be said often enough: Merckx was the greatest, but the men who contested the races with him, and usually lost, were far more than also-rans. They had several things in common with him. They were all part of a highly talented generation that was born in the second half of the Second World War, or just after: Gimondi, 1942; Godefroot, Van Springel, 1943; Luis Ocaña and José Manuel Fuente. 1945; Eric Leman, Lucien Van Impe and Joop Zoetemelk 1946; De Vlaeminck, Guimard, 1947. Raymond Poulidor was the exception, being born in 1936, and having turned professional six years before Merckx. He, Gimondi, Godefroot, Van Springel, Van Impe, De Vlaeminck and Zoetemelk all enjoyed far longer careers than the average, as indeed did Merckx himself. Ocaña's career, at ten years, was definitely one of the shortest, along with that of Guimard, who lasted eight years, and Fuente, who quit after just six. This trio all burned themselves out physically and mentally in trying to match Merckx.

The reason why Merckx is not perceived as having any opposition is that, unlike with Anquetil or Coppi, there was no single specific rival to contrast with him, no figure to be his equivalent of Raymond Poulidor or Gino Bartali. Ocaña's challenge only lasted for three years. Apart from the Spaniard the assault came from disparate sources, like waves crashing on a battleship, and to about as much effect. The boat was rocked on occasion, but no more. There was no other dread-nought on the horizon. However, Merckx's leading rivals forged considerable records in The Cannibal's shadow, winning enough major races to be placed firmly among the greats of the sport. In spite of the number of races Merckx won – and they did not – Godefroot, De Vlaeminck and Van Springel still rate among the top Classics riders of all time. Gimondi ranks fourth in the all-time hierarchy of Italian cycling, while Van Impe, Zoetemelk and Raymond Poulidor have their place among the most prolific and most consistent Tour de France finishers.

They were great cyclists. But they were unable to compete with Merckx on a daily basis. 'I remember the days when I was in the same form as Eddy,' said one. 'There must have been four a year. About as many as Eddy had bad days.' 'At a certain point you just give up. You have no option. If [winning] doesn't happen, it doesn't happen,' said Van Springel. Godefroot recalled being dropped together with Van Springel as Merckx went to the front one day: 'he [Van Springel] looked at me and we just said "welcome to the club".' 'You would be happy to be second in a Classic after Merckx,' said Frans Verbeeck, who went to considerable lengths to try to match Merckx. He would train up a one-in-five hill using a large fixed gear (50x18) to build his thigh strength, tackling the climb forty-five times in one day.

'I never thought Merckx was in a class of his own,' says Walter Godefroot, who felt that some riders tried to avoid direct confrontation with Merckx, but he just went in there 'with his visor open'. 'For me he was a competitor like any other. Now, when I think back, it's clear perhaps I would have won more races if Merckx hadn't been there. But I gave it all I had without being fixated by Merckx. I respected him as a competitor, because you could see what he was capable of. If I did two-hundred-metre turns in a break, Merckx's turns would last a kilometre. If he got away, you would never get him back.' For the lesser riders, merely beating Merckx once was a career highlight. 'To see a photo with yourself in front and Merckx behind is truly satisfying, even if it only happened once and in some chipper of a race,' said the Spaniard Domingo 'Txomin' Perurena. 'Most of the time, you spent looking at his arse.'

Because of Merckx's dominance the opposition had no option but to base their race around him, if only to hang on as long as they could. Most top-level cyclists are attuned to the idea that they will encounter opponents who are better on certain days, and on certain terrains. That is part of the great mystery of road racing. They in turn will be better on their day. What baffled Merckx's rivals was that they had never had to cope with an opponent who was better on a daily basis, and not just in major events. Contemporaries recall secondary races – stages of the Tour of Belgium, one-day races in Italy – when Merckx would race as if he were contesting a Classic. Van Springel recalled a Giro del Piemonte when Merckx attacked sixty kilometres from the finish, and spent the rest of the race 200 metres ahead of the best Italian riders, all of them chasing like fury. He never turned his head, apparently never contemplating giving up.

Luis Ocaña was a man for whom the word mercurial seems to have been coined. 'A volatile rider of undoubted class but uncertain temperament . . . accident prone and understandably anxious,' wrote Geoffrey Nicholson of him. As well as crashing frequently, he was also superstitious, hypochondriac and vulnerable to poor weather, the antithesis of the nervous but robust Merckx. 'He was the cliché of the Spanish nobleman, all pride,' Jørgen Leth recalls. Ocaña was surprisingly similar in appearance to Merckx, if squarer in the jaw and straighter of eyebrow; from certain angles they could have been taken for brothers. But the Spaniard bore a slightly bitter half-smile on his lips, as if no matter the joy of the moment he was always aware of the tragic undercurrents in his life.

'Merckx and I were the same age, twenty-four,' wrote Ocaña, 'but he had had a happy childhood and adolescence, not marked at all by the same privations that I had suffered, and life continued to smile on him.' Ocaña was from the village of Viejo in Castile, where his father worked in a textile mill carding wool, but the family had trouble scratching a living in the years after the Spanish civil war. 'Meat was a luxury, so too our sweets at Christmas,' wrote Ocaña. They moved several times as his father sought work, ending up in the Landes of southwest France, close to the town of Mont-de-Marsan. There he began racing only at the age of sixteen, because his family could not afford a bike for him (he 'borrowed' his first one, without asking the owner). By 1968, after his father's premature death, he was supporting his wife and child and his mother and four siblings. He was a near neighbour of the legendary rugby player Guy Boniface, to whom he was related by marriage. Ocaña was as much French as Spanish, and might well have had a French professional licence had he not been offered a contract with the Fagor team in 1967. These were all connections that endeared him to the French public and press.

Ocaña could climb almost as well as his fellow Spaniard José Manuel Fuente, the supreme mountain specialist of the early 1970s, but he had more all-round talent. He was a stylish cyclist when in perfect health – which was not as often as it should have been – a supreme time triallist on his day, twice a winner of the Grand Prix des Nations, the longest and toughest time trial on the calendar. He was more talented than the best cyclist Spain had produced until then, Federico Bahamontes. 'The Eagle of Toledo' had set the mercurial standard for Spanish cyclists with a series of spectacular mountain victories and dramatic – occasionally petulant – *abandons* during the 1950s and early 1960s. Both Fuente and Ocaña burned brightly but briefly. Their careers lasted seven and ten years respectively, their retirements were premature and their deaths tragically early, Fuente at fifty from kidney disease, Ocaña taking his own life at forty-nine.

Fuente's challenge to Merckx would not gain momentum until 1972, but by 1970 Ocaña was already rapidly emerging as a possible rival. He had won the Spanish national championship in 1968 (and had taken the prized jersey to his father, who was bedridden with terminal cancer). He had been narrowly beaten by Roger Pingeon, the 1967 Tour de France winner, at the 1969 Vuelta a España, and had overcome Raymond Poulidor to take the 1969 Midi Libre stage race. In 1970, after picking up the leader's spot at the French Bic team when Jacques Anquetil retired, he was already being tipped as Merckx's next big rival even before winning the Vuelta and Dauphiné Libéré (at this point known as the Critérium Dauphiné-Six-Provinces). He had crashed out of the 1969 Tour de France but not until he had attempted to race for two days with his wrist and arm in such a state that he could not get food from his jersey pockets and had to be fed like a baby by his teammates.

He had struggled in the 1970 race, where he fell ill in the Alps, but recovered to win the stage at Saint-Gaudens with Merckx's Faemino chasing behind him. Ocaña believed that he was one of the few who made a point of trying to avoid passive acceptance of Merckx's superiority, and he questioned Merckx's decision to chase him that day. Merckx's response was that Ocaña had won the Tour of Spain that year and you could not simply let a rider of his calibre have his head. He might also have been repaying the Spaniard for an episode during the opening week where Ocaña attacked, Merckx responded, but then punctured, at which Ocaña promptly attacked again. This was not the kind of incident that would endear him to the Belgian.

Without either of the pair being aware of it, the stage was gradually being set for a confrontation in the Tour de France of 1971 that remains one of the race's greatest battles. Merckx versus Ocaña in the Tour of 1971 ranks with Muhammad Ali and George Foreman's Rumble in the Jungle for intensity; but although it was Merckx and Ocaña's defining encounter, its particular fascination is that there was no satisfactory resolution. During the three years in which they went head-to-head, 1971, 1972 and 1973, Merckx's campaign against the Spaniard was decisively won by the Belgian. But the pair's relationship is defined by the 1971 Tour de France, and its inconclusive ending.

Faema was dissolved in the autumn of 1970 after the death of Vincenzo Giacotto from lung cancer during the Tour de France of that year. Merckx and the bulk of his entourage moved to the Molteni squad, a longstanding Italian set-up sponsored by a family-run sausage company based in Arcore, near Milan. Molteni had expanded rapidly since the 1950s and their team had been founded in the early 1960s. In 1970 Molteni had won Milan–San Remo through Michele Dancelli – one of the riders Merckx overcame in the finish sprint of his first victory in the race – but Dancelli had moved on when Merckx and company arrived.

Driessens came along as *directeur sportif* – for the time being – sharing his duties with Giorgio Albani. The Italian, known as *Il Professore*, was, like Giacotto, a contemporary of Coppi as a professional and had been a confidant of Eberardo Pavesi, Gino Bartali's legendary manager at Legnano. Molteni's budget was substantial and the team had other leaders, notably Van Springel, who had been signed before the team had landed Merckx. They also hired the sprinter Marino Basso, and the blond Dutchman Rinus Wagtmans, who had finished fifth and sixth in the last two Tours de France. It was a far stronger squad than Faema, although the other leaders would not last long at Merckx's side.

In 1971, Merckx enjoyed a decent enough early spring, winning the Tour of Sardinia with an escape on the last stage in pouring rain that left his adversaries shivering. He added Paris–Nice for the third year running after leading from start to finish, with Ocaña third, and went on to win his fourth Milan–San Remo. This was a fine piece of teamwork in wet conditions: an early 'selection' on the Turchino Pass, a further sort-out along the coast when Merckx himself reduced the leaders to seven, including two teammates, Jos Bruyère and Jos Spruyt. After a brief intervention from Gimondi, the Molteni pair engineered the final break on the Poggio and launched their leader.

A solo escape in Het Volk six days later took the victory tally for March to nine, but April was more fraught, in spite of a victory in the Tour of Belgium, in similar snowy conditions to the previous year. Merckx could be beaten when the opposition were there in numbers and worked together to foil him, as happened in the Tour of Flanders. He was not immune to mechanical problems, such as the five punctures that lost him that year's Paris–Roubaix. There was a certain desperation about the other riders: Merckx noted that when he punctured, they all started racing. When he had ridden back to the field, they would slow up. 'The fifth time, I felt out of breath,' he said afterwards.

The build-up to the Ardennes Classics, Liège–Bastogne–Liège and Flèche Wallonne, was not propitious: a spot of stomach trouble – probably picked up during a flying visit to Italy to negotiate with Molteni over whether he should start the Giro – and a boil on the backside. Merckx was not his usual self in Liège but refused to take it into account. It was yet another diabolical 'Merckx day' – chilly rain, and snow on the higher parts of the Ardennes – and The Cannibal attacked alone ninety kilometres from the finish in typical style. He caught the early break (closing a six-minute gap in just twenty kilometres) but opted to go past, leaving his teammate Jos Spruyt behind, a mistake as it turned out. Victory was apparently in the bag thirty kilometres from the finish, as he had a five-minute lead. Then, however, the seemingly impossible happened and he crumbled, just as the small, pugnacious Belgian Georges Pintens attacked from behind. Merckx's teammates, led by Bruyère, appear to have let him have a free rein on the mistaken assumption that he would only be racing for second place.

Unlikely as it seems, Merckx did not panic as Pintens closed rapidly on him. He made sure he stayed ahead over the final hill, with Pintens breathing down his neck. He then sat up, ate a little and waited for the other man, who caught him 3.5 kilometres from the finish, after which Merckx glued himself to Pintens's wheel, then left him trailing in the sprint. All that made Merckx great is there in that win: the aggression, cavalier bordering on foolhardiness; the disregard for tactical niceties, as using Spruyt to make the pace for a few kilometres would have been the conventional and, indeed, the sensible thing to do; the clarity of mind when things went against him; finally, the absolute need to win. And presumably the despair the opposition felt when their nemesis seemed to be on the ropes, but bounced off with the knockout punch. The press loved it.

That year, Merckx opted for two prestigious stage races in France, the Dauphiné Libéré and Midi Libre, rather than returning to the Giro for a fifth time in five years. He won both races – with Ocaña the runner-up in the Dauphiné – but he displayed hints of frailty against the climbers who had come out of the Tour of Spain in peak condition. In the Dauphiné he was left behind briefly on the Alpine Col du Granier, partly because he was experimenting with a raised pedal to make up for the difference in length between his legs, and had altered his position on the bike. In the Midi Libre he complained of aches in his knee, due to referred pain from the attempts to perfect his position. More seriously, he lost one of his main assistants in the mountains, the domestique Jos de Schoenmaecker, who broke a leg in a crash. He 'massacred' the bunch on the stage from Béziers to Millau, then came close to abandoning in the final stage to Montpellier, run off in chilly rain.

Ocaña, for his part, felt that Merckx was now beatable. Merckx had spent three years more in professional racing but that seemed less significant now. 'Luis was getting closer and closer to Merckx in terms of mindset, professionalism, attention to detail, and the constant urge for improvement,' wrote François Terbéen in Merckx–Ocaña Duel au Sommet. 'Both were rigorously self-disciplined, and had the same meticulousness where their equipment was concerned, to the point of obsession. Luis knew that, however it might look, however flattering his record might be, success had not come easily to Eddy.'

In *La Fabuleuse Histoire du Tour de France*, Pierre Chany wrote that an 'anti-Merckx climate' was prevalent at the start of the 1971 Tour after his crushing wins in 1969 and 1970. 'His repeated victories annoy people and people are muttering that a defeat for him would be to the benefit of cycling.' The race was widely expected to be a walkover for Merckx, so much so that beforehand senior figures within cycling suggested to Jacques Goddet that an extra prize be awarded for 'first behind Merckx'. That race is now famous for a single day, the stage to Orcières-Merlette in the southern Alps, when Merckx was tested as never before.

The prologue was a team time trial at Mulhouse, won by Molteni at over fifty kilometres per hour with Merckx winning a twenty-second time bonus. He experienced minor hassles, such as the fact that he did not get to begin the Tour in the yellow jersey because the organisers had forgotten to bring it to the start. After the first split stage – the first day's racing consisted of three stages in a single hectic day taking the riders first to Basle in Switzerland, on to Freiburg in Germany, then back to Mulhouse – Merckx was told he had to give the yellow jersey to Wagtmans, who had finished twentieth in the sprint and therefore was ahead of Merckx on points. Merckx was, not unreasonably, annoyed by the nitpicking and, fifteen minutes after giving up the jersey, he won it back by taking a time bonus at the first intermediate sprint on the second split stage.

The first major sort-out came on the second day. It was instigated by Zoetemelk, Van Impe and Fuente, a hundred kilometres from the finish in Strasbourg on the Col de Firstpan, with Merckx sensing the opportunity. The 'royal escape' involved most of the race favourites. The fifteen riders came in more than nine minutes ahead of the bunch, and the yellow jersey and De Vlaeminck fought out a dangerous sprint on the flat cinder track in the Tivoli stadium. Merckx diced with disaster on the final bend as he went around De Vlaeminck on the outside, flat out, but won the sprint. By pushing for the stage win like this, he was yet again going against the conventional wisdom that an overall contender should save himself for the key moments.

By the end of the first week the other fourteen riders who he had led into Strasbourg were still all within a minute of him. That led to the inevitable murmurings: was he quite as fresh as usual? The answer came on the first mountain-top finish at the Puy-de-Dôme, the extinct volcano in the Massif Central that had been the scene of the dramatic showdown between Poulidor and Anquetil in the 1964 Tour. Merckx attempted to get away early in the stage, but then struggled to contain an attack from Bernard Thévenet on the lower slopes of the mountain, five kilometres from the finish. Both Ocaña and Zoetemelk sensed an opportunity and made their escape. Merckx had lost fifteen seconds, although not the jersey. It was a major event. 'Thévenet and I had ripped up the notion that no one dared attack the ogre,' wrote Ocaña. The 'ogre' admitted that he had sprinted 'harder than ever before' to limit his losses: expending that kind of effort takes its toll in a long stage race such as the Tour.

For Merckx worse came the next day, as the race crossed the Chartreuse *massif* en route to Grenoble. It began when he punctured his front tyre at high speed close to the foot of the descent from the Col du Cucheron, thirty-two kilometres from the finish. By this time, a sudden acceleration by Ocaña's Bic team had reduced the leaders to just five, and left Merckx isolated from his Molteni teammates. The race leader kept control, however, and stayed upright, partly by pushing against the barrier that ran alongside the road. Because the team cars were a little way back, the wheel change was slow and he lost about a minute. Ocaña had attacked 'like a bullet out of a gun' the second he noticed Merckx had punctured, and he was joined by the other leaders: the Swede Gosta Petterson, Zoetemelk and Thévenet. The descent from the Cucheron was followed by another climb, the Col de Porte, which Merckx began with a forty-second deficit. Assisted by Agostinho and a trio of Spanish climbers who had been dropped on the Cucheron he made his way up through the convoy of team cars to approach the four leaders. At its closest, the gap was all of about eighty metres, but Goddet, regulating affairs from the race control vehicle, had made the line of cars wait behind a rider who had just been dropped. This *barrage*, as it is known, prevents that rider, or any other, from using the convoy's slip-stream to close the gap. For Merckx that eighty metres might as well have been eight thousand.

Merckx could not bridge the gap and crumbled. He was whistled as he finished in Grenoble, one minute twenty-eight seconds behind the four, with Thévenet taking the stage and Zoetemelk the jersey. It was the first time in the Tour that he had lost the jersey to a rival of stature. 'NOTHING CAN BE THE SAME AS IT WAS,' read the headline in *l'Equipe*, where Goddet wrote, not without a certain amount of wishful thinking: 'Has the Merckx era begun slipping away to its conclusion? The least we can say is that it has entered a new period. The glorious bird has lost a little plumage but he will remain the eagle of cycling for some time yet. However, he is no longer in a class of his own.' Blondin noted, somewhat maliciously, that at this point the previous year Merckx had been able to afford the luxury of adjusting his saddle as he opened a massive gap on his floundering rivals. The message was clear: things had changed.

Next day came the stage to the Orcières-Merlette ski station, on the southern edge of the Alps. Merckx had hardly slept that night and acknowledged that for the moment he was merely trying to limit his losses. Maurice de Muer, manager at Ocaña's Bic team, sensed an opportunity. He knew that after just twelve kilometres the race went up the Côte de Laffrey, a relatively short climb but as steep as the side of a house. It would be difficult for a larger rider such as Merckx and particularly tough in this instance because there was barely any time to warm up beforehand. De Muer recognised that the Laffrey would be hard enough to scatter Merckx's teammates and with a further 120 kilometres to the finish any gap opened on the climb could be extended further.

'We set the whole team to work, and the race was hard from the off, because we had seen the day before that Merckx wasn't in his best form,' he said. At the foot of the climb, the Hoover rider Joaquim Agostinho attacked first and Ocaña, Van Impe, Pettersson and Zoetemelk reacted. Initially, Merckx was not even able to stay in the second group, as he was suffering from stomach pains and indigestion. By the summit he was two minutes behind Ocaña, who then set a pace that was too much for the quartet who had remained on his wheel. One by one, they dropped back and the gap widened, with Merckx forced to chase alone, the whole lead group sitting on his wheel. Of his Molteni team, only Jos Huysmans and Wagtmans had been able to stay anywhere near him, but only the former was suited to this kind of terrain. While Van Impe stayed ahead, and raced for second place, Merckx rode with 'a pack of dogs attached to his heels', as Goddet wrote, most notably five of Ocaña's Bic teammates, and Thévenet in his chequered Peugeot jersey.

The 'dogs' did, however, pass Merckx a bottle from time to time when his teammates were no longer there, but no one was willing to share the pace. The price of three years of dominance was that, when the crisis came, Merckx was made to endure it alone: the physical pain, the mental torment of hearing the time gaps shouted from the team car, knowing with each one that Ocaña was carving out a colossal advantage. Gradually the knowledge must have dawned on him that there was more to this than just the humiliation of 120 kilometres, chasing to no avail: he might well lose the Tour. Briefly, he considered abandoning but, instead, he rode his own time trial, with the gap to Ocaña growing and growing. The stage ended with a long gradual climb up the valley to the little ski station: at the finish line Merckx was eight minutes forty-two seconds back. It was an unimaginably large deficit, but he made a point of winning the sprint for third place ahead of the half-dozen who had been able to hold his wheel in the final kilometre.

'THE EMPEROR SHOT TO PIECES,' ran the headline in next morning's *l'Equipe*. Luis Ocaña had managed something which was seen only once in the years when Merckx was in his prime. He had crushed the Belgian and he had done it by the kind of gaping margin Merckx himself was accustomed to open. The speed of the stage was so high that seventy-one of the 109 riders in the race were outside the normal time limit, which had to be extended. It was, said the triple Tour winner Louison Bobet, the finest Tour stage he had seen since his retirement in 1961. As for Merckx himself, he said simply that he had wanted to lose with panache, if defeat was the only option. He had seen no point in inciting the others to help, as it was not clear whether they were physically capable of it. Critically, he emerged with his head high, although the Tour seemed lost. There was no petulance, no excuses: he accepted that Ocaña had taken a firm grip on the race and said he didn't see how the Spaniard could lose now. He was, after all, nearly ten minutes ahead.

There were inevitable rumours that Merckx might quit, but within an hour of the finish he was with his mechanics, fixing up a new bike which had just been delivered from Belgium. He took his teammates out on a brutally hard ride on the rest day, then made his plans for the next morning. The stage looked unthreatening: the route dropped out of the Alps all the way to Marseilles, beginning with the hairpinned descent off the hillside on which Orcières was situated. The stage was 251 kilometres long, starting at 8 a.m., on the grounds that it would take seven hours to complete. After a series of mountain days such 'stages of transition' were usually taken at a steady pace as the field recovered. 'It should be a formality,' Ocaña told reporters. Merckx had other ideas. Wagtmans, the most daring descender in the Molteni team, was ordered to attack from the second the start flag dropped, taking the first hairpins at maximum speed. Later Ocaña accused him of going off before the race was actually under way, although according to one source the Spaniard was busy doing press interviews and had only just got to the back of the bunch when they arrived at the *départ réel*. Wagtmans was joined by Merckx and two other teammates, Jos Huysmans and Julien Stevens, and, with a crash holding up the bunch a little, by the time they had flown down the valley and tackled the little climb to Gap the lead was one minute fifty seconds.

What ensued was probably the longest and most dramatic chase the Tour has ever seen. The pursuit match between Merckx and his two teammates – Stevens did not make it past the only climb of the stage – and Ocaña and the rest of the field, lasted all the way to Marseilles. The most hardened experts in the caravan said they had not seen a battle of this intensity for twenty years, since Hugo Koblet's legendary

Tour-winning attack on the stage to Agen. It was not an equal fight. All the leaders who had been trapped in the bunch assisted Ocaña and his Bic riders, particularly Cyrille Guimard and his Mercier-Fagor team, because Guimard had his eyes on gaining points for the green jersey. In the escape, Merckx received a little assistance from three other riders, not in his team, who could sense a possible stage win, but Lucien Aimar (Sonolor), Robert Bouloux (Peugeot) and Desiré Letort from Ocaña's Bic were all under instructions from their team managers not to contribute. Behind, there was near-disaster for Molteni, as Jos Bruyère punctured in the bunch, and four of the remaining six Molteni riders all waited for him, finishing twenty-two minutes behind at the end of the stage, and coming close to being eliminated.

At one point, sixty-five kilometres from the finish, Ocaña and Bic – with help from another team, the Spaniards of Werner – dragged the bunch to within a minute of the Merckx group, close enough to see the cars behind them. Merckx and company pulled away again, and at the finish the Belgian had gained all of two minutes for 251 kilometres of effort. Those 251 kilometres were covered at 45.351 kilometres per hour, a record speed for a stage at the time, and among the fastest still. The race was ninety minutes ahead of schedule when Luciano Armani outsprinted Merckx by the Vieux Port in front of barriers devoid of crowds. Most of the potential spectators were still at lunch – as was one television journalist, who emerged from his chosen restaurant to see dozens of the Tour field in front of him. He assumed the only way they could have arrived at the finish so soon was by car, so got the idea they had all abandoned the race. Live television slots were missed, and Marseilles' mayor, Gaston Deferre, was so annoyed at the lack of spectacle – in spite of the fact that the racing on the stage was as dramatic as anything the Tour has ever seen – that he did not want the race back. It would not return to Marseilles for eighteen years.

The escape to Marseilles was 'pure folly' in the eyes of Ocaña's manager, Maurice de Muer, but it was also, probably, the ultimate example of Merckx's way of racing. The Tour looked as if it was lost, and for many cyclists the instinctive response would have been to accept that Ocaña was the strongest. As Merckx saw it, however, the race was still there to be won. Ocaña's advantage seemed insurmountable, but he might crack. To that end, he had to be kept on edge, given no respite, no chance to settle into the lead, or to gain any authority within the peloton. Hence the attack into Marseilles: Ocaña was forced to expend energy the day before a time trial at the town of Albi. That would be followed immediately by the Pyrenean stages. By racing all the way to Marseilles, Merckx ensured that Ocaña had not a single second's respite.

In the Albi time trial, Merckx won and regained eleven seconds. That was a small psychological step forward, but it came amid controversy. He claimed live on Belgian television that the Spaniard had been taking pace behind a television car. Merckx made it clear that he was not accusing the Spaniard of cheating, rather the television car of giving him unfair assistance, but the French company responsible for creating the television images warned that unless he retracted the accusation they would not show him on screen. Ocaña, for his part, was offended. The atmosphere of the race was becoming heated. There had already been claims that the race organisers had acted wrongly in permitting several Spanish cyclists who were outside the time limit at Marseilles to stay in the race – the implication being that any Spaniard was a potential ally for Ocaña. In the case of the time trial, the Merckx camp was wrong. The car had been alongside Ocaña simply because for the first time ever the television pictures were broadcast in colour, and a car rather than a motorbike was needed to carry the camera.

Before entering the Pyrenees, Ocaña was warned by Maurice de Muer that he should avoid overreaching himself. The fear at Bic was that Merckx was trying to rattle him to make him push too hard. Ocaña himself was convinced he would win the Tour. The first Pyrenean stage to the spa town of Luchon via the Cols de Menté and Portillon – where his family had moved before crossing the border to France – was nothing to fear. It began in fine weather. The action was started by Fuente, who was out of the picture overall, and was allowed to open a healthy gap, but behind him Merckx, inevitably, attacked early on. He made his first move on the Col du Portet d'Aspet, the incredibly steep little ascent where the Italian Fabio Casartelli was to die in the 1995 Tour; Ocaña, Zoetemelk and Van Impe all went with the Belgian. They came down off the Portet d'Aspet and on to the Col de Menté, a similarly short, steep climb up over a wooded hilltop and straight down again. It was here, at about 3 p.m., that a huge thunderstorm gathered as they climbed. As the thunder rumbled, Merckx continued his attacks.

The storm broke just before they went over the top and on to the descent. Television footage of the climb is surreal: blurred shots through sheets of rain, with the road barely visible among the torrents of water, thunder echoing around the mountain. The sudden rainstorm, the lack of visibility – it was only possible to see for about five metres – and the intense pace produced carnage on the tight hairpins. The riders tried to stay upright by putting one foot on the tarmac as they cornered, spraying fountains of water into the air. Fuente, who was in front, went right off the road at one point and had to crawl back up the muddy slope on to the tarmac. Riders were puncturing left, right and centre and having to change wheels and, if their cars were elsewhere, they had to put on spare tubulars.

Merckx tackled the descent at the head of his little group with Ocaña, Van Impe and Zoetemelk close behind. He fell on one hairpin, but the true drama happened a few seconds later, on the same left-hander, among a knot of spectators in swimming trunks, brandishing umbrellas. Entering the bend too fast, Ocaña whizzed between a motorbike and a car, clearly out of control. Unable to take the corner, he fell heavily in the gutter. As he was trying to get up out of the torrent of flood-water, Zoetemelk collided with him at full speed. The Dutchman could not avoid the prostrate race leader as his front tyre was nearly flat and his brakes weren't responding due to the wet. Immediately afterwards, four more riders missed the bend one by one and piled into the pair in their turn. At least two of them walloped Ocaña as he tried to get up and get back on his bike. That left him semi-conscious, severely winded, suffering from shock, possibly hypothermia, and he had bruising to the chest. He sank back into the mire in despair as the adrenaline that had built over the five days of psychological warfare with Merckx subsided from his bruised body. He was flown away in the race helicopter.

In spite of the photographs that show him by the roadside looking stricken, wrapped in a blanket, it transpired that Ocaña had no broken bones and might just have continued in different circumstances. The decision to pull him out of the race was not made by one of the race doctors as neither of them was on the spot, but probably by Goddet, who was right there, and can be seen in the footage trying to help him to his feet. That sounds peculiar, but it was only eleven years since the horrendous crash that had seen Roger Rivière break his back in 1960, and Tom Simpson's death in 1967 was a recent memory. 'My fear became panic,' Ocaña wrote in his autobiography, 'and I felt I was dying. It was as if my chest was smashed in, but my mental state was simply atrocious.'

That, to Merckx's vexation, ended the Tour as a contest. The Belgian had fallen off twice himself and hurt his knee but was bitterly disappointed that Ocaña had suddenly been spirited away. 'I've lost the Tour,' was his conclusion. 'Ocaña's crash removes any interest from a possible win. I didn't win it by fighting for it. We were going to battle it out all the way.' He was awarded the yellow jersey that evening but refused to put it on when he was presented with it on the podium. He requested that he be permitted to start without the jersey the next day. This gesture was against the rules at the time, but dispensation was granted. He actually contemplated leaving the Tour – 'I would rather finish second than win in this way,' he said – but word came from Molteni that he was to continue. Clearly he saw little point in a victory that would have a question mark against it. He wouldn't forget how this felt. In 1975, suffering from an injury that was far more severe than Ocaña's, he would continue, as if to accord Bernard Thévenet a victory that could never be in doubt.

The next day's stage was a hill-climb to the Superbagnères ski resort, won by Fuente (who had also taken the stage to Luchon, for what it was worth). Merckx did pull on the yellow jersey afterwards, and the following day he and his teammates controlled the brace of split stages over four cols to Gourette, and then on to Pau. The next morning he visited Ocaña – who had been released from hospital the day after the accident – at the start in the Spaniard's home town of Mont-de-Marsan. The race was in the bag, but there were still issues to be resolved. He produced a typically Merckx-esque gesture en route to Bordeaux, where he won from a break in a flat stage that is traditionally a sprint finish. As a bonus, he was able to seal victory in the green points jersey and take his revenge on the French sprinter Cyrille Guimard for the alliance he had formed with Ocaña on the road to Marseilles. Guimard had the jersey as his goal: going into the Bordeaux stage, the Frenchman was only five points behind Merckx in the standings, and thus a threat. So Merckx attacked when Guimard was moving a bottle from one cage to another on his bike. After the finish, the Belgian was twenty-nine points clear, the classification won.

He took the final time trial to Versailles at forty-six kilometres per hour, two minutes thirty seconds ahead of the next riders. Wisely, Ocaña stayed away, although he was invited to attend. 'Thousands of letters [it was estimated that they weighed a total of eighty kilos] had arrived at my home, full of compassion and warmth, but they suggested rather colder feelings towards Merckx. Their vindictive spirit worried me, and I did not wish to lessen nor spoil the triumph of my fortunate rival.' It took several weeks before the Spaniard could breathe without pain from the bruising in his chest.

Merckx's hat-trick of Tours put him level with Louison Bobet. Only Anquetil lay ahead, with five Tour wins. Even so, he was left with the feeling that the Tour win lacked something, because of the contest that had been cut short. According to Antoine Blondin, the 1971 Tour saw the emergence of a new Merckx: 'a measured and judicious adult' – dealing with defeat, first actual, and subsequently moral. Speculation over what would have happened was intense, with opinions divided. Jacques Goddet's view after the race was that Merckx would not have broken Ocaña because he was not a good enough climber, and his showing after Ocaña's departure proved this, particularly the fact that he was unable to win the mountain time trial the day after the Luchon stage.

'Ocaña would have won,' says Jørgen Leth, 'I'm convinced of that. What he had done up to when he fell was so extraordinary, so convincing. He was successful in his attacks and there was no sign that Merckx would come back. There were more mountains and Ocaña could not be beaten easily on the flat or in the time trials.' Merckx's victory was, suggested François Terbéen, a triumph of science over art 'because the ability to avoid falling seriously is one of the breastplates in the armour of a complete, scientific champion'. Another writer, Olivier Dazat, believes 'in the Pyrenees, going through the Landes or in the final time trial, Merckx would have overtaken Ocaña. Why? Because he had to.' Psychologically, Dazat claims, Ocaña needed defeat as a form of self-justification. Perhaps. What is certain is that Merckx needed victory every bit as much, and would have contested the race to the last metre. It remains one of cycling's great unanswered questions.

ACCIDENTAL ATTACKS OF AN ANARCHIST

Luis Ocaña remained obsessed with the 1971 Tour. His house in the village of Bretagne-de-Marsan was named Orcières-Merlette, and in it there were three items he valued: an old photograph of his family at communion, a wooden box made by his father who was much loved and sorely missed, and the yellow jersey he won at Orcières. 'I was wearing it for the Revel–Luchon stage . . . and it has remained just as it was afterwards. Dried blood in the creases, and the scissor marks where the nurses in the Saint-Gaudens hospital cut through to search the wounds in my back. If I live to be a hundred it will never be far from me.' He remained convinced that he would have won the Tour and that Merckx would be beaten one day.

After the inconclusive drama of the 1971 Tour, every contest between the Belgian and the Spaniard would refer back to the disputed race. The world championship at Mendrisio in the Swiss-speaking part of Switzerland was Merckx's first chance to prove a point. The race came seven weeks after the Tour; it was on a hilly circuit and in spite of his stature Merckx wasn't given undisputed leadership of the Belgian team. Even so, he produced the perfect race: a five-man move going into the final laps included another Belgian, George Pintens, and it was Pintens who helped to set up the race-winning attack on the penultimate lap. Archive footage of the sprint shows Merckx stamping on the pedals as the 250 metres to go banner approaches: Gimondi has no answer, the power absent as he attempts to match the Belgian's acceleration; he loses by four lengths. Ocaña was nowhere to be seen. So hard had Gimondi gritted his teeth in order to stay with Merckx as he made his move on the Cormano climb, the Italian gave himself a jaw strain that took two weeks to dissipate.

The duel between Ocaña and Merckx in 1971 continued up to the Giro di Lombardia, the last Classic of the season, and one of the few which Merckx had yet to win. Ocaña was enjoying a good end to the season, most notably winning the Grand Prix des Nations time trial, and attacked early on. Merckx responded, and – showing the same tactic that had worked so well in the Tour de France that July – he ended up making his winning move on the descent from the Intelvi Pass, firing into a hairpin flat out, with Jos de Schoenmaecker marking Ocaña a few yards behind. Once the gap opened, he was never seen again, with the Spaniard chasing behind together with Pintens, De Vlaeminck, Zoetemelk and Verbeeck. It was a chase group of incredible quality, which closed to within a minute, then fell apart, with the next rider home three minutes thirty-one seconds behind at the finish. By then Ocaña had quit the race in disgust, claiming that he was the only competitor who would not submit to Merckx. In the press, he addressed his fellow cyclists: 'you have more to gain by taking on Merckx than competing against me. Where are the anti-Merckx alliances that are announced at the start of every season? So many words, so few deeds. If I had ridden in the Tour as you seem to do, I would never have got rid of Merckx in the way I did. If you keep riding in this way, I wonder what interest there will be in bike races.'

The following day, the Spaniard made a point of winning *A Travers Lausanne*, an invitation time trial and road race through the Swiss city. He then teamed up with Leif Mortensen – the amateur world road race champion in 1969 – to take a scintillating win in the Baracchi Trophy two-man time trial, at an average speed of over thirty miles per hour. The season, however, belonged to Merckx: he had taken the Lombardy/ world championship double, the Milan–San Remo/Lombardy double – last done in 1951 by Louison Bobet – and an unprecedented season-long 'Grand Slam': Milan–San Remo/Tour de France/world championship/Lombardy. Incredibly, the Belgian had won every stage race he started.

Not surprisingly, however, given the massive interest in the Merckx–Ocaña duel in the Tour de France, and its controversial ending, Jacques Goddet and Félix Levitan were already plotting how to set up the pair's rematch in 1972. The intention was to load the scales in the Spaniard's favour. The route was particularly mountainous, with four summit finishes including Mont Ventoux, Mont Revard and the Ballon d'Alsace. Eleven of the twenty stages included mountains of some kind. Most pointedly, however, the race returned to Orcières-Merlette. Generalisations are dangerous, but the Tours of the Merckx years included more mountain-top stage finishes and fewer kilometres of time trialling than in the Hinault era, and certainly the Indurain or Armstrong Tours. Based on what had happened in 1971 – where Merckx was outclimbed by Ocaña in the Alps – the equation was superficially simple. A mountainous Tour would favour not just Ocaña, but also José Manuel Fuente and his group of climbers at the KAS team, who could together give the triple champion a hard time. There was more than a little wishful thinking here, however, as Merckx had gone into the 1971 Tour a little off his best form, and with only a weakened team to support him.

What was building that winter was a head-to-head between two contrasting characters – Ocaña manically energetic, Merckx more clinical; Merckx self-analytical, Ocaña fuelled by raw emotion, which made him as unpredictable as the

Belgian was consistent. The Spaniard was happy to give the press the lurid headlines they loved. Merckx, on the other hand, famously remained withdrawn. That winter, the Belgian took particular care of himself. He had his displaced pelvis treated by an osteopath. He kept away from track racing, which would have involved extra travelling and fatigue, although that in turn meant he did not begin the season in his usual scintillating form.

His start to the year was disrupted by a quite appalling finish-straight crash at Saint-Etienne during Paris–Nice. It was the heaviest fall of his career after the Derny *chute* at Blois. A classic sprint pile-up, with bikes in the air, bodies falling heavily at high speed, it left Merckx with a broken vertebra. But it was also where the psychological warfare with Ocaña began in earnest. There was controversy over whether or not the organisers should have applied the rule that states that a rider crashing in the final kilometre is given the same time as the winner. As Merckx was being treated in hospital, Ocaña's manager, Maurice de Muer, filed a protest, and threatened to withdraw his team unless the forty-two seconds Merckx crossed the line behind Ocaña were deducted from the Belgian's time.

Next morning, Ocaña told the television cameras 'there's nothing wrong with Merckx'. That didn't tally with the view of the doctor who had examined him in hospital. His advice was that Merckx should quit the race – 'It's as if you have fallen from the third floor of a house' was his diagnosis – and that was echoed by his team doctor. That, however, was not Merckx's way: he tested himself by riding flat out behind a team car and believed he felt better on his bike, although he could barely ride out of the saddle. The attacks were immediate as the race climbed the Col de la République straight from the start in Saint-Etienne: Ocaña flew ahead three times but was retrieved. Any doubts over Merckx's decision to stay in the race were dispelled on the stage to Manosque where he left Ocaña 150 metres from the line to win. He simply could not afford to give even the slightest psychological edge to the Spaniard and the press that supported his rival. 'Why hide it? The way Ocaña behaves is deeply annoying,' he said, through a ghost-writer, in his personal account of the year. 'Firstly because he says aggressive things to the press, and secondly because he takes himself for the head of the peloton. He tells all the riders what to do; he gives orders; he calls back those who have escaped and looks daggers at anyone who looks as if they intend to attack. Who does he take himself for?' Who indeed?

A stunning final time trial by Raymond Poulidor left the injured Merckx in second place – by a mere six seconds – when the race reached Nice. Two days later, however, he landed his fifth Milan–San Remo in the space of seven years. He had decided to leave everything to the climb and descent of the Poggio; his team softened up the pack and he got the vital gap on the fifth hairpin going down into San Remo. He was asked, as usual, whether the risks he took going down were 'insane', but replied that in professional cycling risk is always there. As he said, he knew the descent perfectly; he was physically fresh and confident and 'in those circumstances, you gauge it right'.

After San Remo, it was decided that he would ride the Giro and the Tour. There was pressure to race the Vuelta instead; the organisers were offering Merckx a small fortune to start their race, and those around him, such as his manager, Giorgio Albani, knew that the atmosphere at the Tour would be hostile. Paris–Nice had shown how high emotions were running, and any opportunity would be taken to make The Cannibal feel uncomfortable. Merckx, however, felt that after the previous year's events it was necessary to give Ocaña the chance to have his revenge. Pulling out of the Tour would have been seen as cowardice, he said.

Merckx later estimated that it took him two months to get over the Saint-Etienne crash: the cracked vertebra did not show up in X-rays until after Milan–San Remo, but he was never the type to stop racing unless absolutely necessary. The 'Northern Classics' – Flanders, Ghent–Wevelgem and Roubaix – did not smile on him, and in the 'Hell of the North' he took a spectacular tumble on to his left shoulder, fortunately without aggravating the back injury, although the crash ruined his race. The morning after, his *directeur sportif*, Bob Lelangue – newly appointed from the start of the year after Driessens had been removed – phoned his house: Merckx was already out on his bike at 8.30, on a two-hundred-kilometre training ride behind the motorbike driven by Guillaume Michiels.

What followed was special: victory in the Ardennes Weekend for the first time in his career, doubling up in Liège–Bastogne–Liège, held on the Thursday that year (and finishing in the town of Verviers), followed by Flèche Wallonne on the Sunday. There was an additional emotional side to the achievement: only two riders had managed the 'weekend' double. One was the Swiss Ferdi Kübler, the other was his boyhood idol Stan Ockers. Merckx was racing comparatively conservatively by the standards he had set, saving his strength until the key moments and using his teammates to soften up the field so that he could choose his time to make moves such as the forty-six-kilometre lone break that won him Liège for the third time. At Flèche, which finished in the Liège suburb of Marcinelle, the team's work was far less straightforward. This was a tactical race which left the bulk of the favourites in contention in the finale, where a five-rider lead group formed. Merckx attacked late, bridged to the escape which included his teammates Swerts and Van Springel (initially he had thought of leaving them to contest the win, but the temptation to go for the double was too strong).

With three riders from Molteni in the break against three from Ocaña's Bic – Roger Rosiers, Leif Mortensen and Alain Santy – Merckx asked Swerts to lead out the sprint, but his teammate misunderstood him and attacked, setting in train a series of countermoves that made the final kilometre virtually impossible to read. In addition, Merckx's gears jumped to the wrong sprocket three hundred metres out and, rather than risk changing again, he chose to sprint in a gear he would normally consider far too high on this finish, which was uphill, and on cobbles. He still won, of course.

That completed a spring in which the Belgian had been competing against medical advice but had still pulled in three Classic victories in three contrasting styles. Not only were the opposition raising their game, opposing teams were stating openly that they would combine forces against him. But Merckx was now a mature, confident talent, able to call on reserves of experience as well as strength. Winning is not merely a habit: it can be 'learned'. Experience and necessity were making him better able to distinguish between spectacular attacks and winning attacks. This would be seen to best advantage in the Giro d'Italia a month later. Once again, the principal opposition would be Spanish, but from another source: José Manuel Fuente and the disparate band of mountain climbers who made up the KAS team.

Fuente, a child of 1945 like Merckx and Ocaña, was in the line of Bahamontes and Ocaña: mercurial, megalomaniac, a man of extremes. In his native Asturias, his nickname *El Tarangu* (also that of his father and grandfather) means a man of strong character. He would light up a cigarette before a stage start simply to prove he was not like the other riders: he is one of a handful of cyclists to have been photographed smoking during a race. Fuente was a classic 'pocket climber' (as in small enough to put in your pocket) along the lines of Julio Jiménez, Jean Robic, Charly Gaul or, later, Lucien Van Impe and Robert Millar. Tiny, curly-haired, stick-legged, he never looked particularly comfortable on his bike, due to his short arms and bizarrely long legs, one of which had an obscene tangle of varicose veins. He used old-fashioned gear shifters, at the end of his handlebars, a style which had been briefly popular in the mid-sixties. However, he could produce the repeated accelerations in the mountains that are the hallmark of the pure climber. He relied on pedalling at a high cadence whereas an all-rounder such as Merckx used brute strength at a much lower rhythm, shoving the pedals round where Fuente would spin them. It was recorded that Fuente attacked twenty times in one single climb in the 1973 Tour. He had no option: in any stage race, he needed to gain time in the mountains to make up for his losses in the time trial stages. He also lacked Merckx's consummate descending ability and tended to lose much of what he had gained on one side of a hill when the road went back down on the other. 'An anarchist,' Jørgen Leth termed him, determined to spread chaos in every race he rode.

Sponsored by a soft drinks company, KAS was Spain's first serious professional team. They were the first to mount campaigns outside their own borders, but reflected the fact that Spanish cycling was still more primitive. Spain's racers had fallen behind the rest of Europe in the years of the civil war, and were now a generation behind countries such as Italy, France and Belgium. As a result, their teams were less well organised than Merckx's cohesive squads; the riders themselves were lacking in technical knowledge. KAS was crammed with talented climbers – mountain men such as Francisco Galdós, Miguel María Lasa, Santiago Lazcano and Vicente López Carril

– but they never started a race with a plan and, although it might look to the outsider as if on certain days they were ganging up on Merckx, they were racing each other as much as the Belgian.

'Fuente would always attack when you were least expecting it, he didn't have the calculating spirit that says "I'm going to go for it here",' recalled his teammate Txomin Perurena. 'He just went for it without thinking whether Merckx was in good shape or looking bad. He would just feel like attacking. There was no doubt he was affected by the moon. I can't remember whether it was when the moon was waxing or waning but he would suddenly flip and it wouldn't matter whether he had Merckx in front of him or not, he would go haywire.'

El Tarangu was far less disciplined than his great rival, less able to focus on the task in hand. The tale is told that one night during the Giro he was unable to sleep due to nerves about the next day's stage, so he simply stayed up all night in his hotel room smoking one cigarette after another. On one occasion, he crossed the line at a stage finish in the Giro with one foot out of the pedal, to show he was capable of winning on one leg. A journalist wrote that this was crude stuff, so Fuente sought him out at a stage finish and punched him.

The duels between the little Spaniard and Merckx took place from 1972 to 1974, and tended to follow a pattern. The climber and his teammates would all start the Giro in peak form, having come straight from their home Tour. At this time, the Vuelta was held from late April to mid-May. Merckx, on the other hand, tended to start the Giro a little over his best racing weight, a handicap against a mountain specialist who weighed fifty kilos when wet through. To liven things up a little more, the Giro organiser Vincenzo Torriani tended to design routes that would give the Lilliputian Spanish climber every oppor- tunity to ambush Merckx. The 1972 race included short mountainous stages, a finish on the massive Alpine climb of the Stelvio, and one hilltop finish after another. Fuente's early form told: Merckx dropped two minutes thirty-six seconds on stage four, a brief hill-climb up the Blockhaus, ironically enough the place where he had recorded the first Giro stage win of his career back in 1967. However, a stage with just a twenty-kilometre-run-in before the climb was always going to favour an explosive pure climber, rather than an all-rounder like Merckx, who needed time to warm up.

There was only one way to defeat Fuente on courses which included so much terrain that favoured him. That was to keep the pressure on, day by day. This tactic at least ensured that when he arrived at the key stages he would not be fresh. In addition, it was always likely that one so inconsistent, relatively inexperienced at stage racing and without a cohesive team, might be caught napping. So it proved: later that week Merckx made a surprise attack on the short stage to Catanzaro in southern Italy and snaffled the pink jersey. With a mountain early on he was expecting an early move from the Spanish and had the Molteni domestiques warm up for fifty kilometres before the start. Fuente attacked but cracked close to the top of the first climb of the day, the romantically named Pass of the Dark Mountain (Valico di Monte Scuro), and Merckx followed up almost alone, accompanied only by Gosta Pettersson of Sweden. Behind, the Spaniard had a little help in the chase from Gimondi's Salvarani team but the die was cast: Merckx gained four minutes.

According to the journalist Bruno Raschi, one of those who could remember the days of Fausto Coppi, Merckx's triumph led to similar scenes of public adulation: 'I believed I had gone back twenty years and was in the time of Fausto. I saw people kneeling as Merckx went past and beating the ground with both hands, in a gesture which was familiar from the days of the *campionissimo.*' In another episode, there was a near-riot at a hotel in Sicily when fans gathered outside and were determined to see the great man; Merckx and his teammates had to leave by the back door. As in the days of Coppi, the *tifosi* would climb the outside walls of the hotels to get access to the champion's room.

After a brief stay in Sicily the caravan flew to Rome – the organisers having insured Merckx for 40,000,000 Belgian francs – to begin the final phase of the race. He gained a further two minutes in a mid-race day of time trialling in Tuscany, two twenty-kilometre events run off over the same course on the same day, one of which he won, one of which went to Swerts. The last week was mountainous, with three finishes at high altitude. On the fourteenth stage to Jafferau in the eastern Alps, Fuente finally managed to isolate Merckx from his teammates and attacked with Francisco Galdós. Merckx expected to lose two minutes, but on the final climb to the finish he came back gradually, in the classic style of the all-rounder pitted against the specialist climber. He caught Fuente in the final kilometre and put forty-seven seconds into him. A similar thing happened on the stage to Livigno three days later, then came an eighty-eight-kilometre stage ending at the top of the Stelvio, like the Blockhaus finish a stage in its brevity made for Fuente. Merckx had stomach trouble and ate virtually nothing before the start, keeping his condition from the race doctor, as he wanted to ensure none of the other riders found out.

There were echoes of Fausto Coppi's great ride here in 1953 as Merckx climbed past the snowdrifts, limiting his losses to two minutes as Fuente rode to victory in blinding sleet; as at Jafferau, he controlled his pace, with five of Fuente's KAS teammates around him, but he was unable to fight back at the end as he could not see the kilometre-to-go flag – it had been blown away. It did not matter. The effort was enough to clinch victory in the Giro. It had been a classic race where – apart from the one opportunistic move that sealed Fuente's fate – he had ridden more defensively than usual. There were two reasons for this: taking on Fuente *mano a mano* would have been suicidal, but in the back of his mind Merckx probably felt he needed to conserve the maximum amount of energy for the duel with Ocaña in France. It was, wrote the journalist Marc Jeuniau, the victory of a mature rider. 'Merckx is more experienced, he's older, he's wiser. He now has heavy responsibility. All of international cycling is based around him and he is alone in the peloton. He is still furiously in love with winning, bursting with ambition, but more than in the past he knows the difference between what is essential and what is not.'

Ocaña had not ridden the Giro. Instead, he had won the Dauphiné thanks to an emphatic attack in the mountains of the Chartreuse Massif, and backed it up with a dominant win in the Spanish national championship. He looked as good as in 1971. Merckx, on the other hand, was probably in better form even though he had to sleep with a plank under his mattress to keep his back in order. The consensus coming into the Tour and during the first week was that Ocaña would outclimb Merckx; the Spaniard was prepared to lose up to a minute by the time the race reached the mountains, confident he could regain it. But after seizing the psychological whip hand by winning the prologue, Merckx began looking for openings such as the stage to Saint-Brieuc, with a little hill before the velodrome finish, the team time trial at Merlin Plage and a windy stage across the Vendée where the field split and all the favourites bar Ocaña lost three minutes. Here, it was argued, Ocaña had made a mistake, as, having eliminated all the other threats to Merckx's hegemony, he became the sole concern for the Belgian. His counter-argument was that if

Zoetemelk, Thévenet and Van Impe had been level on time, they would merely have waited for him to soften up Merckx before making a move. But Merckx came out of the opening phase in front, marginally: after a battle with Guimard for stage finishes and bonuses he went into the Pyrenees fifty-one seconds ahead of the Spaniard. It had been a classic plan: wear out the climbers by making the opening flat phase 'nervous', high-speed and high-intensity, no time for rest mentally or physically.

As soon as they hit the Aubisque, the first great mountain pass of the Tour, Ocaña began attacking. Merckx held him and they crested the summit together. As they tackled the Soulor, Ocaña punctured, Merckx and the other favourites went ahead and the Spaniard never regained contact. Pushing to the limit on the descent Ocaña pulled the gap down to a mere 150 metres before losing control as he changed direction to avoid some cars parked on a hairpin bend. He crashed, taking with him Van Impe and Thévenet and piling into a wall. At the finish he had lost one minute forty-nine seconds. Ocaña bitterly accused Merckx of taking advantage of his puncture to attack. (There were echoes of this in the dispute between Alberto Contador and Andy Schleck in 2010, when the Spaniard broke away after Schleck unshipped his chain.) Merckx made the point that twelve months earlier it had been Ocaña who had attacked when he punctured in the Alps.

It was meat and drink for the newspapers: one headline read 'VENGEANCE WILL BE MINE SAYS OCAÑA'. That vengeance did not materialise on the next day at Luchon, where Merckx took the stage and won the yellow jersey from Guimard. After this Jacques Goddet began hedging his bets as to an eventual winner, acknowledging that Merckx was in better form than the previous year. For Merckx there were minor issues like losing his teammate Jos Spruyt to a crash, and falling off

himself on a gravelly corner near Montpellier, finishing the
stage cut and bruised on a damaged bike, with a back wheel
so broken that he had to cut the brake cable. On the Ventoux
he simply rode behind Ocaña, the kind of man-marking that
he wouldn't have dreamed of a year or two earlier. Close to
the top, as Thévenet zipped away for the win Merckx left
Ocaña behind to gain five seconds which were a kind of moral
victory in themselves over all the doubters. This was Thévenet's
second Tour stage in two years; in this Tour he was to finish
fourth, a foretaste of the duel that was to come between him
and Merckx in 1975. Merckx marked Ocaña closely again on
the next stage, to Orcières-Merlette – put in the route to titil-
late the media by acting as a constant reminder of what had
happened the previous year – again beating Ocaña for third
place behind Van Impe and Agostinho. The Spaniard was
frustrated, complaining that he and his Bic team were unable
to escape. 'We are treated like lepers,' he lamented. That was
the point: Merckx had to get him under control, put him under
psychological pressure, and keep him there.

The stage to Briançon witnessed another puncture controversy, on the Col de Porte, when Ocaña had to stop on the
descent after Merckx had attacked just before the summit.
The stage turned into a pursuit race between the two, with
Merckx crossing the Izoard alone – in the wheel-marks of
Coppi and Bobet – to win the stage by one minute thirty-one
seconds from Gimondi, sealing overall victory in the Tour.
Ocaña struggled in almost two minutes back and slipped to
four minutes forty-three seconds behind overall. He was a sick
man having suffered a bout of vomiting overnight. On the next
day's split stage the Spaniard fell to bits, first in the morning
in the fifty-one kilometres over the Lautaret and Galibier to
Valloire, where he lost two minutes, then in the afternoon to
Aix-les-Bains through the Chartreuse where Merckx controlled

the head of the race in a nine-man lead group. Ocaña finished five minutes back, coughing up blood because of a lung infection that appeared to have started after he caught cold waiting for his team car when he crashed in the Pyrenees. He quit the race the next morning, his third *abandon* in four Tours. As ever, he was determined to continue at all costs, and it was not until he was formally forbidden to do so by the Tour's doctors that he desisted.

Guimard, meanwhile, was destroying his knees and his entire career in a vain attempt to wrestle the green jersey from Merckx. The little Frenchman had tendonitis from using gears that were too big for his small frame and was taking xylocaine injections every two hours to keep him on the road. He eventually quit two days from Paris. However, in a big gesture that captured the hearts of the French, Merckx presented the green jersey to him on the podium. There were those who charged him with being cold-hearted, but gestures such as this indicated that the opposite was true, as those close to him would reiterate. The difficulties both Guimard and Ocaña suffered suggest that they were simply physically incapable of taking on Merckx, while Ocaña clearly could not handle it mentally. There was a pattern here that was seen later with other greats of the Tour such as Hinault, Indurain and Armstrong. Rivals would take the fight to them once, then submit to their physical and psychological superiority and accept that they were going to be second from then on unless an opening occurred – or they would try to fight again, and fall apart in the process.

Victory in Paris, with Gimondi at ten minutes forty-one seconds, gave Merckx his second Giro–Tour double. The historian Jean-Paul Ollivier describes Merckx's conduct in the battle of 1972 as a 'masterpiece of clear-headed racing'. It was also a masterpiece of attritional racing: he gained time on

Ocaña on all bar four of the fifteen stages that the Spaniard was in the race, ensuring that the psychological pressure never let up. Yet again Ocaña had confirmed the impression of many observers that he was massively talented but terrifyingly fragile, physically and mentally. It was, wrote the French journalist Jacques Augendre, the finest of Merckx's wins in the Tour, with Guimard pushing him hard and the Belgian looking under pressure in the mountain top finishes from new riders such as Thévenet.

It was also the last Merckx–Ocaña confrontation in the Tour, although the following year's head-to-head in the Vuelta went decisively the Belgian's way. In 1973 Merckx opted to miss the Tour de France and the Spaniard – having stopped racing at the end of the 1972 season while his lungs healed – won emphatically, winning six stages and dominating to such an extent that the French press speculated he might even have beaten the Belgian. Merckx himself said that he would struggle if he had to beat Ocaña to win a fifth Tour, but the rematch between The Cannibal and his understudy never happened. As their careers drew to a close, he and Merckx had long buried the hatchet. The two great rivals had found themselves sitting side by side on a plane travelling to Geneva for the *A Travers Lausanne* race at the end of 1973. It was Ocaña who broke the ice, asking Merckx: 'Are we going to glare at each other for all our lives?' A long drinking session and a hangover later, they were firm friends.

In 1974 Ocaña planned to race all three major Tours, but his health got the better of him – it appears he started the Vuelta with a lung infection – and the project was stillborn. Bic terminated his contract, he achieved no more major results and abandoned the 1975 Tour because of an abscess and tendonitis. He then came close to winning the 1976 Vuelta but retired in 1977, after a positive drugs test in that year's

Tour. After retirement, when Ocaña was trying to get his personal venture, a brandy distillery, under way, it was Merckx who helped him find buyers in Belgium. The man who had played a leading role in two of the greatest stages in the history of the Tour came to a tragic end, however: the Spaniard, volatile to the last, committed suicide in 1994 for reasons that remain obscure.

ANNUS MIRABILIS

*'I will never start one again', Eddy Merckx after beating
the Hour Record*

Two voices, two men nicknamed 'Professor', one shared experience twenty years apart. Speaking from his home near Monza, northern Italy, the crystal-clear Lombardian twang of Giorgio Albani belies his eighty-three-years. From the Wirral, Chris Boardman's more nasal tones are scientific, analytical and passionate. *Il professore*, former contemporary of Fausto Coppi and *direttore sportivo* at Molteni, makes one thing very obvious when discussing the Hour Record set by Merckx in 1972. It was largely improvised, and that raised the stakes in the gamble that The Cannibal was taking with his reputation. Boardman comes at Merckx's record from another angle: in today's record books, which demand the same conditions as Merckx for what is now called the 'Athlete's Hour', he is down as the man who beat The Cannibal.

The Hour Record is a sadly devalued concept now, after being revised and rejigged to the extent that no star of cycling has taken it on since Boardman in 2000, but in the early 1970s its mystique and prestige meant it had lost none of its lustre. Fausto Coppi and Jacques Anquetil in particular had helped to forge their reputations by taking up what was, at the time, seen as cycling's greatest challenge. The task was simple: the cyclist rode alone and unpaced on a velodrome, attempting to cover the greatest possible distance in sixty minutes. It provided an absolute measure of what men could achieve on two wheels with the means available to them at any given time. It was a test of pure physical effort, unadulterated by tactical niceties, the presence of any other cyclists, or variables such as road surfaces and gradients.

This was where the purity of the Hour was to be found. There were no half-measures. There was no chance for compromise or debate. The outcome was either success or failure. And whether it was decided by a single metre either way, that success or failure could not have been more public. A cyclist attempting an hour record was on his own on the velodrome, and his progress could be measured against a schedule. Fall behind the split times, reduce the pressure on the pedals however slightly, and it was virtually impossible to regain the lost distance. If the cyclist went too hard, he risked overreaching himself and blowing up.

Riding an Hour, says Boardman, the athlete is constantly on the edge of collapse. 'You have three questions going through your mind. How far to go? How hard am I trying? Is the pace sustainable for that distance? If the answer [to the third question] is "yes", that means you're not trying hard enough, if it's "no" it's too late to do anything about it. You're looking for the answer "maybe". It's that crude.' Fall or fly, it happened right there, in front of the crowd. There was tradition in the Hour, too, dating back to its foundation by the 'Father' of the Tour de France, Henri Desgrange in 1893. Its history included the romance of Fausto Coppi's wartime attempt as the bombs fell in Milan, the intense battles of the 1930s and late 1950s, when one star after another added a couple of hundred metres at a time. But most importantly it was a simple concept that related to the common, shared experience of cycling, based on this fundamental question: how far can I go?

The record stood at 48.653 kilometres, set on 10 October 1968 by the Dane Ole Ritter, who had been the first man to attempt it at altitude, in Mexico City. A specialist in the Hour, he had no knowledge of the demands of altitude. He had added over half a kilometre to the distance posted by Merckx's fellow Belgian Ferdinand Bracke a year earlier in Rome. Merckx had had the Hour Record in his sights for several years; together with the Tour de France, it had been an early dream. He had pondered it earlier in his career, but had abandoned the idea after the crash at Blois. In the spring of 1971, when Merckx opted to miss the Giro d'Italia for the first time in five years, he had told his new sponsors, Molteni: at some point before the end of 1972, he would attack Ritter's record. 'It was a bargain,' Albani says, a straight swap for missing the biggest event on the Italian company's home turf.

The Hour was in Merckx's mind in the August of 1972 – he told a journalist he was going for it after a criterium at the end of the month – but the final decision was not taken until late September. The idea was simple: finish the season flat out on the road as per usual and hope the form translated on to the track. For once, Merckx took a break at the height of the criterium season, ten days rest, to enable a minor inflammation on his hindquarters to heal. The break worried him – he was afraid his form would evaporate – but it probably ensured that he was relatively fresh going into September. Meanwhile, Ernesto Colnago had constructed him a road machine with the same measurements as his track bike so that there would be less discomfort when he took to the track. At his first outing on the bike, the Giro del Piemonte on 9 September, he attacked sixty kilometres from the finish: the plan not to win, but to practise riding flat out in the same position he would use for the Hour. It was one of his less celebrated victories but the battle lasted for fifty kilometres, with a small chase group – Gimondi, Franco Bitossi, Gianni Motta and Wladimiro Panizza, marked by his teammate Herman Van Springel – a few hundred metres behind. When the four chasers cracked in the final ten kilometres, the margins grew to one minute twenty-six seconds on Gimondi and three others; a staggering ten minutes five seconds on the next group.

There were other indications that Merckx was in his best form: a win at record speed in the Montjuich hill-climb at Barcelona, a dominant first place in the Giro dell'Emilia, where only Fuente's teammate Santiago Lazcano could stay with him when he made his move fifty kilometres from the finish, and a spectacular solo victory in the Giro di Lombardia on 7 October. The following morning he was racing *A Travers Lausanne*, where he broke the record for the first stage, a road race uphill through the city, and caught Ocaña, who had started one minute ahead of him, in the time trial which followed. Three days later came the Baracchi Trophy team time trial, where he tested his leg strength with a massive gear – 54x13. Accompanied by Roger Swerts, he pushed his victory tally to fifty for the year.

There was pressure from Molteni for him to attempt the record on the Vigorelli velodrome in Milan. It was partly history, as this was where Coppi, Roger Rivière and Anquetil had set their records, and also a matter of publicity on home soil for the sausage makers. But when Merckx visited in early October the wooden surface was sodden and slow after heavy rain. Instead he opted for the Agustín Melgar outdoor track in Mexico City, a 333-metre velodrome built for the 1968 Olympic Games, where Ritter had set his record that year. Mexico offered the advantage of altitude, where the thin air means less resistance – literally, there are fewer air molecules to have to push the body through.* However, it raised the issue of racing in an atmosphere with less oxygen to power the muscles. Body performance in hypoxic conditions was then a new, relatively unexplored area. The Mexico Olympic Games had shown that endurance athletes suffered in these conditions, while the messages from the most recent Hour attempts were mixed. Ritter had broken the record by a decent margin, having headed for Mexico in order to take advantage of the publicity around the Olympic Games. In 1969 on the other hand, Merckx's fellow Belgian Ferdinand Bracke had tried to regain the record from the Dane in Mexico but had had to give up the attempt due to poor adaptation to the hypoxic air.

At the end of September, with the decision over the location of the record yet to be decided, Merckx had undergone physiological tests at the University of Liège, and in Milan by Professor Ceretelli, whose work with the Italian expedition to K2 made him an expert on the body's potential adaptation to altitude. Ceretelli was, says Albani, suitably impressed. The decision was taken to put Merckx on a hypoxic training programme in between races, and assess his physical reaction using a primitive pulse monitor. This meant training at home using a facemask to replicate the effects of thinner air – he had thirty canisters of air with a reduced oxygen content and trained six times a day on static rollers while breathing in the thin air, with four doctors looking on as he rode. The only glitch came when one of the canisters exploded, injuring one of the doctors and making Merckx believe, for a moment, that his house had blown up. The doctor in charge of the operation, Professor Jean-Marie Petit, said he was 99.9

---

* There is some debate about how much of an advantage is actually gained by riding at altitude, because, although the air is thinner, this is counteracted by the fact that the air tends to be colder, which slows things up to some degree. This was not known in the early 1970s.

per cent confident that the record was possible, but that Merckx should have started preparation sooner.

Albani says this: 'Because of Merckx's racing calendar, there were no tests, nothing on the track, only the physical exams that we did with Ceretelli.' In other words, Merckx set off for Mexico with only his personal conviction to guide him. He was adept on a track, having raced on the boards since his teenage years. He believed he could race 49.5 kilometres in the sixty minutes. He was in the form of his life, as his end-of-season races had demonstrated. But there was no hard, scientific evidence to confirm that when he flew out on 21 October. He did, however, have the best bike he and Ernesto Colnago could dream up. As was customary at the time, they had looked for weight reduction in all areas. The machine weighed 5.9 kilos. It had been two hundred hours in the making, and included titanium parts, at a time when this exotic metal was rarely used. Every possible component – the cranks, the chain, the seatpost, even the handlebars – was drilled full of holes to reduce weight. Ironically in view of the controversy that has dogged modern attempts at the record, Merckx's bike was a standard one in its shape only.

Once on the ground – after the longest flight Merckx had taken since he rode the Olympic Games in Tokyo in 1964 – the issue was timing the record attempt to get the best of the weather. At that time of year the wind tended to rise later in the day. On some days there were tropical deluges. On an outdoor track such as that in Mexico, either was disastrous. The first day's training was encouraging: the track was fast, and he opted for a higher gear than planned, 52x14 rather than 52x15. The next two days were ruined by rain. One morning, he greeted the journalists who had accompanied him from Belgium by joking that it looked as if they would be celebrating Christmas in Mexico. It was an attempt at humour to disguise his nerves: in his memoirs, he confesses to being 'terrified' by the waiting. By day three, 24 October, the track was beginning to dry out, and first thing in the morning of 25 October he decided to go for the record; he breakfasted before seven, and eventually got started at 8.46 a.m.

The impromptu nature of the Merckx record is shown in the debate over the schedule he was intending to ride, which remained in the air until late on. The original schedule would have seen him overcome Ritter's record by a margin of about 240 metres, according to Albani, but according to the manager, 'I advised him to attempt the ten kilometre and twenty kilometre records, because of his lack of references. The plan was that if he got past twenty kilometres and he had the form to go on and beat the Hour, he could continue; we could reduce his speed very slightly. I didn't want him to risk embarrassment. We agreed this. Then overnight, the journalist René Jacobs, who was in charge of the schedule, had to rewrite the whole thing.' The revised schedule was for 49.2 kilometres, far more ambitious than the first one.

Saludo Eddy Merckx said the electric scoreboard; he was greeted by trumpets as he entered the stadium – two thousand people were there, having heard a last-minute alert that had been put out on national radio. The spectators included King Leopold of Belgium, and princesses Liliane, Esmeralda and Marie-Christine. At the end of each lap, Jacobs rang the bell that indicated whether Merckx was ahead of schedule or not, while Albani 'walked the line', stepping forwards in the same direction Merckx was riding as he gained on the schedule, back again if he slipped. 'I was walking forwards three to four metres per lap,' recalls Albani. 'He was constantly ahead of schedule.'

The fast start that Merckx made to his sixty minutes is the stuff of legend. It was probably always going to happen, but a

change to a faster schedule made it more likely. So, too, did
the decision to go for the two intermediate records. Each would
have acted as a 'carrot', with his ultra-competitive nature doing
the rest. From a standing start he went through the first kilometre in 1 minute 9.97 seconds – back then a time good
enough to win a world championship medal at the discipline
– and a colossal five seconds faster than Ritter. The second
kilometre was even faster: 1 minute 9.84 seconds. He covered
five kilometres in 5 minutes 55.6 seconds – in the world pursuit
championship over the distance less than six minutes was
respectable. By ten kilometres he was twenty-eight seconds
faster than Ritter (11 minutes 53.2 seconds to 12–21.76), by
twenty kilometres, the margin over the Dane was thirty-five
seconds (24–6.8 to 24–42.19).

It looked more than promising: it was devastating. It could,
however, have proved his undoing. Peter Keen, who trained
Boardman to his three Hour records between 1993 and 2000,
recalls that his protégé set the same time as Merckx for the
first kilometre but that was en route to the best Hour ever:
56.375 kilometres, almost eight kilometres further than Merckx.
Boardman concurs: 'It's mortal for the record, doing the time
Merckx did. At altitude you never get over it.' Boardman
compares riding the Hour to bailing out a boat with a hole in
it: the body is constantly producing lactic acid from the effort
of turning the pedals, but there is only a certain rate at which
the body can deal with it. 'It's like a balance between what's
coming in, and the speed you can get it out. If you push the
boat quicker, more water pours in but you can't bail it faster.
If you overcook it even slightly it can take a significant time
to recover. You have to ride below optimal speed for a considerable time.'

Keen, who is now Performance Director at UK Sport, says
that Boardman's ride was perfectly paced for his distance and

agrees that Merckx's start was simply way too fast. The aim in an hour, he says, should be to maintain a constant, sustainable speed for the full sixty minutes. 'Not only did Merckx massively overcook the starting effort, hitting a speed getting on for six kilometres per hour faster than he could sustain, he did it at altitude where as a consequence you pay a much bigger price for what some still call an oxygen debt. The torture he must have experienced for most of the rest of the hour as a result of this error must have been considerable. If I had been track-side with him I'd have pulled him up after thirty seconds, got him on the rollers for thirty minutes and gone again – it was that big a mistake!'

The crisis came, recalls Albani, between thirty-five and forty minutes, although the figures show that Merckx's progress against Ritter slowed most dramatically between forty-two and forty-eight minutes, when he put in his slowest five-kilometre split. 'It was ugly. I had been walking forward, but I went from a lap and three-quarters ahead, to just a lap ahead. Merckx said "I'm dead", I told him to calm down, and said "If you're travelling at forty-nine and a half kilometres per hour you must be alive.' Inspection of Merckx's kilometre times shows a dramatic slowing: after the storming first two kilometres the next eight are covered at between 1–11.28 and 1–12.15 (in other words, *slower* than that first kilometre, which included a standing start!). After ten kilometres the kilometre times slow a second time: for the next thirty-six minutes Merckx is generally hitting the one minute thirteen seconds mark. He speeds up in the final twelve minutes, once forty kilometres have been covered, running below one minute thirteen seconds for seven of his last nine kilometres. The last full kilometre is covered in one minute 11.76; the final complete lap – the 148th – in twenty-four seconds. Merckx's memoirs record, 'After a short period of stabilisation compared to my schedule, I began to gain again and finished very strongly'. Albani says, 'the last five kilometres were the best of the lot, he finished *in crescendo*'. He covered the last two hundred metres in thirteen seconds and broke the record by 788 metres, the biggest margin since 1912. His distance of 49.431 kilometres was seen as 'unbeatable' for eleven years.

The Merckx Hour was, wrote the journalist Marc Jeuniau, the most intense experience in his twenty-five years covering sport. Describing the scene while Merckx was riding, he wrote, 'the men intimately concerned with the champion's performance were going through atrocious moments that they will never forget. The face of Jean Van Buggenhout was crimson. Old Piero Molteni was crying. Colnago, who was ready to run over if Merckx had a puncture, looked weighed down by the spare bike on his shoulders. Lucien Acou, the least confident of all of them, had trouble hiding his nerves, and, alone in a corner of the track, Doctor Cavalli was following Merckx with haggard eyes.' Jeuniau underlined the risk that Merckx was running: 'If he had fallen short, the public would have been quick to point out that he had failed where Coppi and Anquetil had succeeded. All his previous prestigious victories would have been pushed into the background and only the defeat would have stuck in people's minds.'

After two laps' warm-down, Merckx had to be carried away. His grimace as he gulped down a bottle of mineral water in the seconds after coming to a halt remains a defining image. 'The pain was very, very, very significant', was how Merckx put it. 'There is no comparison with a time trial [on the road]. There you can change gear, change your cadence, relax even if it is only for a few instants' respite. The Hour is a permanent, total, intense effort, which can't be compared to anything else.' Boardman is in a unique position to compare the two, being the only man since Merckx to attempt the record on both a 'modern' bike, with stretched-out 'triathlon' handlebars, and on one using a drop-handlebar position similar to that of Merckx. 'I watched footage of Merckx being carried off afterwards and was laughing a bit, I thought it was showmanship, but I couldn't walk for four days after the 2000 Hour. There is something about that position that does massive damage to you. It's to do with riding on the drops.' The difference, says Boardman, is that on drop handlebars the muscles of the arm, shoulders and back are supporting the body, whereas on stretched-out bars such as he used in 1993 and 1996, much of the strain is taken by the bones of the forearms. As for Albani, his final memory is this: 'Merckx told me never to mention the Hour Record again.'

Merckx's change to a more ambitious schedule paid off in one sense. In early November 1974 Ritter returned to Mexico for a wholehearted campaign to regain his Hour. At his second attempt he managed 48.879 kilometres, close enough to suggest to Albani that if Merckx had stuck to his original timings, the record might well have fallen just a couple of years after Merckx had taken it. Ritter himself felt that he might have surpassed Merckx if he had not come under pressure from media and sponsors to attack the record sooner than he wanted. After that, the Merckx Hour was considered 'unbeatable', partly because of the massive distance that the Belgian had added, partly because of Ritter's conspicuous failure to beat him, but mainly because of Merckx's physical state when he got off his bike. If the record could do this to the greatest cyclist ever, who could possibly beat it? In the end, eleven and a half years later, it fell to Francesco Moser to take the record into a new dimension, but only after a comprehensive rethink of all the aerodynamic aids on the market, radical innovation in training and equipment, plus a special membrane laid on the track to make it super-smooth. And blood doping, which was not banned at the time, Moser confessed later.

Now, the Hour has changed completely. Like Merckx, Moser was considered to have put it on the shelf. The 1990s, saw its last flurry, with seven attempts in four years, prompted by the innovation of the Scot Graeme Obree and the science of Boardman and Keen. Indurain was the last Tour de France winner to attack it, in 1994, while Boardman achieved the definitive record, 56.375 kilometres, two years later. After that, cycling's governing body muddied the waters when they decided to create two records. One with any scientific aids available such as those attempts by Moser, Boardman et al. was dubbed the Best Hour Performance. For the other – the Athlete's Hour – the cyclist had to use a bike similar to Merckx's, which is the record Boardman broke in 2000.

This rewriting of the sport's history means that, whereas in Merckx's day it was clear that the Hour belonged to the fastest man under the conditions prevailing at the time, now it is no longer clear what it means. Every attempt post-Merckx has been devalued. Merckx himself seemed unhappy with it when I asked him for his thoughts. 'Riders must be able to beat the Hour under the same conditions as their predecessors. I went to Mexico because Ritter did, and there was an advantage. It's as if they had said [afterwards] I couldn't go to Mexico. It's hardly another planet.'

Whatever the debates since, Albani believes that Merckx's record closed an era, as 'the last one to be done by craftsmen', whatever the advantages and the flaws that that may imply. Boardman has a more dispassionate view, having beaten Merckx's record on a similar bike in 2000, by only a few metres. 'Some of what they did was advanced, some was very crude. You look at Merckx riding a treadmill with an oxygen mask at

16 per cent, hypoxic training, and that's quite thought through, pretty scientific. Despite the way he actually rode it, I'm always impressed with how far he went. Doing an Hour is about bringing everything you have together and seeing where it gets you. Merckx's nerves got the better of him and he attacked it full on. But if you look at the disadvantages, it's still as fast as we did with all the knowledge that we had. It shows what an athlete he was.'

In the view of Albani, the vagaries of the Mexican weather prevented Merckx from going even further. The window of time available was small, and the demands of altitude meant that the record had either to be tackled soon after arrival, before his health began to decline, or after a month's adaptation. Ritter, he points out, spent a month in Mexico during his Hour attempt. 'The plan was to do it on the third day, but it rained, so we put it back to the fifth.' By then, he believes, Merckx's form had begun to decline – Merckx himself said afterwards that he was only having an 'average' day – and that in turn meant when The Cannibal eventually did get on the track, he was nervous, knowing that this was his only chance. 'I'm convinced that if he had gone for it on the third day, he would have beaten fifty kilometres,' says the Italian. Keen agrees that Merckx might have beaten fifty kilometres, but for a different reason. 'Had he opened with a one minute thirteen seconds first kilo he would have comfortably surpassed fifty kilometres per hour and probably not reflected on the experience in the way he did.'

Merckx's willingness to chance his arm should be seen in a wider perspective. Of the *fuoriclasse* who have attempted the Hour since the war, only Miguel Indurain went for the record at the height of his power; like Merckx, he did so at a time when the record was in a state of flux, although by then it was clear that it was the province of specialists.

Anquetil and Coppi attacked it at the start of their careers
(Anquetil did try a second time, taking the record in 1967,
but the distance was not validated because he did not undergo
a drugs test). The crucial point is that Bernard Hinault, Lance
Armstrong, Louison Bobet and Greg LeMond never even
tried. There were good reasons for this: firstly, the risk of
damaging their reputations if they failed was too great,
secondly, the logistical demands in terms of planning, cost
and training. This underlines that the Hour was the biggest
gamble of Merckx's career, perhaps one of the biggest gambles
taken by any great of the sport. He could not afford to fail.
The view of his wife Claudine was that he simply had no
option but to beat it. He either went further than Ritter or
fell on his face.

Finally, consider what came before. When he travelled to
Mexico to tackle Ritter's record, Merckx had taken a second
Giro d'Italia–Tour de France double, with ten stage wins along
the way, and pushed his record in the Tour to four consecutive
victories. He had taken a fifth win in Milan–San Remo, then
added the Ardennes Weekend of Liège–Bastogne–Liège and
Flèche Wallonne. He had achieved all that while wearing the
rainbow jersey of world champion (figuratively if not literally
while he had the *maglia rosa* or *maillot jaune* on his back in
the Giro and Tour); the rainbow stripes have never been
honoured in such complete style. Although he had not defended
his world title, he had added a second consecutive victory in
the Giro di Lombardia and had also laid to rest the spectre of
Ocaña's near win in the 1971 Tour de France with a comprehensive defeat of the Spaniard.

The Hour marked the culmination of what was probably the
greatest season of racing any cyclist has ever produced, or ever
will. Most tellingly of all, on the road at least, fifty victories
notwithstanding, that last race of 1972 ended with the sight

of Merckx throwing his bike down in disgust after the finish of the season-closing event at Putte-Kapellen, after Gustav Van Reysbroucke had outsprinted him for what would have been win number fifty-one. That image underlined that, no matter how much The Cannibal won, he remained insatiable. Eight days later the Hour made it clear that, by this stage of his career, Merckx's only true opponents were himself, and Time.

LA COURSE EN TÊTE

'You become a superstar if, having won, you are never completely satisfied'. *Fausto Coppi*

Bob Addy, a British professional of modest reputation, was racing an obscure Belgian *kermis* race as part of his build-up to a world championship in the early 1970s. He attacked early on and built a decent lead. In the peloton behind him, Eddy Merckx learned that the advantage was two and a half minutes; he went to another British cyclist, Barry Hoban, and asked 'what is the Englishman up to?' 'He's just training for the world's', was Hoban's answer. In other words, Hoban told Merckx that Addy wasn't trying to win, he was merely putting in a big effort to test himself. 'The lead is too much,' said Merckx and put himself on the front of the bunch. 'Suddenly the lead went from two and a half minutes to nothing,' Addy would relate, before pointing out that 'it was only a little race.'

Addy's training event might have been 'only a little race' in the great scheme of a calendar including Classics and Tours, but on its given day it mattered to Merckx. This *kermis* event in Nowhere-in-Particular was not a race where he had anything to prove. This was not the toughest mountain stage of the most important race on the calendar six weeks after an unjust doping ban. It was not Mourenx. Above all the victories, the massive winning margins, this is still one of the things that puts Merckx in a different category from all the other greats of cycling such as Bernard Hinault, Fausto Coppi, Jacques Anquetil, Rik Van

Looy. As Hoban famously said, whenever a flag was waved by the roadside Merckx would sprint for it.

It didn't matter what the race was. Merckx was seen to throw away his bike in disgust on various occasions after being beaten in a *kermis* race. Patrick Sercu recalled a national Madison championship in 1967 when he and Merckx lapped the field nine times driven partly by the public's yells of disbelief at what they were seeing, but also by reports that the other riders might combine against Merekx. Guillaume Michiels told the story that on reading in a newspaper that Roger De Vlaeminck had a higher victory count one season, Merckx's response was to grab a copy of the racing calendar and seek out a race to go and win. Bob Lelangue remembered a criterium 'of no importance' where Merckx asked him to lead him out. Lelangue couldn't see Merckx sitting on his wheel and was worried they might give the race away, so he sprinted and won himself. Merckx was not happy.

Winning small races was a matter of professional obligation, Merckx told me. There was always a reason to get focussed for a major event: a previous defeat to be avenged, a point to be made, another little bit of history perhaps. 'For a big race like Milan–San Remo or Paris–Roubaix, it's normal to be motivated. As for less important races, the fact is that you are paid to do something and to do it well. If people come and pay to see a criterium they want to see you win, not just participate. It's part of being a professional. People work to earn the money to see you, you mustn't disappoint them. You have to be conscious of being a professional.'

Winning was a kind of illness, a form of addiction that was stronger than Merckx's better nature. Those who played cards with him on holiday noticed that he would be unhappy if he didn't win, and would switch to something else. Michiels said that he would be seriously fed up if he didn't win a race every week or so. 'He would get to about four days, then start saying "do you realise, Guillaume, I haven't won anything for a while?"' Michiels recalled returning from a Milan–San Remo which Merckx had won; as they drove from San Remo to the airport in Nice, Merckx observed: 'Now I've won, I am *tranquil. J'ai ma course* – I've got my race.' De Vlaeminck observed that you could have a coffee with Merckx and a couple of hours later he would no longer know you when you were side by side on your bikes. There were times when he walked past close friends without seeing them, such was his ability to put himself in a bubble. He was not alone in becoming a man possessed when on his bike. It was the Italian Fiorenzo Magni who said, 'When I start a race I forget about my wife and child.'

At home, Merckx remained quiet, utterly focused, unable to emerge from race mode. Claudine noted that he was never a talker: it affected his concentration. In the early days of their marriage, he was so silent that she wondered if she had done something wrong. Then she realised he was simply concentrating on everything that had to be done. 'When he was grumpy and silent on waking up, it was a good sign.' He would be annoyed by the smallest thing that affected his focus on a given race. On the way home from a major win, the talk would centre on the next race. After the race, the ritual would never change: a massage from Guillaume Michiels and a long discussion.

Roger Pingeon said he did not believe Merckx started any event determined to grind the opposition into the dust: 'I believe it was stronger than him.' Pingeon believed that it wasn't about making other riders suffer or lose; the collateral damage was incidental, never premeditated. Merckx was never arrogant about a victory, was rarely quoted doing down the opposition. Only if he was provoked did he speak up. If he lost, he said

why; some saw this as complaining, not realising that for Merckx winning was the natural state of affairs, any departure from that an aberration. 'He was never angry if he lost because he was not the strongest,' says Michiels. 'But if he was the strongest and he didn't win, he would be really upset.' Mark Cavendish shows similar traits: unable to conceive of anything other than victory, totally locked into his own world when he gets a whiff of it, like a vampire that scents blood.

In 1973 Merckx did something that would be unimaginable now. He turned down the Tour de France. He had contemplated this before. Relations with the Tour organisers had been tense in the past; after the 1971 Tour, he had felt the public might be against him, and the Vuelta organisers were offering a small fortune. By now, he was beginning to cross the t's and dot the i's on his race record: there were events he had yet to win, and the Spanish Tour was one of them. Moreover, it was a further chance to rubber-stamp his superiority over Ocaña – on his rival's home soil.

In the build-up, illness kept him out of Milan–San Remo for the first time since 1966, but he still enjoyed a remarkable spring, with four Classic wins in nineteen April days, to go with his second victory in the Belgian season-opener Het Volk. Four days after a narrow win over Frans Verbeeck in Liège–Bastogne–Liège, he was in Calpe, on the start line of the Vuelta. Amidst the April frenzy, Ocaña had managed to get the better of his old nemesis in the Catalan Week stage race, winning both the mountain-top finish and the time trial but the Vuelta was a different matter. It was an accomplished win, with Molteni dominant, and Merckx taking the points and combine awards in addition to six stages and the overall title. The first blow was struck in the prologue time trial, a second on the hilltop finish to Cuenca, where victory went to his teammate Jos de Schoenmaecker. Molteni won the team time trial, then, with the help of Victor Van Schil and Jos Huysmans, Merckx outpaced the sprinters en route to Ampuriabrava, and finished the race with three stage wins in three days: the individual time trial at Torrelavega, a mountainous leg to Miranda del Ebro and the final time trial in San Sebastián.

Ocaña's challenge came on the Puerto de Orduña en route to Miranda del Ebro, but it was the same scenario as so often in 1972. The Spaniard opened a gap, Merckx didn't panic but reeled him in very slowly, overhauling him seven kilometres from the finish, and then winning the sprint. Afterwards, there were complaints from Ocaña and his camp that the race had been structured to suit the Belgian, with time bonuses on hilltops as well as in finish sprints. 'Using his finish speed, with no real sprinters present, Merckx was able to gain 3min 46sec on Ocaña without ever really dropping him,' wrote one biographer. The Spaniard himself said that 'three decent mountain stages' would have been enough to make a difference.

No one, at that time, had won the Giro in the same year as the Vuelta, because the gap between the two races was a week or less, as it remained until 1995. With only four days to draw breath, then, Merckx was at the start of the Italian Tour, although he was not actually in Italy. That year, the Giro started in Belgium, at Verviers, then travelled through Holland, Germany, Luxembourg and Switzerland, using the Mont Blanc Tunnel to get back into Italy. This was the race immortalised in Jørgen Leth's film *Stars and Watercarriers*, and was enlivened by another duel between Merckx and José Manuel Fuente. The race seemed destined for the Belgian after only the second stage in Italy, where Fuente lost time due to stomach cramps. In classic style, however, the little Spaniard never gave up, putting in continual attacks over high passes that were frequently little more than dirt roads through mountain meadows. The race boiled down to him and his little Spanish climbers against Merckx and his *rouleurs*.

After a prologue win for Merckx, teamed with Jos Swerts in a two-man team time trial, the Belgian added stage one to Cologne, but this was mere manoeuvring. The race was effectively won nine days in after the ascent of Monte Carpegna, a monster of a climb with slopes between one-in-four and one-in-five, on the border between Emilia-Romagna and Marche, known locally as *Il Cippo*.* With Fuente attacking continually, Merckx is seen in Leth's film constantly at the head of the field. Most often he seems to have two men in his slipstream, Gimondi and Giovanni Battaglin, the latter by coincidence the only other rider who would achieve the Vuelta–Giro double before the 1995 calendar change. 'Merckx churns on and on,' says Leth's narrator as the piano soundtrack plays.

The only occasion on which Fuente managed to make one of his attacks stick was late in the race, on the final Dolomite stages to Auronzo di Cadore, and by then the outcome of the race was no longer in question. That reflected Merckx's iron control of the whole three weeks. By the finish The Cannibal had become the first rider to lead the Giro from beginning to end in the post-war era; the only previous riders to manage the feat were Alfredo Binda and Costante Girardengo, *campionissimi* both. He had also managed a run of four Classic and two Grand Tour wins in less than ten weeks. It is safe to say that this feat at least will never be equalled.

Txomin Perurena, who raced for KAS throughout the years of the duels with Merckx, recalls that relations between the Spanish and the Belgian were close in spite of Fuente's constant refusal to give in. On the final stage of that Giro, he says, as

---

* In the 1990s *Il Cippo* was to be a favourite training ground of the legendary Italian climber Marco Pantani.

the race headed towards Trieste through a series of tunnels, the Spaniards in the field, including Fuente, agreed to ride around Merckx together with the Molteni domestiques to protect him because 'he was afraid of certain riders . . . and he was worried they could cause him to crash'.

Merckx and Ocaña would never again go head-to-head in a major Tour, but their soap opera had a couple more twists yet. In Merckx's absence, the Spaniard managed a dominant win in the Tour – a victory so absolute that the French press inevitably hinted that he might even have beaten the Belgian. Once again Merckx was left with a point to be proved. One opportunity was a post-Tour criterium where the pair were both down to ride. Merckx trained hard, turned up at the very last minute so that none of the other starters – and particularly Ocaña, obviously – would have the chance to tell him to take it easy as convention demanded. Just before the start, the Spaniard made a vague attempt to ask the Belgian to ride steadily, but too late, as Merckx recalled in the book *Homme et Cannibale*: 'I pressed the pedals down violently. You should have seen it. They were all over the place. Ocaña abandoned. I won.' Point made.

On the other hand, the world championship on the Montjuich circuit in Barcelona – on Ocaña's home soil – was a disaster, and gave rise to lasting controversy. Gimondi won in dazzling sunshine on a course that should have suited Merckx, and a new rival appeared. Freddy Maertens was in his second professional season and only as yet showing hints of the talent that would blossom spectacularly and briefly in the mid-1970s. He had finished second to Eric Leman at the Tour of Flanders and had won the Four Days of Dunkirk. He was faster than Merckx in a sprint and could time-trial at least as well, although he climbed as if he was pushing a barrel of brown Belgian beer in front of him. Merckx raced Montjuich in his usual style, throwing caution to the winds in the final hundred kilometres, dislodging the entire field bar Maertens, Gimondi and Ocaña, but it was Maertens who responded to his teammate's most incisive attack, on the final lap – bringing Gimondi and Ocaña in his wake.

There are several different versions of what actually happened. There were unfounded accusations that Merckx might have come to a deal with Gimondi to keep the emerging Belgian rival in his place, but the most likely explanation has Maertens offering his services to Merckx in the finale, then realising belatedly that his leader had run out of steam and just failing to get to Gimondi himself. Viewing the television footage today, that's certainly how it looks: Maertens leads out the sprint, constantly looking at Merckx, driving harder and harder, but at the critical moment his leader simply cannot come past him. Merckx was bitter about the fact that Maertens had pulled the other two up to him, and noted that something similar had happened in the amateur worlds in 1971. He was completely devastated when he returned to the Belgian pits, where he sat with his head in his hands for half an hour. Maertens felt he himself should have won: he visited a restaurant not far away a few years later, and, on seeing a picture of Gimondi in the rainbow jersey, he said 'that jersey is mine'.

Merckx's version of events was as follows: 'I attacked and Maertens chased me down two or three times, then told me to stop attacking as he'd lead me out in the sprint. I wanted to save him a bit as he is a young rider. Coming up to the sprint he launched the sprint too hard instead of leading it out normally; I lost a couple of lengths, tried to make up the ground but Gimondi passed me.' 'Merckx tried too hard, he gave too much of himself' was the verdict of the Italian manager, Nino Defilippis, the old pro from the 1950s who had been at Vincenzo Giacotto's side when he had tested the Belgian out for Faema in spring 1967.

After that disappointment, Merckx filled in two more gaps in his *palmares*. Having won his first and only Vuelta, he added Paris–Brussels – which finished near his home after going over the little hills to the south of the Belgian capital – and the Grand Prix des Nations. The celebrated time trial, that year run at the Vendée resort of Saint-Jean-de-Monts, presented another opportunity to put Ocaña in his place. The Spaniard finished two minutes forty-eight seconds behind at the end of the eighty kilometres: a crushing defeat. Merckx closed the season with five wins in a week, following the Nations with victory in both legs of *A Travers Lausanne* and a criterium.

Or it would have been five wins if he had not been disqualified after a stunning win in the Giro di Lombardia thanks to a positive drugs test. His team doctor, Angelo Cavalli, took responsibility: he explained that it was down to a mistake with cough medicine, sold under the name Mucantil, but including a small amount of the stimulant ephedrine, something of which he had been unaware. Merckx was not the only rider of the time to whom something similar happened; with the more lenient climate then prevailing, and given that ephedrine was very much at the light end of the drugs spectrum, the explanation of human error seems reasonable. Unlike after Savona, there was no benefit of the doubt this time and the test remained on Merckx's record.

At the start of his career, Merckx had stated his ambition to achieve something new every season, to give his fans fresh pleasure. He managed that until 1974, but 1973 was the end of the peak of his career. It was the last of the four consecutive seasons in which he managed more than fifty victories, the last in which he won both Classics and major Tours. It was the last of his truly great years; the following season he would show unprecedented physical vulnerability as he nudged up against the limits of what his body could stand. By the end of 1973, now twenty-eight, he had set the standard for his career and had changed the entire way in which fans and press viewed their sport. He had become the first rider to dominate three-week Tours, consistently, day-by-day; the first and last rider to dominate for so long, on so many terrains, without a break. The Tour triumphs of Hinault, Indurain and Armstrong are sometimes compared to those of Merckx or considered greater, but the Merckx wins have to be seen in the context of domination of an entire season.

Moreover, he had raced in a new way, always attacking, taking every race on from start to finish. He had adopted an approach that brooked no compromise, no matter where the race, what its context, and no matter the weather. This was what became known as *la course en tête*, the term immortalised in the film of that name, produced by Joël Santoni. There is no English equivalent that completely captures the sense of the term, but the one that comes closest is 'racing from the front'. That is shorthand for a tactical approach to racing in which the entire focus is on what happens at the front of a given race. That is not as simplistic as it sounds. It is possible to race defensively. For example, a team with a strong sprinter might do so in a one-day race or a stage of a Tour, permitting an escape to gain a certain margin before pulling together to reunite the field in time for the finish. In a tough stage race, defensive racing is the norm: traditionally, the prime objective is not to lose time on the other contenders, while waiting for an opportunity on two or three target stages. For Fausto Coppi, Bernard Hinault or Lance Armstrong these would be mountain stages or time trials; for Jacques Anquetil or Miguel Indurain they would only be time trials. Once the lead has been acquired, it is defended, from behind.

As practised by Merckx, *la course en tête* turns that on its head. As a way of racing, it is pro-active. It is centred on the premise that as much physical and mental energy is used in chasing down moves as is spent in making them. Attack becomes the best form of defence: you need to crack a climber such as Fuente, so you harass him on the flat then frustrate him in the mountains; you have to beat a sprinter so you burn him out beforehand. A star's team is there not merely to control the race but to destroy rivals' minds and bodies before the leader puts in the *coup de grâce*, or to be sent up the road to act as decoys: the leader bridges to them when he makes his move or forces the opposition to tire themselves out chasing. *La course en tête* calls for resourcefulness, inventiveness, complete determination, total concentration.

It also calls for presence: the leader has to be constantly in view at the front of the bunch, to demonstrate physical mastery, even if on occasion he may be bluffing. 'I remember in one Paris–Nice watching Anquetil jump from one echelon to the next to get to the front,' said Walter Godefroot. 'That would never happen with Merckx because he would always be in the front echelon.' In fact, it was impossible for Eddy to be anywhere else. Patrick Sercu recalled that, during one Tour of Italy, he and Rudy Altig made an attempt at showing Eddy life at the back of the peloton, where on occasion even the best riders would spend a little time to relax and save energy. 'We tried and tried to get him to drop back by talking to him and distracting him so that he wouldn't notice as we slipped back down the line. But it was useless. Every time he got to about twentieth in the bunch, he would whizz back to the front to see what was going on in the race.' Other leaders such as Raymond Poulidor or Bernard Thévenet were far less vigilant.

The hallmark of Merckx was constant presence of mind, readiness to use anything that might destabilise the opposition to launch an attack. 'With Eddy, you never knew when the racing would start: he might escape in a side wind, on a cobbled section, after a big crash or just the minute the flag dropped,' said one opponent. 'You'd be waiting to see when he attacked. Many times you'd be almost hoping that he would wait as late as possible, but he was unpredictable.' Merckx felt his philosophy was that nothing could be left to chance – the course, the weather, the opposition's teams. 'In a race I tried to be everywhere at once, wherever an opportunity appeared, when the weather changed suddenly, when echelons formed, when an unexpected hill appeared. There are a lot of things in a race that you can't control although you have to be aware of them. The main thing you can count on is yourself. And that's what I always put emphasis on.'

It helped that his domination produced a by-product. Merckx won so much that his rivals were more concerned with salvaging what they could than with actually beating him. 'It wasn't easy to work out why Merckx, so superior and with the team he had, would attack two or three mountain passes from the finish, or with a hundred kilometres to go,' said Txomin Perurena. 'Perhaps he would whittle it down to three or four riders, and they would cooperate, because they knew that way they would make second or third, which was a lot better than nothing, and then next day he'd go off again with another three or four and they'd work with him again because they'd want that second or third place. It was divide and rule. Logically we should have all ganged together and tried to beat him. But that never occurred to anybody because he was so superior all we wanted to do was finish second.'

La course en tête also reflected another fact about cycling's development, which Merckx himself had seen: the eclipse of specialist climbers such as Fuente and the pre-eminence of strong all-rounders such as himself. 'Our sport has always called for huge amounts of stamina, but from now on physical strength will become all-important,' he had said in an interview with Swiss writer Serge Lang in 1970. 'We are in a time when average speeds have risen and bigger gears are used, which will exclude from the first rank riders who do not have certain physical size and athletic ability. We've already seen the last of the great climbers. Riders who possess the same basic qualities as Bahamontes or Jiménez still exist in the peloton, but with one essential difference: when they get to the mountains they have lost part of their potential because of having to use big gears in the flat part of the race. They may not be defeated in the mountains in the strictest sense but they are no longer able to create huge gaps.'

Of course Merckx could race defensively, and sometimes did, most notably in his duels with Fuente in the Giro, but the starting point was offensive racing. It was conjectured that the best way to beat Merckx might be to ride slowly deliberately, to make him lose patience with the bunch and waste his energy attacking fruitlessly. 'I believe in hard racing for one reason,' said Merckx. 'If I do the work I am controlling the rhythm of the race and that is particularly valuable in the mountains. I wear down the others and am no more tired than they are at the finish. I avoid surprises and crashes.'

The post-war greats – Coppi, Anquetil, Hinault, Indurain, Sean Kelly, Armstrong – have always been able to race *en tête* on more days than the lesser men, but what set Merckx apart is that he could do it on so many more days than the other greats and on so many different terrains. Coppi had many off days, when his head simply failed him. Van Looy never showed his true worth in the Tour de France, because he was a man from a cycling culture in which the Classics were everything. Anquetil limited himself to what he knew best: time trialling, and his home Tour. The writer Roger Bastide said he felt that the Frenchman was probably worth fifteen minutes more than his opponents in the Tour de France but he would keep it in reserve for when he needed it. Merckx would get the fifteen minutes first up then try to get more.

Hinault was the best practitioner of *la course en tête* post-Merckx, but even he restricted himself to certain races. Indurain and Armstrong restrained their ambitions to the Tour de France, while Sean Kelly could be Merckx-esque in short-stage races and Classics – as his nickname 'The New Cannibal' suggested – but he was limited in the three-week Tours by his lack of climbing ability.

La course en tête can also be seen in a wider sense. Giving his utmost in every area, be it equipment, extra training or aggressive racing, was clearly a matter of duty for Merckx, which can only have stemmed from his upbringing. In the terms he put it to me, not making full use of the talent he had been given would have been bordering on the criminal. 'I believe, sincerely, that I am better at my profession – I mean I do it more scrupulously, more methodically – than most of my rivals,' he said in 1970. Like father, like son: think of Jules Merckx's perfectionism, his Stakhanovite work ethic, his Victorian maxims.

La course en tête is the product of an obsessive nature. Claudine Merckx recalled that, before a major race, her husband's mind would be relentlessly focused on whichever rival he perceived to be the most important. He would find the chink in the armour: Fuente's inconsistency; Ocaña's mental fragility; Thévenet's lack of finesse on the descents. Nothing could be left to chance. Merckx's first lieutenant Jos Bruyère recalled that he and Merckx must have gone up and down the Poggio, the last climb in Milan–San Remo, 'hundreds of times, even though we knew it by heart'. The twist there is that Bruyère turned professional with Merckx in 1970, by which point he had already won the race three times and had already seen enough of the Poggio to last most cyclists a life-time.

Watch the loving detail in the film *La Course en Tête* with which Eddy gently puts a transfer on his track bike; give a wry smile as time after time he checks his saddle height or adjusts the seatpost while on the move using an Allen key carried in his back pocket for precisely that purpose. There was only one occasion on which he forgot that Allen key, according to Guillaume Michiels, who was with Merckx for most of his career, post-Blois. It was a stage of the Tour of Belgium in Wallonia; Michiels had to find a bike shop, buy a new one and hand it up to The Cannibal with his race food in the *musette* at the day's feed station.

His incessant worrying would make him get out of bed the night before a race to check his bikes were properly adjusted and led to his obsession with his position and his equipment: the 110 spare wheels and 200 spare tubulars, each one seasoned for two years. At the 1970 Giro he travelled with eighteen bikes, all with components that he had personally drilled out for lightness. There were limits, however. Once, he was asked if it was true that he had dismantled a bike to see how many pieces it was made up of; that was not the case, but he had, he said, found out that a bike had 1125 individual components. Ernesto Colnago told me of one year when he supplied twenty-seven bikes, while two hundred hours went into the making of his Hour Record machine.

Guillaume Michiels recalls two examples of Merckx's atten-tion to detail. During a reconnaissance of the 1970 Tour de France route with Belgian television they looked over the finish of the innocuous stage to Châlons-sur-Marne. 'There were four corners in the last kilometre, he rode it and said "if we are sprinting for first, I'll win the stage. I'll get going before that corner, and because there is another one two hundred metres later, they will never catch me." He took that corner flat out, gained half a dozen metres, and that was that.' There was a ruse the pair used on occasion, in hot weather, to supply Merckx with extra water bottles in the days when riders were not allowed to receive water from their team cars. For these secret roadside handups, Michiels would place his wife two hundred metres before a corner: she would shout to Merckx that a bottle was waiting, and he would drop back in the field so that he could not be spotted by the race referee sitting in a car in front of the bunch. Michiels, always shirtless so that he could be recognised, would hand up the bottle.

Sometimes his approach bordered on the masochistic, taking professional obligation to extremes that baffled his contemporaries. Patrick Sercu tells a story which he believes shows the level of Merckx's obsession. 'Liège–Bastogne–Liège was a race which didn't have a course that suited me, so I rarely rode it. One year I had a call the day before from the team manager, Franco Cribiori, to say that Roger De Vlaeminck, the star of the Brooklyn team, was ill and wouldn't start. That meant I had to race as I was the No. 2 in the team. I left Ghent on the Saturday afternoon with my father to drive down: a slow drive as there was no motorway. We were driving down the main road from Brussels to Liège, it was raining and snowing together, the worst possible conditions for riding a bike. A long way up ahead we spotted a cyclist on the road: we couldn't work out who would be riding in such weather. It was so bad that there was no one else outside. When we passed the bike rider we saw it was Merckx: he was riding the hundred kilometres from Brussels to Liège, all alone, because he had not won Flèche Wallonne during the week. He won Liège–Bastogne–Liège the next day five minutes ahead of the second rider: I climbed off after forty kilometres.'

In the first week of the 1970 Tour de France Merckx was asked why he and his team had expended energy bringing back escapes by riders who were no threat overall. 'I couldn't let them gain half an hour on the field. What would they have said in Belgium? People worry too much about the energy that I expend. My teammates and I are here to work, to do all the work.' And he responded to accusations that he won too much, leaving too little for the rest, with these words: 'The day when I start a race without intending to win it, I won't be able to look at myself in the mirror. I'm not saying that every time I race I go to the very limit of my strength. But when the opportunities appear I consider it immoral not to take them.'

His willingness to shoulder responsibility was felt to have restored a certain purity to the sport, after a period when children of the pre-war era such as Van Looy, Anquetil and Van Steenbergen had seen the sport in far more commercial terms. It was said that Rik I would only win a Classic if Van Buggenhout was standing on the start line and pointed out that his contract value was dropping. As for Anquetil, in one criterium the organisers refused to pay him as he sat in and had done nothing to merit his fee. So the following year he returned, ripped the race to shreds and said, 'See that? You can pay me last year's fee as well as this year's.'

'When Anquetil turned professional he understood that it was an excellent way of earning money. It was as if he had calculated in advance the number of pedal strokes it would take to earn a certain amount,' wrote Pierre Chany. 'Merckx, on the other hand, has set himself no limits. He rides for the pleasure of glory; praise from fans and media is sweet. He earns money but his soul has remained pure. Being acclaimed counts more for him than the money he may or may not make.' In *Eddy Merckx and His Rivals*, François Terbéen struck a similar chord: 'Eddy Merckx's particular strength is his intransigence, his thirst for truth. Eddy gives no gifts to the opposition. In this way he has restored the most absolute rigour to the act of cycle racing, whether that race is a classic, a stage race or a standard criterium. This scrupulous honesty cannot be overemphasised, because it is the expression of an integrity which is perhaps without equal in the long saga of the Giants of the road.'

Claudine, had a more succinct way of saying the same thing: 'Eddy was driven on by a power that was unique to him. He never looked for glory. He just wanted to be at peace with himself.'

SERVING THE CANNIBAL

'Merckx is like a feudal chieftain', *Geoffrey Nicholson,*
The Great Bike Race

What Jos Bruyère really wanted to do was play football. That might seem like a strange admission from Eddy Merckx's first lieutenant, a man who wore the yellow jersey for most of the 1978 Tour de France and whose record in the one-day Classics would stand up well thanks to two victories in Liège–Bastogne–Liège and three in Het Volk. But Bruyère now gives the firm impression that he became a cyclist in spite of himself. He was talented on a bike, good enough to win major races in his own right, and he played a key role in many of Merckx's greatest wins. Even so, that was not enough for him to hang up his wheels and live comfortably. At sixty-three he is still working, in the Sports Service of the Province of Liège, and it's obvious he would like to stop and live quietly on his pension, if that were possible. The reference book *Gotha* describes him as 'a magnificent athlete' but now he is not in the best of health – he is overweight and walks awkwardly due to a hip replacement operation dating back to a crash he suffered in 1975 – and he doesn't seem overjoyed with the hand life has dealt him.

Bruyère's father, a factory worker, took his son from their home on the Dutch border into the nearby city of Liège one Sunday morning in 1961. There was a vast market in the city centre, 'La Batte', the locals called it, and there Jos was bought a racing bike as a reward for getting a good school report. 'I rode it home, and, once I had it, my brother said he would buy me some shorts, and so on.' He began racing against lads ten years older, and held his own. A few years later, with his military service out of the way, decision time came: his father was ill, the family were short of money, his mother was working as a cleaner, and they wouldn't be able to support a young racing cyclist for long. Joseph had a year to prove he could earn a living on his bike. He won seventeen races that season and, after his second amateur classic win, he had the offer that mattered: it came from Eddy Merckx, then twenty-four years old and building his own team at Faema. He would stay with Eddy until the end came for The Cannibal. Bruyère spent eight years in what he called a 'twenty-five hours a day job, keeping him out of the wind, taking him to the front and using my elbows, then leaving him two hundred metres from the finish'.

Joseph was put in the Tour de France at the age of twenty-one. He gained a kilo by the end of the Tour, and that was enough to prove that he was suited to stage races: most cyclists come out of the three-week marathon far lighter than they go in due to the daily demands the Tour makes on the body. 'I was always eating, eating. I was the first at the dinner table, the last to leave,' he recalls with a smile. But you had to earn your crust with Eddy; it was not just a matter of eating what was on the table. There was a pool of twenty riders in the team, and the best eight or nine got to accompany their leader in the big races. The riders who rode the Tour would come home rich men, because Eddy would share his prize money with them. 'I had a small contract but I rode the Tour de France and earned 120,000 Belgian francs.' The riders who stayed at home went without. The upshot was that the riders fought among themselves to race at Eddy's side. 'You had to be in the ten best riders or the director would take someone else. I did the Tour de France so young because I absolutely had to be part of it. I needed to take money home, because the year before I had earned nothing. It was a fight to be in the team. It was like a soccer team where the best eleven players played every week and they would bring in a reserve from time to time.'

'Here as elsewhere (apart from at bike races) he is always late, but his twenty "domestiques" don't go to the dinner table before he gets to the dining room,' wrote Marc Jeuniau in *Face to Face with Eddy Merckx*. 'They don't get out of their seats until he rises and they only get on their bikes when he finally turns up, always the last.' Life in the team was straightforward, Bruyère recalls, as long as you were in the Praetorian Guard around Merckx. 'Everyone knew how to do their work, that's why I learned so fast.' That was reiterated by another of the inner circle, Jos Huysmans: 'Merckx wasn't that bothered by tactical considerations. Anyway, we knew what we had to do. It was fairly obvious. Everything was decided around Merckx. And as he never stopped winning, we never wondered about it.' There would be a briefing from the *directeur sportif* in the morning before the race with some details of the route, but there was no real need for a tactical plan. 'We made sure there was always a rider in every break, so it would be easier for those of us behind. If we were in the break and any of the other guys were dangerous we would soft-pedal, if they weren't dangerous we'd ride with them.'

The riders were constantly at the front of the bunch, because that was where Eddy spent the race; as their leader was usually the strongest in the race, there was no need to go into much detail beforehand. There was no need for a *capitaine de route*, the senior rider some teams appointed to watch what went on and decide the tactics. It was a small world, so the riders knew all their colleagues by sight without memorising their race numbers. They knew how they rode, their style on the bike, whether their shoulders moved as they pedalled, whether one leg or the other stuck out. When the attacks came and riders sped away from the bunch, it was clear who was ahead. The team manager, Giorgio Albani or the Belgian Bob Lelangue, might fill in the details when they dropped back to the team car for water bottles; they would pick up the rider numbers from the race's internal radio system, look at the standings and confirm that the rider who had broken away was twenty minutes down on the overall standings, so he wasn't dangerous, for example, but by and large Merckx's men knew what was happening. That was their job.

An account of how Merckx and his teammates could dominate a race is given by Léon Zitrone's description of the Ballon d'Alsace stage in the 1969 Tour. Faema took up station at the head of the bunch well before the climb, giving rise to what Zitrone described as 'a strange and fascinating spectacle. On roads which were still flat, the selection of the strong and the weak took place through a series of little chopper blows. For a few minutes, one of the Faema team would ride in front. Everything went as usual. Merckx, hands on the bars, spun his big gear. But each time he moved to the front of the bunch to take over from one of his teammates and "pushed", someone, behind, would show signs of distress, and, having gone as fast as he could go, would suddenly give in, and sit up as if the line joining him to the bunch had been cut, defeated, with no chance of remission.'

The team's tactical plan was relatively simple even on a mountain stage of the Giro or Tour, explains Bruyère. 'There were the Spanish climbers, who would attack constantly so we would always ride at the same steady tempo to keep them within reach then bring them back. Over the last two cols of the stage Merckx would attack and for us the race would be over then. We just had to get to the finish within the time limit.' There were times when the team's strongest climbers, Bruyère and Jos de Schoenmaecker, would be ordered to set the tempo on the climbs to discourage the opposition and to soften their legs up. As they rode, Merckx would whistle from behind if the tempo was too high. But once their leader had delivered the *coup de grâce*, their work would be over, and it would be a matter of surviving until it all began again the next day.

Sometimes things went wrong, and then there would be a reckoning. 'On the road, Eddy is a demanding and authoritarian leader,' wrote Roger Bastide. 'He's been seen, sometimes, to lose his temper spectacularly while gathering his lads around him to get a chase going. In the evening, at the dinner table, he criticises each one without skirting around the subject. But when it's all been said, the slate is wiped clean and the discussion often ends with a few bottles being opened.' 'If things hadn't gone well, it would be sorted out quickly afterwards because we needed to get it out of the way; some days it didn't work out and things needed to be rectified,' says Bruyère. He notes that it was always Merckx who took the lead in the discussions. 'It was always Eddy. The *directeur sportif* would always follow Eddy.'

From 1972 onwards, that *directeur sportif* was most often Bob Lelangue, burly, balding and round-faced, a former professional only five years older than Merckx and another *Bruxellois*. They had trained together when Merckx was a young amateur riding with the local professionals, they had raced together at Faema, briefly, and Merckx had asked Lelangue to join him as team manager for the first time in 1968. Shortly afterwards Van Buggenhout imposed Driessens on his protégé but in 1971, as

Driessens' star waned during Ocaña's incredible Tour, Merckx again approached his fellow *Bruxellois*. Lelangue had retired and was working as a press driver, but from the following season he became a key part of Molteni.

Lelangue's priority was to sharpen up the organisation. Cycling in the 1970s had hardly moved on from the 1960s in that the *directeur sportif* was a factotum, a one-man operation running every aspect of the team. He booked flights, sorted out bikes and clothing, hired and fired the riders and ran the team on the road, all the while managing the budget, and probably doling out training advice. It was no surprise therefore that in many teams travel arrangements were often primitive. Riders might drive from Brussels to Paris for a 9 a.m. start, leaving at three or four in the morning. They also frequently preferred to buy their own kit and bits because team issue was not always to be relied upon. There were occasions such as the one Lelangue remembers from his racing days, when, being the eighth rider back to the team car to ask for a cape on a rainy day meant there was no cape: the manager had brought one too few.

There are still performance gains to be made in cycling teams from a tighter focus on the logistical side, but, in more primitive times, the potential advantages from getting certain basics right were even greater. So at Merckx's Molteni the hotels had to be just right, the travel arrangements precise, and the riders had to be punctual, because the leader hated to be late. Lelangue recalls one Paris–Nice when a fellow Belgian team manager whose squad were staying in the same hotel asked if he could follow Molteni to a start somewhere in Burgundy, as he had no idea where it was. The agreed departure time was 10 a.m., Merckx was in the team car on the dot 'tapping his fingers', but the other squad was nowhere to be seen. Molteni did not wait. The other team got lost, never found the start and were out of the race.

There were other details Lelangue worked on. It was customary in those days for riders to use their own wheels as well as those supplied by the team; many bought their own tyres and got local wheel builders to make what they wanted. To avoid mix-ups, and make sure that all the kit was of a guaranteed standard, Molteni's riders brought only their bikes to a race, leaving their wheels at home: they raced team issue wheels, meaning the tyres and gears could be compatible. That mattered: if Merckx needed a wheel from a teammate during a race, he knew exactly what he was getting.

Lelangue echoes Bruyère: tactics weren't an issue. Interviewed by Stéphane Thirion in the book *Tout Merckx*, he went further: 'There were no tactics with Merckx. He was so strong that he would improvise during a race and his teammates had to be prepared to back him up in every decision. He was like an artist, a filmmaker or a painter. You could guess which way the work of art was heading but you didn't know quite how he was going to get there. He just followed whatever inspired him on the day.'

The *directeur sportif* only had a tactical role in special circumstances, for example on the afternoon when Bruyère ended up winning his first Liège–Bastogne–Liège, in 1976. If the domestique was to be given his head, he had to be in the company of the right rival – not too strong, not too fast – and Merckx, the eternal worrier, had to be certain that Bruyère would win, otherwise a potential victory was going to waste. 'I was shuttling up to the break and back to the bunch time after time in that race,' recalls Lelangue. 'Eddy kept asking me, "is he strong, is he going to win?" so I had to keep going to look, then going back to tell him.'

Where the manager's job got demanding was when Merckx's perfectionism took him to extremes. There was one occasion when they were racing in Switzerland, not far from Basle, when the leader dropped back from the bunch to the team car and specified that he wanted two new frames that were hanging in his cellar in his house near Brussels. 'He gave me the measurements, I always had a wallet with change in it just in case, so I stopped at a phone box and phoned a local mechanic, gave him the measurements so he knew which ones they were, he wrapped them up, took them to Sabena, got them sent on the next flight to Basle-Mulhouse airport.' At the feed zone Lelangue swapped cars with the soigneur, Guillaume Michiels, who drove the team car for the rest of the day while he drove hot foot to the airport to collect the frames. Basle-Mulhouse has a French side and a Swiss side, and the Swiss customs man would not surrender the frames without seeing Lelangue's documents. 'I had no documents, so he refused, I waited until he was reading his newspaper, went out and came in from the other side and took the frames.' He is not actually sure whether his team leader used them. 'He was happy, but two days later he would change again. It's hard to tell if it was all in his head or not.'

The team would take seven or eight frames for Merckx to the Tour or the Giro, all of them subtly different – five millimetres here or there, a fraction of an angle between the tubes – carrying one on each of the two team cars just in case. Additionally, Lelangue's team car was crammed with spare parts: half a dozen stems of slightly different lengths fitted to handlebars of various dimensions, all fitted up with brake levers and cables (the gear changers being on the downtube of the bikes in this prehistoric era). 'My favourite episode was one day in the Tour of Italy. It was early in a mountain stage, pretty quiet as usual, all the favourites down the back talking. Eddy came and asked us to swap the stem and the bars between his race bike and his spare.' It had to be done on the spot: Lelangue believes it took him and the mechanic Julien De

Vries – later famed as spanner-man to Greg LeMond and Lance Armstrong – less than three minutes to swap the bars around, including loosening, undoing, rerouting and refixing the brake cables. Their boss's immediate reaction was anger: he could not imagine them carrying out his orders so quickly, and assumed they had merely pretended to do it.

Merckx was intimately involved in the day-to-day running of the team, who rode which races. The Tour de France team would be selected early in the year, and would ride a different programme from that of their leader, because, says Lelangue, if they had tried to keep up with him they would have found it physically too much. He would keep tabs on their form, for example making Lelangue push Jos Bruyère to ride the Tour of Switzerland against his will in 1974 (Bruyère had just got married and his wife wasn't keen on the idea). Bruyère had attempted to pull out; Lelangue had to make him an ultimatum: I won't replace you, the plane for Zurich leaves tomorrow, you can be on it or not. Merckx's idea was that, rather than staying at home and putting on weight, Bruyère needed to race himself fit. So it proved, as he pulled on the yellow jersey in the 1974 Tour, and helped Merckx to his fifth win.

The team system in cycling had moved on since its foundation by Fausto Coppi in the post-war years. Coppi and his successors would have a bevy of humble *gregari* or domestiques devoted to their service, but in the great days of the *campionissimo* these were most often obscurities who had no interest in winning. Those who had ambition would often leave because there wasn't room for them. Co-leaders tended to be foreign stars such as Louison Bobet or Raphael Geminiani, hired on a very occasional basis for certain races. Merckx's predecessor Rik Van Looy had refined the system by bringing in riders who were capable of winning in their own right and persuading them to subordinate their interests to his. The argument was simple: they would earn more as part of his 'Red Guard' helping him win large numbers of races, and using his contacts to get lucrative appearance deals, than they would in their own right winning one or two events. Merckx used a combination of both systems: a bevy of good riders, most of whom were capable of winning, all devoted to his cause.

Lelangue, who rode for Van Looy and managed Merckx, believes that Faema and Molteni were far more cohesive than Van Looy's 'Red Guard'. The transformation from the days when Merckx was fighting for position alongside Van Looy, Simpson and Pingeon was rapid, and took place the day he moved to Faema in 1968. He ended up heading the most expensive team in the world: Molteni had a monthly wage bill estimated at about one million Belgian francs, and an annual budget put at twenty-five million. There were complaints that Merckx's system killed off individual initiative, but this was not quite the case. There were teams that tried to emulate Faema/Molteni – Ocaña's Bic being one example – but most squads had more than one leader, because no other *kopman* could race as much as Merckx, all year long. Although Hinault, LeMond, Indurain and Armstrong would continue the phenomenon of the sole leader surrounded by *gregari*, other systems were being developed even as Merckx was at his best. At TI-Raleigh, the former 'Red Guard' member Peter Post was already formulating a more modern team structure, with a variety of strongmen who would decide leadership as a given race dictated. This in turn would be built on by legendary managers such as Cyrille Guimard, Jan Raas and Giancarlo Ferretti.

'Merckx is like a feudal chieftain,' wrote Geoffrey Nicholson in 1976. 'He is the sole leader and all the other members of the team are there to support and protect him. They have few

complaints for they live very well on the spoils he wins them.'
The philosophy of *la course en tête* also meant that they had
chances to win. A domestique had to feature in every escape
if possible, and that created openings. The best of Merckx's
teammates tended to win races in their own right. Bruyère
explained to me, 'It would happen that Merckx had everyone
sitting on his wheel, so I would get ahead to oblige the others
to ride and Eddy would wait behind. Then, if they worked in
the chase, Eddy would win, and some days I won.' It was
classic cycling team tactics: a decoy out front, a teammate
behind monitoring the chase, ready to take advantage of the
chasers when they tired or when the junction was made. For
the opposition it was the stuff of nightmares: big strong Jos
out front riding away, the strongest rider in the world watching
them chase, albeit with a worried frown rather than a smile
on his face.

The flipside of the iron discipline was that sometimes Merckx
would positively try to ensure a teammate won, and according
to Bruyère, 'if I won, Merckx was just as happy as if he won'.
Merckx had learned early on at Peugeot that a good leader
doesn't take it all for himself, so he took what he wanted –
which was most of what there was – and gave the occasional
handout. One example came in spring 1970 when he tried to
engineer wins in Flèche Wallonne and the Polymultipliée circuit
race for Bruyère, neither time with any success. There were
occasions when it simply did not fit in, though. Merckx was
not happy when his great friend Italo Zilioli rode his socks off
to take the yellow jersey early in the 1970 Tour. The issue was
not that Zilioli had upstaged him, but that he had ridden so
hard so early in the race although Merckx had a plan to keep
the Italian at his side in the mountains so that he could push
for a place in the top three.

In the early 1970s, Bruyère was offered twice his Molteni

salary to ride alongside Ocaña at Bic, but he turned it down. 'It never came into my head to be the leader at another team. I was very friendly with Eddy so I didn't look at the money. It was about friendship first of all, but you can't live off friendship. He liked me riding for him, and I think he preferred to have me riding for him rather than against him.' Not everyone saw it that way. 'Merckx is appallingly professional,' said Guido Reybroeck. 'With him, all that matters is cycling and racing. He talks of nothing else.' Van Springel complained that in Merckx's teams life was 'cold and professional', for example the champagne did not flow after a major win, and that contact with the leader was 'superficial'.

Bruyère does not remember it as being like that. 'There was good team spirit – we laughed, we joked, we were good friends. If anyone felt competitive [in their own right] they put it to one side.' The riders all had their own tricks for keeping up morale during the long spells away from home with no communications to distract them. Bruyère's speciality was to pretend to hypnotise one of his teammates, turning off the lights and rubbing a finger across a plate that had been blackened using soot or burned cork or ink, then drawing the finger across the victim's face as he worked his 'magic'. At the end of the session the 'hypnotised' teammate's face would be black. He did the trick once or twice a year, and each time the response would be similar: the plate would end up on the floor once the victim realised he had been taken in.

'He doesn't treat his teammates as domestiques. He tries to make friends of them but doesn't always manage,' said Jean Van Buggenhout of Merckx. He went on to explain that being the boss didn't come naturally to Merckx, because until he emerged as a star he had never had to direct anyone else. He found stardom at an early age, and as Van Buggenhout said 'being authoritarian is not his way. He likes to be understood, to be helped, but without having to intervene himself in an abrupt way.' The point was that service was on Merckx's terms, and loyalty had to be absolute, as Martin Van Den Bossche discovered. The lanky climber worked tirelessly for Merckx during the 1969 Tour, and was given the right to look after himself at one point to improve his overall placing. The trouble was, he had decided to leave Faema. Merckx had no problem with that, but was offended that Van Den Bossche had opened negotiations during the race, which was why he did not let him win the Tourmalet *prime* during the stage to Mourenx. Tellingly, when his closest friend in the bunch, Italo Zilioli, opted to go to Ferretti in 1971 rather than moving with Merckx to Molteni, Merckx had no problem with him taking the higher offer.

Van Den Bossche apparently did not like the atmosphere of conformity that surrounded the leader: 'when he ordered a Trappist beer, everyone ordered one. You lost all your personality alongside Merckx. I didn't want that.' There was simply no room for a co-leader or a personality that even began to look as if it might be as large as Merckx's, as Van Springel found out. He signed for Molteni in 1970, only to find out that Merckx was coming too. Assurances were given that he would get openings but he feels they never really happened: 'You had to race Merckx's way. It was an honour, but I never felt good there. I was capable of riding the Giro d'Italia but Merckx wanted to ride it. It was the same with the Tour de France.' Van Springel, for one, went his own way, as did Patrick Sercu – until the end of both their careers – and there were some riders who turned Merckx down, for example Johan De Muynck. He was asked to join in 1971 but refused because he didn't want his liberty curtailed.

The money they earned was not outstanding. Bob Lelangue said of his time at Faema that the wages were so meagre he might as well have paid the team to let him race. But cycling was a poorly resourced sport: in the late 1960s and into the 1970s there were plenty of riders on zero contracts, riding for a bike, a jersey, and expenses if they were lucky. Roger Swerts raced with Merckx from 1968 to 1973, earning 25,000 Belgian francs a month, ten months a year, a big increase on his wages as a new pro at the French team Mercier: 8000 Belgian francs. At Faema all the *gregari* earned the same basic wage to avoid jealousy, and their salary was bumped up with win bonuses. Van Buggenhout refused to increase Swerts's money, Gimondi offered him 50,000 after he placed twelfth at the 1971 Giro and he accepted. Merckx wasn't happy and eventually arranged for the transfer of two Italians to Gimondi's team, so he could keep Swerts at his side.

Merckx was no easy taskmaster, but his teammates accepted his demands partly because of the rewards, partly because he appreciated their services, but also because he was equally hard with himself, if not harder. 'He got the best out of us thanks to a bit of whipcracking and his personal example,' said Swerts. 'He kills us because he constantly wants us to make the running at the front, and to smash any attempts by our rivals to take the initiative,' said Victor Van Schil. 'But he is well able to smile and let us off the hook when we are worn out. So he ends up doing the bulk of the work himself, to the point where we actually feel ashamed about it.'

Teammates and managers came and went, but there was one constant presence throughout most of Merckx's career: the burly figure of Guillaume Michiels. During his brief career as a professional – his three seasons were roughly average for a métier that takes in new men and spits them out constantly – Michiels had put up television aerials and made coffins for a living. He had also worked on the 1967 Giro as a factotum at Peugeot: in 1969, he mentioned to Merckx that the aerial-installation business was going to decline as companies used cables instead, so Merckx suggested he take a massage course and help him out. From 1970 he was employed directly by the great cyclist, an unusual arrangement: clearly Merckx felt the need to have someone at his side who could be trusted absolutely and who would ensure that he had only to think about training and racing. The right man was worth a little investment.

Michiels's brief was a wide one. It started with driving: Merckx had to get from *kermis* to *kermis*, and, particularly after the Tour de France, from criterium to criterium. Forty years later, he can still rattle off the after-Tour schedule. The distances they covered in The Cannibal's Mercedes were immense, and this in the days before the motorway network had spread around Europe: 60,000 kilometres in one year, 2700 kilometres in one weekend, Friday to Monday morning. They would leave races in France late in the evening – after the start fee had been collected and a meal eaten – then drive through the night to Brussels, crossing the centre of Paris via the boulevards, getting home at dawn. Additionally, Michiels went to all the bigger races as a soigneur, where he worked alongside the other soigneurs in Faema or Molteni making food, giving massage and doing anything else that was needed. The teams would reimburse Merckx for his service on the races. It was a task of epic proportions, requiring considerable sacrifice: in 1970, recalls Michiels – not without a certain amount of pride – he spent 340 days on the road in the service of The Cannibal.

Back home in Brussels, in between races, the daily routine was for Michiels to leave for Merckx's house about 8 a.m., buying fresh rolls known as *pistolets* – pistols – from a local baker en route. While Merckx was having breakfast, he would prepare the bike and food for the day's training. Then he would wheel out the motorbike, which Merckx had bought specially. There is a whole sequence in *La Course en Tête* showing Merckx and Michiels training with the motorbike, and many pictures of Michiels with Merckx in his slipstream. What is not widely known, however, is that Michiels was there to provide company and shelter. What he and Merckx did was not conventional motor-paced training, where the bike is used to replicate the intensity and speed of a race. 'He never went fast behind the bike. The idea was not to ride alone, not to have to ride into a headwind by himself.' The only time Merckx used the bike for motor-paced *training* rather than merely riding was in June 1969, when he had left the Giro prematurely and was short of racing.

Buzzing along, Michiels would keep the bike in third gear. 'I would hit eighty kilometres per hour on the descents, twenty-five kilometres per hour up the climbs.' They would cover huge distances in this way – he talks of outings to Namur, Huy, deep into Wallonia – often talking as they went, safe in the knowledge that no one could hear them over the buzzing of the motorbike. He has fond memories of those days. They would pass groups of amateur cyclists pedalling in the opposite direction, and then The Cannibal and his driver would play a little game. 'They would stand up and point, say "it's Eddy Merckx", and I would keep an eye in the mirrors. They would turn in the road, I would say to Eddy, "they're coming". He didn't like anyone to sit behind him as he rode so I would slow down a little and we would say "let's see what they are made of". They might get to twenty metres behind, then I would open up a bit. It would be "there is a strong pair here, they're not giving up", that kind of thing. Sometimes they would get to within ten metres, then I'd just go faster and faster until they cracked.'

The old soigneur has fond memories of a similar episode with the racing driver Jacky Ickx, who was one of the few

permitted to accompany Merckx when he rode. Ickx did not
like to ride in front of The Cannibal, for fear he might make
him fall off; he ended up getting less shelter than he might
otherwise have done. One day, Michiels and Merckx took him
east, with the wind blowing from the side – making for tough
riding – then turned south, towards Namur, with the wind on
their backs. That meant a high speed on a road which rose
and fell: soon they could see Ickx struggling. Soigneur and
cyclist knew that when he fell apart, as he was clearly going
to do, and as he eventually did, he would have to turn into
the wind to go home. 'He didn't know where he was coming
from. He had to call his wife to come and collect him. We
had him brilliantly.'

Perhaps most telling of all is the point in the conversation
with Michiels when I ask whether they did this kind of thing
on rest days, or on training days. Modern cyclists might distinguish between the two, as might amateur cyclists: for Michiels
and Merckx, there does not appear to have been one or the
other. In between Merckx's 120–150 races a year, they just
rode, motorbike in front, 'half man, half bike' behind. Kilometre
after kilometre, rain or shine, frosty weather or fine.

The core of Merckx's team remained with him for 1974: Victor
Van Schil, Spruyt, Huysmans, Bruyère, De Schoenmaecker. At
the start of the season the leader dispatched Bruyère to win
the Het Volk Classic; the team were as strong as they had ever
been, but that spring was when the cracks started to appear
in their boss's carapace. For Merckx, it was a disastrous early
season. He went without a single Classic win for the first time
in his pro career due to a series of illnesses. In Paris–Nice he
caught a cold, and came up against the Dutchman Joop
Zoetemelk, who was in the best form of his career. (Zoetemelk's
purple patch ended early that summer when 'the eternal second'

fractured his skull in a horrific crash in the Midi Libre, a pile-up that prevented him from giving Merckx a run for his money in the Tour de France that year.) Viral pneumonia kept The Cannibal off his bike on doctor's orders for the best part of a month that spring, leaving him short of form at the start of the Giro d'Italia, where José Manuel Fuente was to enjoy one of the best races of his life, taking five mountain-top stage wins having, as usual, come straight from the Vuelta, which he had won that year.

Fuente had good enough form to win that Giro, which would have matched Merckx's double from the year before. Having taken the lead on stage three to Sorrento, *El Tarangu* turned the screw with two more stage victories, at the ski resort of Il Ciocco in Tuscany, and at Carpegna. That win came over the same climb, Monte Carpegna, where he had lost the Giro the previous year. Fortunately for the Belgian, the Spaniard was as inconsistent as ever and contrived to lose the race on a single day. Merckx pulled back time in the time trial at Forte dei Marmi in Tuscany and he found the opening on a rainy but otherwise innocuous stage up the Ligurian coast to San Remo two days later. His attack came not long after the start. 'Everyone thought he was crazy, for sure, because there were still two hundred kilometres to go and [Fuente's] KAS team would obviously chase him,' recalled Patrick Sercu. 'The weather was bad, rain and lightning: he hung on and won the Giro. Behind, we didn't even know if we were on the right road.'

Fuente lost ten minutes, blaming his bad day on an attack of hunger knock. With the little Spaniard out of the reckoning, the Giro boiled down to a narrow fight between Merckx and the up-and-coming Gianbattista Baronchelli. Merckx would, however, remember it for something darker: the death of Jean Van Buggenhout. The manager had been close to him since his first pedal strokes on the Brussels velodrome and had also been his confidant and father figure. Merckx was told during stage sixteen to Mendrisio, and rode the rest of the race in a state of shock (there was a report that on one of the stages that followed, he barely noticed when he broke a toe strap). There was talk of abandoning but he decided to carry on as a tribute to Van Buggenhout.

Fuente made several attempts to regain the lost time, winning the stage to Mendrisio along the way and closing with the cliffhanging stage at Tre Cime di Lavaredo, two days out from the finish in Milan. Between the penultimate pass, Passo Mauria, and the start of the ascent to the Tre Cime, Fuente sprang out of the peloton in an attempt to close down his five minute nine second deficit on Merckx, who had no option but to chase together with Jos de Schoenmaecker. Three miles from the top, in between massive snowdrifts, it was Baronchelli who attacked, putting Merckx on the ropes. In freezing temperatures and the beginnings of a snowstorm, he hung on to his pink jersey by just twelve seconds, the narrowest victory ever in the race and the closest finish of any of his ten major Tour wins. He believed it was the hardest of all of them. Given the importance of the Tre Cime at the start of Merckx's career, the comparisons have to be made. The Merckx of 1968 was a youth setting off to conquer the world, with all of cycling at his feet; The Cannibal of 1974 an ageing champion clinging on to what he could as the pure climbers did their utmost to unseat him. For Fuente, however, this marked the end of his three years trying to upset Merckx, as a kidney disorder was to end his relatively short career. In the following year's Tour de France, he finished outside the time limit on the first day, his racing days all but over before he reached thirty.

Three days after the Giro, Merckx was in the Swiss town of Gippingen to start the second leg in a now-legendary triple:

Giro, Tour of Switzerland and Tour de France, forty-three days of racing between 16 May and 21 July; three days recovery after the Giro, five between the finish of the Swiss Tour in the north-western town of Olten and the Tour de France start in Brest. The ten-day Swiss event – the hardest stage race on the calendar behind the three Grand Tours – was won in essentially defensive style, in which Merckx landed the prologue time trial, then rode tactically until the final time trial to seal victory by fifty-eight seconds from the Swede Gosta Pettersson. But he came out of the race with a sore backside, a small sebaceous cyst precisely where his crutch sat on the point of the saddle. Watch the old television footage and it's no surprise, given the way that The Cannibal throws himself around the bike as he chases Fuente through the mountains in the Giro. He was to have problems in this area for the next couple of years, like Louison Bobet, whose career was ended by a crutch wound.

The operation to clear up the cyst took place the day after the Tour of Switzerland finished, 22 June; recovery was expected to take five days, precisely the interval before the start of the Tour de France on Thursday 27 June. Merckx travelled to Brest for the Tour start a day late because he was having his stitches out. When the race started, the wound was small, but it was still open, which did not bode well for a three-week event. All he could do was pray for dry weather. As it was, he could never get comfortable, and the whole thing reawoke the referred pain in his left leg dating back to the crash in Blois. He won the prologue with his shorts bloodied as the wound opened further; for the next three weeks it needed constant care, constant bathing, the application of cream and sterile plasters, and cushioning with bits of foam and bandages.

Merckx's crutch was the biggest threat to him in that Tour. Ocaña was absent, having been sacked by Bic; Zoetemelk was recovering from the meningitis that had followed his crash; Fuente was resting after his efforts of April and May; Lucien Van Impe had a broken wrist; and Bernard Thévenet was off form after a series of crashes in the Tour of Spain. Poulidor was to be Merckx's principal rival, although he was now heading for retirement at thirty-eight, while Fuente's teammates at KAS threatened sporadically. Merckx rode strongly from the off, and so too did Bruyère: third in the prologue time trial behind his master, then part of the stage-winning escape en route to Saint-Pol-de-Léon in Brittany on the first stage. That earned the domestique the yellow jersey, not that he really wanted it. Typically for a team man, he felt he had risen above his station; he recalls that after being given the *maillot jaune*, he covered it up with a Molteni jersey. 'I was embarrassed to wear it, because I had taken it off Eddy Merckx.' He held the lead for three days, through the brief transit to England for a stage in Plymouth, before giving up the jersey – one suspects with considerable relief – to his leader.

Much like Bernard Hinault in the 1985 race, Merckx was riding with his aura, his reputation and his experience as well as his head and his legs, bluffing the opposition that he was stronger than was actually the case. From the very first intermediate sprint of the race he was out to snatch every time bonus he could; that was the early pattern. Hence a superb late attack to take the flat stage to Châlons-sur-Marne, sweeping into the town's main square a few yards ahead of the bunch, taking the right-angled bends with his bike leaned to perfection and the entries and exits calculated to the inch. It was his twenty-sixth stage win: he was now ahead of the record held by André Leducq. He was riding more conservatively than in the past and the Alpine stages were essentially a defensive operation against the KAS trio of Vicente López Carril, Francisco Galdós and Gonzalo Aja.

On the Col du Télégraphe, the day after the rest day in Aix-les-Bains, Bruyère put the field to the sword and Merckx dislodged Poulidor on the Galibier en route to Serre-Chevalier. The evergreen Frenchman lost five minutes and that effectively decided the race, with Merckx's only other rivals Aja and López Carril, that day's stage winner. He was climbing out of the saddle most of the time, to avoid putting pressure on his crutch; it was a handicap but it did not alter the outcome. Twenty-four hours later came the Ventoux, where it was De Schoenmaecker who did the work, with Merckx controlling the opposition in classic style: the climbers attacked, he kept at his rhythm and limited his losses. It was what Anquetil had done before him, what Hinault, Indurain and LeMond would all do in Tours to come. Jos Spruyt won that day's stage to Orange; three days later, his leader landed the first Pyrenean stage over the Envalira to Seo d'Urgel in Spain, and then came the finish at Pla d'Adet.

It was the first time the Tour had climbed up the steep mountainside to the ski station above the town of Saint-Lary-Soulan and the finish immediately earned a place in Tour history. It remains celebrated for the rebirth of Raymond Poulidor, who took his first stage win since 1967. Merckx's team had finally fallen apart by the time the race arrived at the climb, and it was 'Poupou' who made the running together with the Spaniards. Merckx's old leg and back injuries were playing up, and he had to change his bike. 'The yellow jersey holder looked awful, his head lolling and nodding, obviously suffering . . .' said one account, adding, 'he finished in as near a state of collapse as made no difference.' Poulidor took his first Tour stage win for eight years, twelve months after quitting the Tour due to a life-threatening crash, and France was in ecstasies. Merckx, however, had the Tour won. The French press were more interested in Poulidor's second youth, ten years after his epic duel with Anquetil on the Puy-de-Dôme, than the state of Merckx's undercarriage.

The only man Merckx had to watch was Vicente López Carril. After losing a little more ground to Poulidor, he added the Bordeaux time trial and took the stage to Orléans with a surprise attack ten kilometres from the finish – gaining one minute twenty-five seconds on the bunch in a move that nowadays would be unthinkable by a Tour leader, and even then earned him accusations of leaving nothing for the minnows. He was then awarded the final stage win on the Cipale velodrome in Paris after Sercu was disqualified for moving off his line in the sprint. It was his fifth Tour win out of five starts, with another eight stages added to his total of thirty-five along the way. That remains the record. While The Cannibal's body may have been on the edge of surrender, his mind was as competitive as ever. He had no need to compete in the final sprint, just as he had had no need to attack at the finish in Orléans, but he did so nonetheless, with the spirit of Mourenx alive and pulsating in his veins.

TWILIGHT OF THE GOD

'He is a prisoner of his persona, of his legend, a victim like every star of the reputation he carved out for himself. He has to win all the time and keep the public happy every day. His personal tragedy is that he is incapable of saying no, really saying no', *Théo Mathy*

Via Roma, San Remo, 19 March 1976

Jean-Luc Vandenbroucke has got rid of all the press cuttings from his racing career, apart from one that tells the story of a race where he came second, a race he did not expect to be in a position to win. Milan–San Remo 1976 was a race the rider from West Hainaut considered as good as a victory, because he came second to Eddy Merckx. At the age of fourteen, he had asked for Merckx's autograph at a criterium after his victory in the 1969 Tour de France; back then, he had never imagined that he would end up here, in this position.

Vandenbroucke was a new professional with the Peugeot team, wearing a jersey with the same chequerboard design as the one on Merckx's back when he won this race in 1966. By the time Milan–San Remo came round, he had been on the road for six weeks solid, travelling to one race after another. His wife was lonely back in Belgium, and was expecting their child. He was so desperate to get home that he had spent 10,000 Belgian francs – two-fifths of his wage – on the last place on a charter flight after the race.

En route to San Remo, he survived the initial sort-out among the massive field, over 250 of them. He made the cut when the final selection was made over the *capi*, the little headlands between Alassio and San Remo. And when Eddy Merckx finally forced himself clear of the leaders, *in extremis*, as The Cannibal was no longer as strong as he used to be, and the host of Classics specialists in the lead group were not willing to let him go, he chased hard to get to Merckx's wheel.

He hung on as Merckx did his best to dislodge him on the Poggio – 'it was terrible, because I didn't know the climb, my effort to get to him was so brutal, and there were still two kilometres left' – and fought back grimly each time a gap opened as the great man drove hard through every corner on the descent. If Vandenbroucke did not expect to be in a position to beat the great man, it was typical of Merckx that he feared the youngster might manage it. He told Vandenbroucke of his fears many years later, but the upset did not happen. The new-pro – who had been tipped as a possible successor to Merckx during his prolific amateur career – did not sprint. 'I led him to the Via Roma. I didn't try to beat him. Second to Merckx was a victory to me.'

In the finish photograph, he is a distant figure, hidden among the motorbikes several yards behind Merckx as The Cannibal punches the air in obvious delight. As good as a victory it may have been for Vandenbroucke, but it was also a milestone for Merckx, the last major win of his career. It came ten years after he had sprinted up the Via Roma ahead of Herman Van Springel to claim his first major professional victory. His years of dominance closed just where they had begun.

Merckx's decline was gradual at first. The Giro–Switzerland– Tour de France treble in 1974 gave the impression that the nonpareil was still superhuman; a few cracks had shown but the edifice remained unassailable. The world championship in

Montreal in September 1974 did nothing to dispel that. Merckx led perhaps the strongest Belgian team there has ever been, including seven possible winners such as himself, Van Springel, Freddy Maertens and Roger De Vlaeminck. But team support mattered little on one of the toughest courses ever: twenty-one laps, each including two climbs. Merckx had to take matters into his own hands, making one definitive attack late in the race, escaping with Raymond Poulidor after being closely marked by the Italians and the French for most of the race.

'There was war with Maertens,' recalls Bob Lelangue, who managed the Belgian team. Maertens was Flemish, young and massively talented, meaning for some of the Flandrian press he was a more attractive prospect than the reserved, French-speaking Merckx. Another issue was the accommodation on offer from the race organisers: school dormitories. Merckx wanted to stay somewhere better; the organisers said there was not a hotel room in town, so Lelangue used his contacts to find a hotel 'where all the stars had fallen off the sign'. The accommodation was not the only culture shock when the world titles were contested outside Europe for the first time. The team cars were massive pick-up trucks; the television cameras were carried on bizarre flatbed vehicles. The backdrop was new, but the picture of Merckx dominating was familiar.

Only eighteen men managed to complete the course, and the medals were contested by a lead group of five: Merckx, the Italian Giacinto Santambrogio and three Frenchmen: Poulidor, Bernard Thévenet and the bespectacled climber Mariano Martínez. The French team were the biggest threat, with Thévenet making a lone move that lasted a hundred kilometres and ended only seven from the finish. When he was caught, Poulidor attacked, and Merckx accompanied him. Given the Belgian's finishing speed and Poupou's ageing legs, there was only ever going to be one winner in the two-man sprint. Merckx's third world title put him level in the history books with two other greats, Alfredo Binda and Rik Van Steenbergen. It was not quite his final flourish, but it ensured that during his final brief spell of domination in early 1975, Merckx was wearing the rainbow stripes.

Asked about retirement later that year, Merckx had this to say: 'When the wind is favourable, that is not the time to stop sailing. I became a racing cyclist to express myself, so I must go to my own limits. What I have to avoid, above all, is hitting a decline, the beginning of mediocrity.' There was no sign of impending mediocrity in the spring of 1975. Here Merckx pulled together his last great string of consecutive victories. In late March and early April he landed Milan–San Remo for the sixth time in nine years, Amstel Gold, and Catalan Week, but in that race he lost the services of Jos Bruyère, who broke his leg in a particularly unfortunate crash. Another rider asked Bruyère how many kilometres were left to the finish, Bruyère took his route card out of his pocket and was passing it over to him when he touched a wheel. The loss of his strongest domestique was probably fatal for Merckx's chances of taking a record sixth Tour de France. Indeed, that spring Bruyère had been going almost as well as his master, winning the Tour of the Mediterranean and Het Volk and playing a key role in Merckx's Milan–San Remo triumph. It was an epic victory, forged when Merckx, Bruyère and Jos Huysmans formed part of a nineteen-man group that escaped after a hundred kilometres. In the finale, Bruyère got away himself over the Poggio, with Merckx letting him go, before linking up to him when Francesco Moser counter-attacked. Victory in the sprint enabled Merckx to equal Costante Girardengo's record of six wins.

Two days after his victory in Catalan Week came the Tour of Flanders, where Merckx made an early attack, as soon as the *monts* were reached. In weather as vile if not more so than when he had first won *de Ronde* in 1969, he finally went clear eighty kilometres from the finish with Frans Verbeeck, carving out a four-minute lead over the Mur de Grammont. He got rid of Verbeeck five kilometres from the finish; 'the Flying Milkman' was grounded, unable to get off his bike without assistance, in a state of complete exhaustion. Afterwards, Verbeeck had visibly aged. 'I have to tell it like it is,' he said. 'He goes five kilometres faster than the rest of us.' As far as Merckx was concerned, this was one of his best Classic wins: the gulf between him and the rest summed up by the photographs of him flying past lapped riders on the finish circuit in Meerbeke.

In Paris–Roubaix Merckx was desperately unlucky, puncturing eight kilometres from the finish when the race was set to come down to a sprint between him, Marc De Meyer, De Vlaeminck and Ludo Dierickx. The other three didn't wait for him, but he regained contact after a three-kilometre chase. Not surprisingly, however, he didn't have enough left to beat 'The Gypsy' in the sprint. De Vlaeminck believed this was the best of his four victories in 'Hell'. A week later, however, Merckx landed his fifth victory in Liège–Bastogne–Liège, a sprint finish after he had constantly attacked in the closing kilometres to tire out the younger, faster men.

The results looked similar, but The Cannibal had changed. At Paris–Nice that year it was noticed that he no longer 'ran' the race. His mechanic Marcel Ryckaert explained: 'You would need to be blind not to notice the change in Eddy. As far as technical stuff goes he's always sought out the last little detail if something doesn't quite work but he's less demanding now. Now everything is always OK or nearly. He's incredibly undemanding.' Merckx himself said he was fed up with the way that the other leaders would wait for him to take on the race, let him get tired, then attack him. He admitted that he was more reflective, less willing to take risks everywhere to gain a few seconds. In other words, he had finally grown up.

Merckx's body had been feeling the strain the previous year, but that was not the only thing that was changing. To make life harder for The Cannibal stage race organisers were increasingly making their races more difficult by including summit finishes that favoured younger riders. There was also a feeling among race followers that mentally he might be tiring after ten years at the top, and after the incredible efforts he had to make to win so much in 1974, his best year in terms of Super Prestige Pernod points (the season-long points' award which rewarded the best rider each year) since 1971. On the road, fresh blood was appearing in the peloton: Maertens was hitting his brief peak, as were his burly sidekick Marc De Meyer and the squat, balding third man in the Flandria trio, Michel Pollentier, while in Italy Francesco Moser had emerged. At the same time, rivals from the past such as De Vlaeminck, Verbeeck and Godefroot were still going strong. The other vital change was the loss of Jean Van Buggenhout. Although Molteni continued through 1975 and 1976, Merckx now felt personally under pressure to make sure his team sponsorships carried on, because there were twenty-five people earning a living from him.

Later that spring, there was another hint that he was not as voracious as he had been. In the Tour of Romandie in early May, he refused to help Joop Zoetemelk defend his race leader's jersey – the Dutchman was in a rival team so there was no reason for Merckx to make his team chase the moves – and the pair lost fourteen minutes in a curious stalemate. 'When I refuse to work for the other guys, the race becomes a promenade,' he said afterwards.

Bernard Thévenet is a gentle man who always looks a little overwhelmed, something which is hardly surprising given that he has spent nearly forty years trying to live up to the events of one week in July 1975. Like Raymond Poulidor, he has apple cheeks that make it look as if he is permanently smiling. Like Poupou, 'Nanard' is a fixture at the Tour de France, having worked first as a *directeur sportif* when his racing career ended, then commentating for French television. Thévenet was never hard enough or political enough to be a great team manager; as a commentator he never quite matched Laurent Fignon – another double Tour winner – for incisiveness and opinionated wisdom. That matters little: now in his early sixties, the Burgundian has his place in cycling history. He will always be celebrated as the man who ended Eddy Merckx's winning run in the Tour. He was, indeed, the first man to beat The Cannibal in a major stage race since Merckx rode his first Giro d'Italia in 1967. A modest person, he finds it a source of constant surprise that, thirty-six years on, people are still talking about the events of July 1975: even, that a journalist might call from England wanting his story.

Thévenet was born less than three years after Merckx, in January 1948, and spent his early childhood on a small farm in a village appropriately called *Le Guidon*, the handlebar, a name commonly given to settlements at a turning in a road. He was inspired to race a bike after the Tour de France passed through his village in 1961, and recalled watching the mass of moving toeclips shimmering in the sun, approaching from a distance for at least forty seconds. They were like stirrups on the horses of medieval knights, he said. He turned professional in 1970 and took Merckx's scalp in one of his first races, up Mont Faron, the great hill that rises above the port of Toulon. It was his first victory, with Merckx second after a crash.

'You would be honoured to be near Merckx in a race. It was admiring a film star, reading about them, seeing the pictures, then meeting face-to-face. I didn't dare speak to him. I was happy just to be next to him.' Nanard moved gradually up the hierarchy through the early 1970s, improving a little every year: fourth in the Tour in 1971, second in 1973 behind Ocaña, half a dozen stage wins along the way. He was a dogged man, who didn't have De Vlaeminck's panache, Gimondi's elegant pedalling style, Fuente's anarchism, or Ocaña's manic-depressive willpower. He was 'strong and self-willed, but not particularly adroit on a bicycle; he could climb efficiently, but on the descents lost time manoeuvring round the corners,' as Geoffrey Nicholson said.

The Cannibal came into the 1975 Tour low on form after a bout of illness. His hitherto rude health had deserted him, a pattern which had begun in 1974 and was to continue from now on. He had caught a cold at a nocturne in Copenhagen and it had turned into tonsillitis. That meant he was unable to start the Giro, which he was planning to use as a build-up to the Tour. There was speculation that he was staying away because the organisers were fed up with him winning, but this seems unlikely since he had given his wife a list of things to put in his bags and had his team waiting for his arrival in Milan. Instead he had to ride the Dauphiné where he suffered as Thévenet flew up the mountains – one writer observed that he finished one stage 'yellowish, livid in the face' – then the Tour of Switzerland where De Vlaeminck was at his best, fresh from the Giro, and pushed him into second.

Thévenet had begun to sense that there might be an opportunity after the Dauphiné: 'I was getting better, he didn't seem to be quite as good. I wondered if our trajectories might cross. But no one had beaten him before in a major Tour, and he was as competitive as ever. In Liège–Bastogne–Liège that April, when I was in the lead group of strong riders at the finish – with guys like De Vlaeminck and Godefroot – I attacked at a kilometre to go, thinking that the others would follow Merckx and that might inhibit him. But he managed to get clear of them, get ten metres on them, held it all through the final kilometre and beat me. He wasn't just strong physically, but mentally and tactically as well. Psychologically it was impossible to be at his level.'

When the Tour started 'his rivals [were] moving out onto the high plateau of their season's form, Merckx still grinding up the slope' in Nicholson's words. It was a route which was 'sadistic' in Jacques Goddet's view, and it could have been designed for Thévenet: five summit finishes, no time bonuses for stage wins, and a serious climb inserted into the final time trial. Merckx had two key rivals: the Frenchman, who had dominated the Dauphiné, and Zoetemelk, the latter still recovering from his horrendous accident and illness of the previous year. Thévenet's team manager at Peugeot, Maurice de Muer, came to him before the start with a piece of paper, on which he had written how much his protégé needed to gain at each of the mountain-top finishes: one minute at the Puy-de-Dôme and so on. The critical target was this: when the race reached the Pyrenees, eleven stages in, Thévenet needed to be less than three minutes behind The Cannibal.

Merckx came second in the prologue in the south Belgian town of Charleroi, behind Francesco Moser. He then went on the attack in a typical improvised move on the Flandrian hills the next morning, taking with him the young Italian, Zoetemelk and Van Impe and stealing a march on Thévenet and Poulidor. That afternoon as the race headed from Belgium to France, Poulidor made his move and Zoetemelk lost time due to a puncture; within twenty-four hours, both Merckx's biggest rivals had slipped behind. On the west coast of France, at Saint Jean-de-Monts, Merckx won the time trial, putting another fifty-two seconds into Thévenet with Zoetemelk even further behind.

At Auch four days later, in another time trial, Merckx took what was to be his last individual Tour stage win, the 352nd road win of his career, but this time the Frenchman was breathing down his neck after Merckx had lost time to a puncture. By now Zoetemelk was almost five minutes back so the overall battle boiled down to Merckx, the Peugeot leader, and his old rival Felice Gimondi. As far as Thévenet was concerned, he had achieved his first objective: he was only two minutes thirty-five seconds behind Merckx. 'I was in with a chance. It was do-able.' On the key Pyrenean stage to Pla d'Adet, Merckx made two crucial errors: he asked his team to make the pace too early, on the Tourmalet; without Bruyère's horsepower they wore themselves out, leaving their leader isolated in the final kilometres. He then made the mistake of trying to follow Zoetemelk's attack on the climb to the finish. Usually, he followed the classic tactic of letting the climber gain a small advantage, then pulling him back gradually without going too deep. Staying with a climber as he makes his initial acceleration leaves a rider open to a counter-attack and on this occasion it came from Thévenet. Merckx lost two minutes eighteen seconds and with it the initiative, which passed to the Frenchman, who might actually have gained more time had he not punctured 400 metres from the line.

Gimondi, however, had slipped to five minutes behind and was out of the picture, so Merckx's strategy switched to marking Thévenet. His plan was to wait, then make his attack on the stage through the southern Alps to Pra-Loup, which came eight days from Paris. On the summit finish at the Puy-de-Dôme, the day before the rest day – thirty-six hours before Pra-Loup – he had only to control the race and that is what he managed to do until five kilometres from the summit, when Thévenet and Van Impe attacked. There was no need to panic; he had been in this situation with both Fuente and Ocaña in the past.

He maintained the gap at about a hundred metres but, as he was about to sprint 150 metres from the finish line, the incident that defined the race took place. A spectator, Nello Breton, emerged from the packed crowd and slammed his fist into Merckx's lower back.

He crossed the line thirty-four seconds behind Thévenet, who closed to just fifty-eight seconds behind overall, but that was the least of the damage. The punch left him with a bruise on his side close to his liver; as he got his breath back, he vomited bile. As he was going down the mountain escorted by police he identified his attacker. Breton claimed he was pushed forward, but it doesn't look like this from the television footage. His right arm can be seen emerging from the crowd as Merckx passes through the tight corridor of spectators – Merckx rides into the arm and a few pedal strokes later he is clutching his side. It doesn't look as if Breton is simply pushed off balance, because he seems to strike Merckx with some force. Merckx sued for damages and several months later he travelled to Clermont-Ferrand for a court ruling which awarded him a symbolic one franc.

Merckx's explanation was that the French press had been stoking up the opposition to him. 'It was a conscious gesture,' he said. Merckx's popularity is now taken as such a given that it can be hard to appreciate or understand the strength of feeling against The Cannibal among some cycling fans. It's easier, perhaps, to translate into a modern context if we remember the comments, slogans and spittle that were directed at Lance Armstrong in his later years of dominating the Tour. To start with, the press had mixed feelings about Merckx's domination, torn between admiration for it and a desire to see him laid low. The public disliked the fact that he never courted their popularity. As has been established, he did not play to the gallery. Astonishingly, a film-maker interviewed spectators at the Tour and found that nine out of ten disliked Merckx 'because he is the only one who ever wins'.

There were others who had stronger feelings, however. Belgian journalists on the Puy-de-Dôme stage had felt that the crowd was incredibly hostile; their cars had been walloped by spectators and insults shouted. The journalist Théo Mathy published a series of letters from a Frenchwoman received by Merckx during the 1971 Tour. The woman, apparently from Lorraine, was an admirer of Poulidor. She attacked Merckx's 'pride' and 'pretensions', related her joy upon hearing him being whistled during the stage finish in Nancy ('I would have whistled at you myself if I had been there'). She wrote: 'I hope that one day, you crack beautifully, because Bobet, Coppi, Kübler and Koblet all cracked in their time.' She described her delight at his loss of time on the Puy-de-Dôme – 'I danced the Twist when I heard' – and amidst her gloating over the defeat at Orcières-Merlette she admits, 'I like you a bit more now that you have shown you are not superhuman, a sort of God . . . cycling was losing its interest.'

Merckx was examined during the rest day at Nice and found to have mild inflammation around the liver area – he had to be given a blood thinner before the start of the next stage. But he was confident enough, having limited his losses. The Pra-Loup stage, immediately after the rest day, was the one where he reckoned he could win the Tour – four cols, each with a brutal descent, followed by a climb to the finish which is easier than either the Puy-de-Dôme or Pla d'Adet. On the third col of the day, the Col des Champs – sixteen kilometres, 1053 metres in altitude, very steep at its foot and a typical exposed, bleak southern Alpine col – as a selection of ten riders was forming, Merckx felt pain in his right side where the punch had landed. He asked his teammate Ward Janssens to slip back to the Red Cross ambulance and get an analgesic. At which point Thévenet began to pile on the pressure. 'I went five or six times, but he got me every time,' recalls the Frenchman. 'It annoyed me, because I had thought I might get some time on him.'

As the gradient eased near the summit, Merckx responded with his own move, taking the descent flat out. This was not unexpected. Thévenet remembers now that the Belgian attacked on every descent in that race (apart from one, of which more later). 'He knew I wasn't as good a descender as he was, and he had won the 1971 Tour like that, when Luis Ocaña tried to stay with him and fell.' The Frenchman had to change a wheel as the road plummeted down, getting back to Merckx after a long chase with his teammate Raymond Delisle.

Merckx, having worked out that his Peugeot rival might be vulnerable – and, according to his *directeur sportif*, Bob Lelangue, feeling under threat himself – put Molteni to work on the next climb, the Col d'Allos, longer than the Champs and higher, running through a bleak backdrop of high meadows, and with another appallingly tricky descent. Less than a kilometre from the summit Merckx made what he hoped would be the race-winning move, getting rid of Thévenet and Gimondi before the downhill. It was, says Thévenet, the most impressive moment of the stage. '*Oh la la, du grand Merckx*. I wasn't feeling great, because I had made a big effort to get back to him, and he knew it. It was really quite something. Quite amazing. He was very very strong. I just couldn't follow. He was really going well at that point.'

At the foot of the descent, Merckx had thirty-one seconds' lead on Gimondi, one minute thirteen seconds on Thévenet. The Tour should have been won, with only the 6.5-kilometre climb to the finish remaining. But suddenly the great man cracked, on what was a far easier ascent than any of the other finishes that year. Thévenet doesn't remember any key moment, just the sense that the race was turning again as the time gap got smaller, each time he heard it. 'I felt I was coming back to him, then I saw the cars in front of me. But of course I didn't know where he was in relation to the cars. To be honest, I rode so hard up that climb that it wasn't a surprise when I caught him. I was flat out, but I had no idea he had slowed as much as he had. I didn't think I was going to take nearly two minutes out of him. I was actually worried he might stay with me so I accelerated so he couldn't take my wheel.'

'The most incredible reversal the Tour has ever seen,' wrote Pierre Chany. As Thévenet passed Merckx, four kilometres from the line, neither looked at the other. It is a telling image: the eyes of both men are fixed on the road ahead. Thévenet has the hungry look of a man who wants to devour the final kilometres as he lifts himself out of the saddle to accelerate past. Merckx has an air of pure desperation as if he dreads what may lie ahead. Thévenet admitted later he had no idea of the implications of the moment: Merckx losing the Tour for the first time.

He described that moment to *l'Equipe* in 2003: 'It's stupid, I was there, but I didn't see it. If I had known all that, I would have looked at him as I overtook him.' He was thinking only of the shining band of melting tarmac between the two of them, that, if he went to the right of it, Merckx would not want to ride across to take his wheel because he might get stuck. 'It was as if we each had half the road, with a great gulf between us. I wasn't thinking about him. He couldn't catch me now. I didn't know it was a historic moment, that this was the last time he would wear the yellow jersey in the Tour. I can only remember the shining band of tarmac. And the fact that I'd stuffed him.' He heard his manager, Maurice de Muer, shout, '"he's cracking, he's cooked". I didn't hesitate.'

One by one, Gimondi, Thévenet and Merckx's old rivals Zoetemelk and Van Impe had all gone past him; Merckx finished fifth, one minute fifty-six seconds back, a spectacular time loss, given that one minute per kilometre is about the norm for a non-climber compared to a mountain specialist. The image as he came up the finish straight left no room for doubt: he was hunched, uncomfortable, arms straight rather than pulling viciously on the bars as they did when he was pushing hard on the pedals. He looked resigned to defeat, tired mentally as much as physically. He was at a loss to understand why, having been in a position to attack Thévenet, he ended up losing the lead. It was not hypoglycaemia – the bonk, as cyclists call it – as he had no memory of devouring food afterwards, as cyclists do when they run out of fuel. The only conclusion that he could come to was that it was related to the medicine the doctor had given him before the start, plus the fact that his back muscles were full of tension from the punch. Perhaps a younger rider, more supple, who hadn't pushed his organism to the limit for years, might have recovered more quickly.

The following day the Tour travelled to Serre-Chevalier over the Vars and Izoard passes. Merckx's plan was to attack Thévenet on the Izoard, using the twenty-kilometre descent to Briançon before the uphill finish to put his rival under pressure. But he threw his plan to the four winds. Again he was forced to take a painkiller during the stage because of the aching in his back from the punch, and again he attacked, this time following an early move on the descent from the Vars – where again Thévenet was not at his ease – joining a lead trio of Zoetemelk, Francisco Galdós and Mariano Martínez. They refused to collaborate with him on the valley leading to the Izoard, although they had a minute's lead, and Merckx sat up to wait for the bunch. Over the Izoard Thévenet made his move, gained over two minutes, and the Tour was as good as won. It was, says the Frenchman now, the critical day, rather than Pra-Loup, but it is Pra-Loup that is talked about now. 'I won the Tour at Serre-Chevalier, that was where I opened the gap. I was lucky, as Eddy was stronger at the start, I was a bit better in the mountains, but we were pretty much at the same level in the final week. I wasn't that good at Pra-Loup, but over the Izoard, he had a not-so-good day, I had a good one.'

Merckx's sufferings, however, were just beginning. The next morning came the crash with Ole Ritter, in the neutralised zone between the start in Valloire and the *départ réel* outside the ski station, as the peloton prepared for the brief climb up the Col du Télégraphe, followed by the far longer descent into the Maurienne valley.* 'I remember this stage clearly,' the Dane told me. 'Everyone wanted to get to the front, and pushed and shoved for a better position before the twenty-one-kilometre-long descent. Eddy Merckx yelled at me "Ole, move over!" but I too wanted to get ahead so I remained where I was. This resulted in Eddy's front wheel hitting my rear wheel and he went down on the tarmac.' Thévenet first had an inkling that something might be amiss on the descent, when Merckx did not put in his usual attack going down the lengthy series of steep hairpins. He recalled that this was so unusual – 'I said to myself, "*tiens, c'est bizarre*"' – that, once they arrived in the valley, he went to find the Belgian at the back of the bunch. 'His cheek was covered in ointment. I didn't know how bad he was. The thing was, he often complained, and often when he said something was wrong with him, that meant he was going well. I didn't know what state he was in for the rest of the race, whether he was good or bad, and it wasn't until after the Tour finished that I found out he was in a really rough

---

* The stage had started in Valloire, which lies between the Col du Galibier and the Col du Télégraphe. It had taken the brief climb up the Télégraphe in the opposite direction from the Galibier; after the Télégraphe came the far longer descent to the Maurienne.

state. I was used to him trying to kid us a bit, exaggerating a bit so that we would all let him race as he wanted to. What I remember from the end of that stage is that I was really annoyed when he took those two seconds from me. He hadn't managed to attack me before. I felt overconfident, and that put me back in touch with reality.'

Instead of going home as common sense and the doctors suggested, Merckx regained a little more time during the time trial stage from Morzine to Châtel – although his silk world champion's jersey, with race number pinned on, was stolen from the bed in his hotel room, so he had to use a less aerodynamic cotton one. He regained fifteen seconds on Thévenet, who was suffering the after-effects of a crash while warming up, but the time trial was probably the most painful experience in his racing career since the Hour Record. 'When he got off his bike, his jerky gestures, livid skin, strangely focused look, his eyes sunk too far into his skull and the tic on one cheek twitching gave him the look of a madman. He was frightening to see,' wrote Théo Mathy.

Half an hour after the finish the same journalist went to visit him in his room, only to find him lying on his bed, unconscious, in the foetal position, still in his dirty race kit. It was another hour before he found the strength to take a bath. He could not eat solid food. He refused point-blank to take any antibiotics, on the grounds that he had taken thousands of units to get rid of the throat infection he suffered in May, and they would weaken his system.

He pulled back another sixteen seconds on Thévenet before the finish in Paris, when the Frenchman fell near the stage finish in Senlis, but the victory was pyrrhic. Thévenet triumphed overall by two minutes forty-seven seconds, the first time Merckx had failed to win the Tour in six starts. The race finished on the Champs-Elysées for the first time, and the

100,000 crowd that had come to see the first French winner in eight years instead got to see a final act of panache from the fading champion. 'He had never known as much sympathy in France as when, beaten for the first time in the Tour, he completed the final laps on the Champs-Elysees,' wrote Nicholson. 'He [Merckx] has not lost the Tour, he has finished second,' said the French President Valéry Giscard d'Estaing as he awarded Thévenet his final yellow jersey.

The effects of the 1975 Tour were long-lasting. Merckx regretted the courage he had shown. One teammate claimed he stayed in the race for their sake, because he knew they would lose money if he pulled out. 'I was dumb,' said Merckx later. 'I could have compensated my teammates.' It was one of the few things in his time in cycling that he would have done differently if he had the chance. It was, he believed, a turning point in his career, the moment at which he started to go downhill because he had asked too much of his system. 'But what made me go on? That time, it was pure madness. But I wasn't suicidal by nature, and I had no desire to die on the bike.'

Although early in his career Merckx had been adamant that he would not race beyond his thirtieth year – because as early as 1970 he had recognised that his extravagant racing style would not permit him to last long – at the start of 1976 he was convinced he could win that sixth Tour. That was under-standable: two outside incidents – the punch and the crash – had contributed to his defeat the previous year, and he had still finished 1975 at the top of the Super Prestige Pernod standings. It was his seventh consecutive win in the Pernod, a record, naturally.

The year 1976 started promisingly, but went downhill rapidly. Milan–San Remo was his final masterpiece but also, according to one of the riders present that day, a win taken when he was actually struggling, the successful attack made in spite of the fact that his strength was running out, and Vandenbroucke was actually the stronger on the road. The rider who told the story did so as an example – yet another – of the physical extremes to which Merckx could push himself as he sought a win, no matter how unlikely eventual victory might seem.

By now his system was so fragile that it took only the slightest reverse to throw him entirely out of kilter. He was still suffering from violent headaches as a result of the crash in the previous year's Tour. His position on the bike was so delicate that when he hurt his arm in a crash the slight shift of position brought on back pain. He still had trouble with his crutch dating back to the 1974 Tour. 'Every time I had a health problem or some little difficulty I realised how much I have asked of myself for so many years.'

Mentally and physically he was close to the end of his tether, although he was too proud to realise it. In the final stage of Catalan Week, which he won overall, he fell when a bag got caught in the chain of his bike. He landed on his elbow and spent the whole Classics season trying to race and get over the injury. Meanwhile, Maertens was enjoying the form of his life, winning three Classics, and clearly attempting to throw off accusations that he was a mere sprinter by racing in the style of Merckx. He was attacking well before the finish to win by large margins, as he did in that spring's Amstel Gold, and that summer's Belgian national championship.

Merckx regained sufficient health in time to start the Giro, where he finished eighth, the first time he had gone through a major Tour without winning a stage. But he was suffering from a saddle boil. He had the option of stopping the Giro – which he had no chance of winning, and which he had to ride in considerable pain – to have the boil lanced. That might have enabled him to heal in time to race the Tour de France, and possibly win it for the sixth time.

As Nicholson writes, Molteni may have wanted him to finish the Giro – the final day's time trial was in the company's home town, Arcore, just north of Milan – but the decision came down to the rider himself. 'Merckx can make his own terms. It was just as consistent with his own stubborn nature that he should see the race through to the end.' Abandoning was not his way, as he had shown the year before in the Tour. A few days after the Giro finished he surprised no one by announcing his and Molteni's withdrawal from the Tour. In the event it turned out to be a curious race, where Thévenet was out of form and neither Lucien Van Impe, the eventual winner, nor the runner-up, Joop Zoetemelk, was at first willing to take the initiative. It is not certain that Merckx would have won it, but he would certainly have changed the race's complexion.

For the first time since 1968, the Super Prestige Pernod Trophy went elsewhere, to Maertens as it happened. And for the first time since 1966, Merckx ended his season before October. After a full August, including fifth place in the world championship at Ostuni, won by Maertens, he struggled in Paris–Brussels and came down with desperate back trouble after winning the criterium at Bourges in central France in the last week of September. He had to spend six weeks lying down, part of the time on a sheet of wood. So much pain, so little reward: it was hardly surprising that, yet again, he contemplated putting an end to his career, as Molteni pulled out of sponsorship.

ALL PASSION SPENT

'Thinking of the day he would have to retire would be
simply too tough for Eddy'. *Claudine Merckx, in the film*
La Course en Tête.

In the 1990s, I rode occasionally with a former professional,
Ian Banbury. He had been British national champion during a
golden age for the sport, when Robert Millar and Sean Yates
were in their prime. He had won an Olympic medal on the
track in the days when few Britons managed it. He was one
of the best British track cyclists ever. He had plenty to boast
about. But the story he liked to tell wasn't about one of his
many achievements. It was about the day he saw Eddy Merckx
give up.

It happened somewhere in the South of France, some time
in the spring of 1978, in a training race, most probably the
Grand Prix de Montauroux on 19 February, the first of the
five races Merckx rode that season. The way Banbers told it,
Merckx went to the front of the bunch, did a massive stint
at the head of the line of riders, stretched them out like elastic,
then turned round and looked at them all. Then he swung off
to one side, slammed on his brakes and pulled into the edge
of the road. It was obvious, Banbury believed, that Merckx's
heart wasn't in racing any more, notwithstanding his five wins
in the Tour, five more in the Giro and who knew what else.
He quit the race.

As I used to hear the story, it sounded like Merckx's

illustrious career came to an end there and then, but it wasn't that neat. He raced for the last time on 19 March 1978. But the point for Banbury wasn't that he had been present at a landmark moment, when history was made. That was precisely the thing. What he saw was a portent. He just felt in his waters that Merckx wasn't going to last much longer when he saw that little incident. It was of minor significance, but it was his personal Merckx moment. And it meant a lot. As Banbury told it, that little episode seemed more vivid to him than any of his victories or medals.

The greats of cycling rarely make exits that are truly worthy of their careers. Fausto Coppi faded away into nothingness before premature death; Rik Van Steenbergen and Jacques Anquetil frittered away their final years making lucrative appearances. Rik Van Looy just stopped one day because he was fed up. Miguel Indurain rode a Vuelta he didn't want to be in and simply upped and quit. Lance Armstrong couldn't keep away and made a comeback to ride one Tour de France too many. Raymond Poulidor, on the other hand, wound up with a Tour podium place at forty before quitting the following year after eighteen years as a professional, but Bernard Hinault achieved the classiest retirement ever, setting the date years in advance and having a massive party in the autumn of 1986. Sean Kelly went out in similar style, with Merckx, De Vlaeminck, Hinault and many more racing around his home village in Ireland to celebrate the last of the old-style champions.

The question through 1977 was how and when Merckx would call time. He had his obligations to fulfil: a new sponsor, FIAT, who wanted to see him race, and an entire team of domestiques dependent on him for their income. In a curious twist, the team was managed by Raphael Geminiani, because it was sponsored by FIAT France. Geminiani had wanted to direct Merckx at the start of his career, but in the long term 'The Big Gun' and The Cannibal did not make a winning combination. The season started well enough when Merckx took the Grand Prix d'Aix en Provence and the Tour of the Mediterranean. It was not the stuff of dreams but enough to make him dream. Another win followed, the Paris–Nice stage finishing in Digne, where he ran in one second ahead of the bunch sprint won by Patrick Sercu from Freddy Maertens, who took five of the twelve stages that year. He was unable to finish Paris–Nice, however, although he made it to the final stage, then came down with sinusitis – which was linked to the crash at Valloire in 1975 – then glandular fever, which was never truly diagnosed, at least not until he had virtually recovered.

As in the previous spring, he was merely coming close to winning races he had dominated outrageously in the past: 9th in Amstel Gold Race, 11th in Paris–Roubaix, 6th in Liège–Bastogne–Liège. At the criterium in Camors, Brittany, on 10 April, he finished first, ahead of a young Breton with a brutally determined face: Bernard Hinault. Another criterium, a couple of months later, took him to the newly opened circuit at Temple Mills in London's East End, a race instigated by the boxing promoter Mike Barrett, where he finished second.* Merckx rode respectably in the Dauphiné Libéré and Tour of Switzerland, where he won the stage into Bellinzona, his last major victory, all of which was just enough to suggest he might

---

* The 'Merckx meeting' at the Eastway circuit in Temple Mills, London, is a legendary British cycling occasion, on a par with the 'Fausto Coppi meetings' at Herne Hill in the late 1950s. The Glenryck Cup was put up by Barrett as part of a brief promotional push into cycling, and also included stars such as Poulidor and the winner, Dietrich Thurau, as well as professionals from the British scene. The Eastway circuit is now buried under the London Olympic park.

be able to challenge in the strangely structured 1977 Tour de France.

At the start of the Tour he told journalists that he was not confident about his form, and was worried he might relapse into the poor health that had stalked him in the spring. It was, wrote the journalist Joël Godaert, 'another fear on top of all those that had haunted his tortured mind since he began racing'. He hung on in second place behind the German Dietrich 'Didi' Thurau – a talent as ephemeral as Merckx had been durable – for two weeks but the reason he managed that was because the race dipped into the Pyrenees in the first couple of days, then had a long, flat hiatus until the Alps in the final week. After stage two, when the race crossed the Tourmalet, Peyresourde and Aubisque, there was no major change to the overall standings until stage fifteen, the time trial from Morzine to Avoriaz.

It later emerged that he and others in his team picked up a stomach bug later in this phase, which included a passage through Belgium and an air transfer to Freibourg in Germany. Merckx had struggled over the Tourmalet, and lost time as soon as the race entered the Alps, but confirmation that he was not going to feature in the race to win came the next day, on the stage to Chamonix over the Col du Forclaz. Merckx was dropped; he wasn't far behind at the top, thought he might regain contact on the descent, but felt he had too small a gear. He accepted his fate with dignity, 'too bad for lovers of melodrama,' wrote Robert Silva in l'Equipe in a piece which sounded the end of the Merckx era. 'No tearful scenes, no nervous crisis. A new life has begun for the champion who marked an entire era.' He accepted he had lost the Tour – the only time in the seven he had ridden that he had been defeated so early on – and said his plan was that this would be his last.

Tuesday 19 July, the stage from Chamonix to l'Alpe d'Huez,

was the champion's final ordeal. It was hot, six hours long and included the Col de la Madeleine, and the Col du Glandon. Merckx's system had finally given best. He had barely slept the previous night due to food poisoning and, although he led the chase behind an early escape in his old style, he fell to bits on the Madeleine, vomiting as he rode. He came round a little on l'Alpe d'Huez, overtaking a fair few backmarkers to come in twentieth, more than thirteen minutes behind the stage winner, Hennie Kuiper of Holland. Underlining that this day marked the end of a generation, Ocaña was suffering as well, not far behind. It was one of the Tour's most brutal days, a torrid stage when Lucien Van Impe sparked action from the off and the high speed meant thirty riders were eliminated. Afterwards, Godaert interviewed Merckx in his hotel room, where he delivered a monologue in which two sentences came up time after time: 'I've never suffered like that' and 'I could not abandon'.

The very next day, however, he was on the attack into Saint-Etienne, moving up to sixth overall, the position he held in Paris, twelve minutes thirty-eight seconds behind Thévenet.* He had started seven Tours and never abandoned one. He said he would return to the Tour, and explained later: 'I said it because I really believed it, I didn't feel I was beaten on my true quality. I was ill. I was unlucky. I wasn't convinced it was all over.' What he did not understand was that he was getting ill and unlucky because he was aging – in cycling terms, after a twelve-year pro career – and his body could no longer keep up with the demands he made on it. In the context of the rest of his season – Did Not Finish in Paris–Nice, 5th in Catalan

---

* The stage win was not awarded as the two riders who finished first and second, Joaquim Agostinho and Antonio Menendez, both tested positive. Merckx was not given the victory as he had not been tested.

Week, 8th in the Dauphiné, 11th in Switzerland – 6th in the Tour was actually a decent performance, but it was not Merckx as the cycling world knew him, or as he knew himself.

At the world championships in San Cristóbal, Venezuela, six weeks later – after a round of criteriums and track meetings that entailed racing twenty-two times in forty days – his old rivalry with Lomme Driessens and Flandria reared its head, with the man in the middle Sean Kelly. The Irishman had not been expecting to travel to Venezuela – the Irish Federation would not have dreamed of paying his fare – until Driessens, his manager at Flandria, phoned up a couple of weeks beforehand and offered to fly him out. Kelly travelled with the Belgian team, stayed with them and trained with them before the race.

'The day before I remember Driessens said to me that if Merckx got in a break I should ride on the front, I wasn't to get in a break with him, but if a group with Merckx got a few seconds ahead, I was to get on the front and ride. I think the feeling was that if Merckx was in the break no one from the Belgian team could ride, and if he got away with five, six, seven riders, it might be difficult. After halfway he went off the front with two or three riders, I put my head down and chased.' There was nothing particularly irregular in Kelly's action: he was sponsored by Flandria, they had paid his fare and expenses, so it was perfectly reasonable for him to do what his trade team director requested. Driessens' manipulation availed his Flandria riders not a whit: the gold medal went to Francesco Moser of Italy. Merckx finished thirty-third and last, just behind Raymond Poulidor, who was riding the last race of his career.

Thirteen days later, on 17 September, came Merckx's last win in a road race – although no one was aware of it at the time – in the *kermis* at Kluisbergen, at the foot of the Oude Kwaremont climb in the heart of Flanders. A week after that, he raced the Classic Tours–Versailles – nowadays the event is run in the opposite direction, from the Paris area to Tours – where he attacked right at the start and stayed away alone for 113 kilometres in a break that no one believed would last to the finish, but that no one dared chase because the man in front was Merckx. In his book *Eddy Merckx, La Roue de la Fortune*, Joël Godaert, writer at the Brussels daily *La Dernière Heure*, described his feelings: 'A few years previously, everyone would have raved about another Merckx exploit. Who thought that on this day? The initial reaction was curiosity. Why was he making such an effort, that everyone knew was in vain? Then the feeling was that the scene we were witnessing was pitiful. Some asked this cruel question: should we praise the attitude of an athlete refusing to capitulate or deplore the fact that a champion of Merckx's stature was reduced to the kind of stunt usually reserved for those making up the numbers?'

That solo escape across the plains north of Tours amounted to Merckx's goodbye. As French cycling writers would describe it, it was his *baroud d'honneur*, the dying fighter's last thrust of the rapier.

Even though he refused to acknowledge it at the time, Merckx was burned out, both physically and mentally. That was hardly surprising given the rate at which he had competed and the pressures it created. The statistics are mindbending. For eleven years, 1967 – 77, he had raced between 111 and 151 races a season, totalling 1413 races. One estimate was that he trained for 15,000 miles a year, raced about 30,000, travelled by car, rail and air another 80,000. The constitution of an ox was needed to live at that pace. In his peak years, 1969 to 1973, he would usually begin racing in mid-February, most often with the Lagueglia Trophy in Italy or the Tour of Sardinia. After the Giro di Lombardia, he would push on with criteriums – or in

1972 the Hour Record – until the second half of October. Then there were the track meetings, the Six Days, and, in 1974, the odd cyclo-cross race in January and December.

There is a telling breakdown of his road programme in Rik Van Walleghem's book *Eddy Merckx Homme et Cannibale*. In 1969, after the Tour de France finished on 20 July, he raced ten times in the next nine days, and added another twenty-four races, mainly criteriums, in August. This was probably the occasion Guillaume Michiels cited when Merckx raced fifty-four times without a day off. He told the soigneur towards the end of the summer as he took off his shorts, 'you realise I've spent fifty days with grease on my backside?', a reference to the cream on the chamois leather insert in his shorts. His programme had not lightened noticeably by 1975.

Part of the reason was that he was trying to reconcile demands from two sources. Jean Van Buggenhout was in charge of Merckx's racing but he couldn't prevent Faema or Molteni asking their leader to ride a heavy programme of Italian races. Van Buggenhout wanted him to ride criteriums and track races anywhere and everywhere for appearance fees, while his commercial sponsors would ask him to race in Italy above all because that was their market. Unlike today, the Giro was probably at least as important as the Tour in terms of cash and prestige, because so many of the best riders raced for Italian teams and the Italian sponsors weren't particularly interested in winning the Tour. Merckx had to ride the Giro and he wanted to ride the Tour. Hence his saturated racing calendar. Many of the other races were Belgian *kermis* events, which were local to him, but he still had to pin a number on and perform. And there were countless occasions when he pushed himself to a state of exhaustion, such as the 1971 Liège–Bastogne–Liège, after which he had to shower in a chair, because he could barely stand. He would come back too soon after injury and illness – think of 1972 and the broken vertebra, 1969 and the serious head injuries at Blois. 'You start from the principle that it will be OK, there are no limits and that anything can be solved by willpower.' But there is only so much that body and mind can take.

'Heavy' race programmes were the norm from the 1940s into the 1980s, when the culture of cycling gradually changed: primarily because wages increased, the riders became more selective in what they rode so the criteriums, *kermis* races and track meets gradually declined in number. But Merckx's programmes were heavier than most and he started most events wanting to win, unlike today, when those stars who race all year will have periods when they back off, events they ride merely for the miles. Even in 1974 and 1975, as his physical powers started to wane, he did not lighten up – they were his 'heaviest' years, with 140 and 151 races respectively – so it was no surprise that in 1976 and 1977 he went downhill. Later, he felt he had been too malleable when managers asked him to chase appearance money here, there and everywhere. He accepted that he needed to race the criteriums to earn a living but later wondered whether his career 'would have been longer or better without that'. Claudine, however, was not convinced that her husband truly regretted racing as much as he did. 'When he wasn't racing and was sitting in an armchair, he would be ill from not being on his bike.' He needed to compete, and he needed to race flat out; so he did.

The racing was not the only pressure. Success did not make The Cannibal's life easy. Once he had become public property, the demands of media, fans, the whole cycling world, were immense. The writer Marc Jeuniau noted that it could take up to two hours to get through to the single open phone line in the Merckx house. (There was a private line for talking to his sponsors in Italy.) His number was available through directory inquiries; most of the calls were fielded by Claudine, who would filter media demands as well. The line usually received about fifty calls a day; Jeuniau counted seventy-five calls in five hours one day when he was with Merckx not long after his accident in Blois. The demands were multifarious, one example being a call from a woman a few days after the accident, with this to say: 'I hope that now that Eddy is unwell he will have time to answer me at last. I want my son to be a professional cyclist and a message from Eddy would help.' Further inquiries revealed the son was three and a half. There were continual requests for money, appearances, logistical demands.

Merckx rarely turned away television crews who would turn up at his house. In 1970, between the Giro and the Tour he had signed a contract with Belgian television to look over a dozen of the Tour stages, a staggering commitment, at the same time as he was receiving intensive treatment on his troublesome left leg.

Not all the contact with fans and media was pleasant. His garden was invaded time after time by souvenir hunters, who once stole his racing jerseys as they hung on the washing line. He was accosted in restaurants, his house was burgled, he was phoned up in the dead of night, received verbal and written threats – one clearly unhinged letter from 1971 threatened to cut the throats of his wife and child with a razor – and was accused of killing off the sport. Notoriously, he was photographed naked in the showers after a race by a photographer whose cameras 'went off accidentally' and who then published the pictures.

'Physically I don't believe he was in bad way when he retired, I think it was a mental thing. It was just very difficult for him in his head,' says Jean-Luc Vandenbroucke. Merckx told me that he had become 'saturated. It was all too much.

Psychologically I couldn't handle it, my nerves had blown a fuse. I had asked too much of myself. I wanted to train but I couldn't. I had lived on my nerves for too long. When the wires are cut, you can't repair them.' He drew the contrast with Raymond Poulidor and Joop Zoetemelk, both of whom raced into their forties. 'There wasn't the pressure on them to make their presence felt all the time. If you are number one, you end your career more quickly.' In the end, he said, the constant worrying had got to him. 'I was worn out by it.' On another occasion, he told me: 'I was mentally exhausted. I was tired of always racing.'

By the end of 1977 Merckx was raging against the dying of the light, but events were moving around him. FIAT had changed their strategy after the Tour: they wanted a young French team, which might have included Merckx, but that would have entailed sacking most of his older teammates, which he would not countenance. With Jean Van Buggenhout no longer at his side to manage his affairs, it was up to him to look for a sponsor to shell out the twenty million Belgian francs it needed to back him and his henchmen. That must have been humiliating for a champion of his stature, but it was also unfamiliar, stressful territory. Hitherto, all he had done was race and deal with things that related to competition, but suddenly he was plunged into the commercial world. Wilkinson razors appeared to have signed up, but they pulled out in December, when everything had been prepared, including getting jerseys made.

Late in the day, in January 1978, the department store C&A agreed to sponsor him, after a chance meeting between their owner and Merckx at a football match between Anderlecht and Liège. But after the worry of putting his team together, Merckx admitted 'mentally I was worn out'. His plan, initially at least, was to race the Tour de France, then hang up his wheels without a lengthy round of 'farewell appearances'. Physically he believed he was in good shape, having 'lived like a monk' and won the European Madison championship along with Sercu. After quitting at Montauroux in the incident that made such an impression on Ian Banbury, he finished fifth in the Tour du Haut Var but that was as good as it got: shortly afterwards he set off with his team to train on the course of Het Volk, but had to stop after seventy-five kilometres, in a state of exhaustion. He was diagnosed with colitis, an infection of the colon. Haut Var was one of just two races he finished that spring. The second and last was on 19 March at Kemzeke, a *kermis* race in a suburb of Sint Niklaas, north-east of Ghent, where he came in twelfth. This was the day after Milan–San Remo, and he was there rather than in Italy: that in itself spoke volumes.

If there was a moment when he finally accepted defeat, it was here, when he turned to the soigneur, Pierrot de Wit, and said it was his last race, in spite of De Wit's protestations. After that, reality set in for the first time in seventeen years. He returned from training sessions worn out. He got one cold after another. He went on holiday to the Swiss ski resort of Crans-Montana, where he put in long cross-country ski outings. The rest availed him little: on his return, his training rides became shorter and shorter. He was at the start of the Tour of Romandie, but it was to sign autographs in a C&A store. On 8 May he was seen training on the course of the Grand Prix de Wallonie and watched the race pass. It was, Godaert told me, open knowledge that he would quit; the only question was when he would make it public.

He announced his retirement at 4.08 p.m. on 18 May at the Brussels International Press Centre, the press having been summoned the day before. 'We had been waiting for it since March. Everyone knew why we had been called there,' Godaert says. 'There were a lot of us; he was very emotional, everyone was a bit emotional. There was a massive silence as he read out his statement. He didn't take questions; he repeated the statement for the radio reporters in Flemish, English, French. He said it was mental fatigue due to having to look for a sponsor all winter, rather than physical. But there is no doubt it was physical fatigue as well.'

Merckx had set himself a deadline of 15 May to begin preparing seriously for the Tour but had realised that he could no longer recover from the slightest effort on the bike; Godaert also believes the delay was necessary for him to negotiate his exit with C&A, who had come into cycling to sponsor Merckx, not to watch him quit. In his statement, Merckx explained that the doctors had told him that he could not race and that meant he could not prepare for the Tour de France. Physically he could not do it anymore, which is pretty much what would be expected given his ability to push his body to places others dared not venture for far longer than any other cyclist had managed.

Ironically, in view of Van Buggenhout's assertion in 1969 that his protégé was already figuring out what to do after he stopped cycling, The Cannibal had quit the sport by the back door without preparing for what was to come. 'The first weeks were appalling. I didn't know what to do with my time.' Claudine recalled going out in the car together and wondering what normal couples did on Sundays. 'When I stopped cycling, psychologically I stopped too. I didn't feel I fitted my skin.'

He took occasional outings on his bike, but only because his doctors had advised it would be wise to do so for the sake of his heart. The agreement with C&A stipulated he had to work with the team by turning up at certain races, but it was not the best place for him, 'in a world where I knew the riders, I was at the dinner table swapping stories with them, and it wasn't really good for me'. On the 1978 Tour he could be seen

applauding Jos Bruyère from a team car as his former domestique, now his team leader, defended the yellow jersey in the
first long time trial. 'MERCKX FOLLOWS BRUYÈRE AS HE DID
BEFORE' ran the headline in that July's *Miroir du Cyclisme*,
one of the first French cycling magazines I read as a teenager.
That year's Tour went to Bernard Hinault, the next great cycling
champion. As the French say, the page turned rapidly.

Merckx's career did not have to end in this way. He could
have gone on, as Rik Van Looy, Jacques Anquetil and Rik Van
Steenbergen did before him, milking the start money from
criteriums and six-day races, eschewing the road races which
would show his true standing in the hierarchy. 'He had a
proposition from Tuborg which would have involved some six-
days and criteriums, and would have been well paid,' revealed
Patrick Sercu, who would probably have partnered Merckx in
the track races. 'But he didn't want it if he couldn't do the
Classics and Tour de France. He could have done five years
as a tourist, just being Merckx.'

But simply turning up for the money had never been Merckx's
style. Nothing less than being the best had been good enough
for fifteen years, and, when he could no longer be the best,
he no longer wanted to compete. Interviewed after his defeat
in the 1975 Tour de France to Thévenet, he said that, when
the decision to quit was made, there would be no compromise:
'It will not be a matter of reducing my activities by cutting
such and such a race from my programme. If I broke away
from my normal schedule I would feel I was cheating the
others and cheating myself.'

Lelangue feels, like Sercu, that Merckx could have gone on
if he had been prepared to compromise, but wonders whether
his sensitivity explains his decision to quit. 'He stopped relatively early. He was afraid of being beaten, afraid of what people
might say, the fans, the press, people at the races.' Herman

Van Springel concurs: 'Actually he wasn't that bad when he stopped, but he just wasn't what he had been, all the time, and being just another rider wasn't good enough. He had to be better than anyone else. Only that would do.'

Merckx had always intended to stop racing when he was thirty. In 1973 he reiterated that it 'would be a mistake going on beyond that'. The reason why he made the 'mistake' and the greatest cycling career of all time ended with a whimper not a bang might seem puzzling to the outsider, but it was quite simple. From the day when he had opted to quit his studies at the age of fifteen, Merckx had spent seventeen years defying the 'reasonable', safe, rational view of things. It would have been 'reasonable' for him to finish school; safe for him to knuckle down alongside Rik Van Looy for a year or two rather than break out and move to Peugeot; logical for him to have ridden defensively during the stage to Mourenx – not to mention hundreds of other races – and sensible for him to have had three months off the bike after crashing at Blois. By 1976 or so, after so many years defying reason, it would have been impossible to expect a man to change.

When I met Merckx, he was nineteen years into retirement, and had spent seventeen years running his bike factory in the former pig farm at Meise, on the outskirts of Brussels. He felt he had created a reasonable substitute for the unity among his old cycling team among his thirty employees, who then included his former *directeur sportif*, Bob Lelangue, since retired. I was struck by two things. At 5 p.m., a little procession of employees came into the office of the *kopman* to say good evening at the end of the working day. That, and the paint sprayer who was delegated to drive me back to the airport: he had nothing but praise for his boss, who he believed was too indulgent, if anything.

Only the pictures on the wall, the trophies in the cabinet, reminded me that the avuncular, well-rounded figure in front of me in the well-appointed office was The Cannibal, the greatest ever cyclist. Merckx was happy to discuss cycling of the time. He didn't like the trend in the 1990s for the stars to target only the Tour de France, wasn't happy with the way that the world championship had been moved to October, felt the Hour Record was being devalued. Compared with other champions I'd met such as Hinault and Armstrong, there was far less edge to him, less combativity. I wrote then: 'Merckx doesn't talk about the racing past with the same dismissive arrogance as Hinault, but it doesn't seem to hold that much interest for him, perhaps because it's been ploughed over so many times.' The only regret I could detect in him was the decision to finish the 1975 Tour, broken jaw and all. That was just a hint: he seemed a man happy in his skin.

It had taken him a while to feel that way. Post-retirement, Merckx went into the doldrums due to the suddenness of the change, and only really re-emerged when he built his bike factory with the help of the Italian constructor Ugo de Rosa in 1980. De Rosa, who had built bikes for Merckx during his Italian years – as well as Colnago – taught him the basics and trained the staff at his factory in Italy. Even this was not without its difficulties: like many other ex-cyclists, he had trouble setting up in business – the bike company almost went bankrupt at one point, and he became embroiled in a tax repayment case.

He was helped, after retirement, by two friends from outside cycling: the footballer Paul Van Himst and the motor racing legend Jacky Ickx. Van Himst had retired at roughly the same time, and persuaded Eddy – a more than passable player in his youth – to join him in the Anderlecht veterans' team. Initially, recalled Van Himst, Merckx was not keen, because he did not know anyone else; once playing, naturally, his sporting instincts took over. That began a strong link between The Cannibal and the Brussels star footballer. Van Himst was trainer when Merckx's son Axel played in the youth teams. For several years, Merckx accompanied Anderlecht to European Cup ties as part of the president's delegation. When Van Himst's son Paul took up cycling, naturally he turned to Eddy for advice. More recently, Van Himst's son-in-law took a job at Merckx's bike factory, and Van Himst himself played a role in organising Merckx's sixtieth birthday celebration in 2005. Ickx, six times a winner at Le Mans, and like Merckx and Van Himst one of the greatest Belgian sports stars of the 1970s, had been friendly with The Cannibal since the early 1970s, had ridden alongside him behind the motorbike driven by Guillaume Michiels, and got Merckx back on his bike after retirement, persuading him to go on cycle-touring trips in the South of France. Merckx protested that he wouldn't ride a bike again, but eventually accepted.

Initially he didn't want his new life to have much to do with the old, then he came to realise that was impossible. You could take the man out of cycling; you couldn't take cycling out of the man. Gradually he became more involved. He had an eleven-year spell (1986–96) managing the Belgian team at the world road race championship. He put in time as race director at the Tour of Flanders and now works running the Tour of Qatar alongside the Tour de France organisers, ASO. His son Axel, born in August 1972, took up cycling after several years playing football – and the decision was a difficult one: not surprisingly, he was worried his father might not approve. Axel began at Motorola and forged a long and much more than respectable professional career – fourteen seasons – in spite of the obvious difficulty of being the 'son of'. The highlights were a Belgian national title, a bronze medal at the Olympic Games in Athens in 2004 – an Olympic medal being a feat that eluded his illustrious father – a stage win in the Giro d'Italia, and tenth place in the Tour in 1998.

Merckx *père* briefly sponsored a youth development team of his own together with the CGER bank. It included Axel, but also such talents as Rik Verbrugghe and Marcel Aerts. The Grand Prix Eddy Merckx was organised from 1980 until 2004, as an invitation time trial run around Brussels in August or September, first as an individual event, then one for two-man teams. It succumbed, ironically enough, to changes in cycling which went totally against the Merckx ethos: the stars were no longer prepared to race such one-off events. Merckx himself retired from his bike business and sold the majority of his shares in 2008. There are still connections: when I visited Guillaume Michiels in November 2011, he was working for a team named Mercator, which rode bikes supplied by his old boss.

It has taken a long time for Belgian cycling to get over the departure of The Cannibal and his generation: Godefroot, Maertens, De Vlaeminck et al. There was a constant search for the next Merckx, and the pressure scarred the careers of many notables in the 1980s and 1990s – Fons de Wolf, Eric Vanderaerden, Frank Vandenbroucke. Merckx is now close to the world no. 1 Philippe Gilbert, with whom he spends time in Monaco and to whom he gives the occasional nugget of advice. If Gilbert displays 'cannibalistic' tendencies at times, perhaps that's no surprise.

It is also hardly surprising that the most voracious champion of recent years, Lance Armstrong, should become close to the great man. Like Merckx, Armstrong was unmatched for the depth of his competitive obsession, or *rage de vaincre*, as the French term it; from 1992 to 1996, Merckx supplied bikes to Armstrong's Motorola team, and the pair remained close when Armstrong was struck down by testicular cancer in 1996.

Armstrong insisted that The Cannibal accompany him when he went out on his first bike ride after leaving hospital. Later, Merckx was one of the few who told him he was capable of winning the Tour. In terms of style, however, Merckx told me in 2005 he felt he had been more aggressive than Armstrong. 'I would attack more often. He waits for the other guys, then counter-attacks. [He] races more in the style of Jacques Anquetil or Miguel Indurain.'

Without Armstrong and Merckx's influence in the noughties and the seventies, the sport of cycling would now have a totally different look about it. While Armstrong turned cycling into a celebrity-driven sport focused on a single event, the Tour de France, Merckx, on the other hand, has done more to define this single sport than any other champion, because of his ubiquitousness. There is only one major race in the calendar that does not have his unique imprint – Paris–Tours – and even the 'sprinters' Classic' could be said to be in a class of its own because Merckx never won it.

Every bit of ground covered regularly by the sport's monumental events has its associations: Tom Simpson and Mont Ventoux, Eugène Christophe and the Tourmalet, Louison Bobet and the Izoard, Fausto Coppi and Gino Bartali on the Galibier, Coppi at the Stelvio and Madonna del Ghisallo in Italy, Ocaña on the Col de Menté, De Vlaeminck, Moser and others on the cobbles of Paris–Roubaix. But the whole of cycling's topography can be seen in reference to Merckx: his imprint is everywhere, from the Côte de Stockeu, near Liège, where his statue stands, to the Ventoux, and the heel of Italy. Every race in the cycling calendar that has any history refers back to Merckx. If there is an irony, it is that as the calendar is being globalised, the European events that are being downgraded and are disappearing are ones where Merckx built his legend.

Merckx's legacy is not one of innovation. He did not create

anything new in terms of the technical side of cycling, compared, for example, to Francesco Moser or Greg LeMond, both of whom pushed the boundaries of the sport in terms of going faster. The bikes he rode didn't look very different in 1978 compared to how they looked in 1965. That came later. But you don't have to be a great innovator to be a genius.

What Merckx has given the sport can be seen in the way bike racing on the road has been perceived since his retirement. *La course en tête* as Merckx forged it remains the benchmark for the entire sport. The way he raced is the gold standard to which all professional cyclists and all their victories are compared. Today, whenever journalists and fans criticise a star for not racing aggressively enough, or praise an *offensif* such as Thomas Voeckler or Jens Voigt for attempting to defy the odds or seizing on a perfect moment to attack, the benchmark – conscious or subliminal – is one man: Merckx. The touch of Merckx was there when Bernard Hinault raced in the snow from Liège to Bastogne and back in 1980, when Sean Kelly raced the final kilometres of the 1991 Giro di Lombardia like a man possessed, when Miguel Indurain put the Tour de France field to the sword in the Ardennes in 1995, when Lance Armstrong won an Alpine stage into Le Grand Bornand in the 2004 Tour de France, simply because he could, not because he needed to. The ultimate accolades for any cycling champion are *Cannibalesque*, *Merckx-esque*. The former is an attitude to racing a season in which the cyclist tries to win every prize on offer; the latter an individual victory that has echoes of the mastery Merckx showed. These are traits *suiveurs* have admired, at various times, in Hinault, Kelly, Laurent Jalabert, Armstrong, Gilbert.

'Never in my life have I met another man like him, a man who constantly wanted to be the best, wanted to be the first,' wrote Jean-Marie Leblanc, who encountered Merckx first as fellow racer, then as a journalist, and later went on to run the Tour de France. 'You may say: Hinault? But there were times when Hinault would let a break go, as all other cyclists do. When a move went and he was five minutes behind he would take a reasonable view. But Merckx never saw it in a reasonable light.'

The purpose of this book was to explore how and why Merckx remained 'unreasonable' from his teenage years until March 1978. There is no single 'why', but a variety of influences and character traits which combine to create that 'why'. The list would begin with an upbringing that indoctrinated young Eddy with a sense of duty and a work ethic. The list would include the following: guilt at subverting these by dropping the studies that meant so much to his mother; the chronic fear of failure; the addictive joy of winning, the habit of winning and the many ways of winning all acquired young; the threat that every victory might be the last after the body blows of Savona and Blois; the pressures from a hostile press and adoring fans.

The ingredients of the 'why' can be thus identified. What cannot be explained is how all those elements combined in one man's mind, how that mind happened to exist in a body that could support the demands of that mind, how they came together at the time that was most propitious. What can be said, however, is that it is unlikely to happen twice. The likes of Merckx will not be seen again. Cycling and sport may well be the poorer for it.

EDDY MERCKX'S MAJOR VICTORIES

1964 World amateur road race championship, Sallanches, France

1965 (team, Solo-Superia, professional from 1 May)

69 races, 9 wins

1966 (Peugeot) Milan–San Remo (20/3); stage of GP Midi Libre (14/6); overall Tour de Morbihan + two stages (11–14/8); Baracchi Trophy (with Ferdinand Bracke, 4/11)

95 races, 20 wins

1967 (Peugeot) World professional road race championship, Heerlen, Holland (3/9); Milan–San Remo (18/3); Ghent–Wevelgem (29/3); Flèche Wallonne (28/4); two stages of Giro d'Italia (31/5+2/6); two stages of the Tour of Sardinia (4+5/3); two stages of Paris–Nice (9+13/3); stage of Paris–Luxembourg (17/9); Baracchi Trophy (with Ferdinand Bracke, 4/11)

113 races, 26 wins

1968 (Faema) Paris–Roubaix (7/4); stage of Tour of Belgium (3/4); overall Giro d'Italia + four stages (20/5–12/6); overall Tour of Sardinia + two stages (24/2–1/3); overall Tour of

Romandie + one stage (8–12/5); overall Tour of Catalonia + two stages (8–15/9); stage of Catalan Week (28/3); Tre Valle Varesine (10/8); Lugano GP time trial (20/10)

129 races, 32 wins

1969 (Faema) Milan–San Remo (19/3); Tour of Flanders (30/3); Liège–Bastogne–Liège (22/4); four stages of Giro d'Italia (18/5–30/5); overall Tour de France + six stages (28/6–20/7); overall Tour of Levant (Spain) + three stages (3–9/3); overall Paris–Nice + three stages (10–16/3); overall Paris–Luxembourg + one stage (5–6/8); stage of Tour of Majorca (1/4)

129 races, 43 wins

1970 (Faemino) Belgian national championship, Yvoir (21/6); Ghent–Wevelgem (1/4); Paris–Roubaix (12/4); Flèche Wallonne (19/4); overall Tour of Belgium + two stages (6–10/4); overall Giro d'Italia + three stages (18/5–7/6); overall Tour de France + eight stages (26/6–19/7); two stages of Tour of Sardinia (23–26/2); three stages of Paris–Nice (11–16/3)

138 races, 52 wins

1971 (Molteni) World professional road race championship, Mendrisio, Switzerland (5/9); Milan–San Remo (19/3); Het Volk (25/3); Liège–Bastogne–Liège (25/4); Henninger Turm (1/5); Giro di Lombardia (9/10); overall Tour of Belgium + three stages (11–15/4); Tour de France + four stages (26/6–18/7); overall Tour of Sardinia + three stages (27/2–3/3); overall Paris–Nice + three stages (10–17/3); overall Criterium du Dauphiné + two stages (18–25/3); overall GP Midi Libre + two stages (3–6/6); GP Baden-Baden (with Herman Van Springel (26/9)

120 races, 54 wins

1972 (Molteni) World Hour Record, Mexico (25/10) 49.431kilometres; Milan–San Remo (18/3); Liège–Bastogne–Liège (20/4); Flèche Wallonne (23/4); GP de l'Escaut (1/8); Giro di Lombardia (7/10); overall Giro d'Italia + four stages (21/5–11/6); overall Tour de France + six stages (1–23/7); three stages of Paris–Nice (9–14/3); Fleche Brabanconne (26/3); Giro del Piemonte (9/9); Giro dell' Emilia (4/10); Baracchi Trophy (with Roger Swerts, 11/10)

127 races, 50 wins

1973 (Molteni) Het Volk (3/3); Ghent–Wevelgem (3/4); Amstel Gold Race (7/4); Paris–Roubaix (15/4); Liège–Bastogne–Liège (22/4); Paris–Brussels (26/9); GP Nations (6/10); overall Vuelta a España + six stages (26/4–13/5); overall Giro d'Italia + six stages (18/5–9/6); overall Tour of Sardinia + one stage (24/2–1/3); stage of Paris–Nice (11/3); overall GP Fourmies + one stage (22–23/9); Lagueglia Trophy (18/2)

136 races, 51 wins

1974 (Molteni) World professional road race championship, Montreal, Canada (25/8); overall Giro d'Italia + two stages (16/5–8/6); overall Tour de France + eight stages (27/6–21/7); overall Tour of Switzerland + three stages (12–21/6); three stages of Paris–Nice (9–14/3); Lagueglia Trophy (20/2)

140 races, 38 wins

1975 (Molteni) Milan–San Remo (19/3); Amstel Gold Race (29/3); Tour of Flanders (6/4); Liège–Bastogne–Liège (20/4); stage of the Tour of Switzerland (19/6); two stages of the Tour de France (2–5/7); overall Tour of Sardinia + one stage (22–26/2); overall Catalan Week + one stage (31/3–4/4); two stages of Paris–Nice (9–14/3); two stages of Tour of Romandie (7–11/5)

151 races, 38 wins

1976 (Molteni) Milan–San Remo (19/3); overall Catalan Week + two stages (22–26/3); stage of Tirreno–Adriatico (13/3); stage of Tour of Romandie (4/5)

111 races, 15 victories

1977 (FIAT) stage of Tour of Switzerland (21/6); overall Tour Mediterranean (19–23/2); stage of Paris–Nice (14/3)

119 races, 17 victories

1978 (C&A) 5 races, 0 victories

Last professional race Circuit du Pays de Waes (Kemzeke, Belgium), 19 March

Bibliography

Rider statistics and Merckx's victory margins are taken from *Vélo-Gotha*, by René Jacobs and Harry Van den Bremt, published in 1984, which was also my reference for Merckx's palmares. For detailed references to the Tour de France, I have gone back to *l'Equipe*'s *Tour de France à 100 Ans*, published in 2002. The website www.cyclingarchives.com was a useful resource for the results of other races. The website www.INA.fr was a good source of archive race footage.

Also of reference were the following books, in no particular order:

Eddy Merckx l'Epopée, Théo Mathy, Editions Luc Pire, 2007; *Maglia rosa, triumph and tragedy at the Giro d'Italia*, Herbie Sykes, Rouleur Ltd, 2011; *Eddy Merckx, La Veridique Histoire*, Jean-Paul Ollivier, Glenat, 1996, from which is taken my translation of Roger Pingeon's account of an evening with Merckx in 1969 in chapter six; *Eddy Merckx, Cet Inconnu*, Roger Bastide, Marabout 1972; *Eddy Merckx, Homme et Cannibale*, Rik Vanwalleghem and Joël Godaert, Pinguin/Dernière Heure, 1993; *Faema Espresso 1945–2010*, Collezione Enrico Maltoni, 2009; *Cycling Classics 1970–72*, Noel G. Henderson, Pelham Books, 1973; *Pedalare! Pedalare! A history of Italian cycling*, John Foot, Bloomsbury, 2011; *The Great Bike Race*, Geoffrey Nicholson, Magnum, 1978; *Het Wonder Van Vlaanderen, de Epos van de Ronde*, Rik Van Walleghem, Pinguin/Het Nieuwsblad, 1998; *Tours de France*, Antoine Blondin, La Table Ronde, 2001; *Toute l'Histoire du Cyclisme Belge sur route*, Théo Mathy, Editions

Arts et Voyages, 1978; *Een Klein Dorp, een Zware Tol*, Stefan van Laere, Frans and Josef Craeninckx, Manteau, 2004; *Eddy Merckx en ik, Herinneringen aan de Kannnibal*, Stefan van Laere, Bola Editions, 2010; *Les Géants du Cyclisme Belge*, Théo Mathy, Editions Arts et Voyages, 1975; *Qui Êtes-Vous Eddy Merckx?*, Marc Jeuniau, Editions Arts et Voyages, 1969; *Le Phénomène, Eddy Merckx et ses Rivaux*, François Terbéen, del Duca, Paris, 1970; *I Miei Campioni*, Nino Defilippis and Beppe Conti, Graphot Editrice, 2000; *Tour de France 1974*, David Saunders, Kennedy Bros Publishing, 1974; *Pour un Maillot Jaune*, Luis Ocaña and François Terbéen, Calmann-Lévy, 1972; *Luis Ocaña, Le Soleil des Pelotons*, Bernard Loizeau, private publication, 1978; *Merckx–Ocaña duel au sommet*, François Terbéen, Calmann-Levy, 1974; *Merckx ou la rage de vaincre*, Léon Zitrone, Editions Planete, 1969; *Eddy Merckx, l'Irrésistible Ascension d'un Jeune Champion*, Pierre Thonon (translation of original biography in Flemish by Louis Clicteur and Lucien Berghmans), De Schorpioen, 1968; *Tout Eddy, le plus grand champion cycliste de tous les temps raconte sa vie d'exception*, Stéphane Thirion, Jourdan, Paris, 2006; *Face à face avec Eddy Merckx*, Marc Jeuniau, Editions Arts et Voyages, 1971; *Merckx Intime*, Philippe Brunel, Calmann-Lévy, 2002; *Plus d'un Tour dans Mon Sac: Mes Carnets de Route 1972*, Eddy Merckx with Marc Jeuniau, Arts et Voyages, 1972.

Newspaper and magazine articles referred to include:

Author interviews with Eddy Merckx, *Cycle Sport*, 1997; *Observer*, 2005; Sandra Laborde's profile, *Vélo*, November 2000; interviews with Eddy Merckx and Bernard Thévenet in *l'Equipe* magazine, 21 June 2003; 'Eddy, Walter, Patrick, Herman et les autres', *Vélo*, October 2005; Patrick Lafayette on Merckx's first race in *l'Equipe* magazine, 1 October 2011.

Index

EM indicates Eddy Merckx.